Canada Amon

Canada Among Nations 2005

Split Images

EDITED BY
ANDREW F. COOPER
DANE ROWLANDS

2x/05/06

Published for the Norman Paterson School
of International Affairs, Carleton University,
in cooperation with
The Centre for International Governance Innovation
by
McGill-Queen's University Press
Montreal & Kingston · London · Ithaca

© McGill-Queen's University Press 2005
ISBN 0-7735-3026-6 (cloth)
ISBN 0-7735-3027-4 (paper)

Legal deposit fourth quarter 2005
Bibliothèque nationale du Québec

Printed in Canada on acid-free paper that is 100% ancient forest free
(100% post-consumer recycled), processed chlorine free

This book has been published with financial support from the
Norman Paterson School of International Affairs, Carleton University,
and The Centre for International Governance Innovation.

McGill-Queen's University Press acknowledges the support of the
Canada Council for the Arts for our publishing program. We also
acknowledge the financial support of the Government of Canada
through the Book Publishing Industry Development Program (BPIDP)
for our publishing activities.

Library and Archives Canada has catalogued this publication as follows:

Canada among nations.

Annual.
1984–
Produced by the Norman Paterson School of
International Affairs at Carleton University.
Publisher varies.
Each vol. also has a distinctive title.
Includes bibliographical references.
ISSN 0832-0683
ISBN 0-7735-3026-6 (cloth);
ISBN 0-7735-3027-4 (paperback)
(2005 edition)

   1. Canada—Foreign relations—1945–   —Periodicals.   2. Canada—
Politics and government—1984–   —Periodicals.   I. Norman Paterson
School of International Affairs.

FC242.C345   327.71   c86-031285-2
REV
F1034.2.C36

Typeset in 10/12 Sabon by True to Type

Contents

Foreword

Split Images is the twenty-first consecutive annual instalment of the *Canada Among Nations* series. The series was founded by two professors in the Norman Paterson School of International Affairs, Carleton University: Brian Tomlin and Maureen Molot. The first volume in the series, which was subtitled *1984: A Time of Transition* brought together some of Canada's leading international affairs experts to review international events and Canadian foreign policy in the calendar year. From the outset, however, the volume was never intended to be merely a review of recent policy initiatives. Nor was it the editors' intention to offer a comprehensive package of priorities and policies for Canada. Rather, the hope was "to provide a better understanding of important developments in Canadian policies and the environments that shape them and, in the process, to promote a more informed public debate about appropriate policies and priorities for Canada."[1]

This volume remains true to the spirit of the original enterprise. It contains a wide ranging series of essays written by some of Canada's leading scholars, journalists, and practitioners on the multiple and critical challenges that Canadian foreign policy decision-makers confront in an increasingly turbulent world. The volume explores key trends in the international environment, including the rise of new powers in the global economy and the opportunities and challenges they pose to Canada's trade, investment, and cultural relations abroad. It examines some of the key aspects of Canadian foreign policy including the recent International Policy Review process and the mechanics of foreign policy implementation. And, like many of the previous volumes in the series, it pays close attention to Canada's evolving and complex relationship with its neighbour to the south.

Unlike previous volumes in the series, which were edited by the School's faculty, this year's volume is the result of a new, collaborative partnership between the School and the Centre for International Governance and Innovation (CIGI). I am most grateful for the generous support that CIGI's executive director, John English, has given to this new partnership and the personal enthusiasm and extraordinary good will he has brought to our new, joint venture. I also want to thank Professor Andrew F. Cooper of CIGI and the University of Waterloo who kindly agreed to join the editorial team and work with my colleague Professor Dane Rowlands in producing this year's volume. Both of them have brought their formidable talents and industry to the task. The end product is a real credit to them both.

Over the years, the *Canada Among Nations* series has developed a loyal and dedicated readership among the growing number of Canadians who are interested in international affairs and Canada's role in the world. Our new partnership with CIGI in producing the series ensures that our readers will not be disappointed.

Fen Osler Hampson
Director
The Norman Paterson School of International Affairs
Carleton University
Ottawa, Canada

NOTES

1 Editors' Introduction, *Canada Among Nations, 1984: A Time of Transition* (Toronto: James Lorimer and Company, 1985).

Acknowledgments

Canada Among Nations 2005, Split Images has emerged through a perfect combination of circumstances and collaboration. As co-editors we endeavoured to put together a volume that reflected a diversity of views about Canadian Foreign Policy and that reached our audience in a punctual manner. The individual chapters capture the scope and immediacy of the contentious debate about Canadian Foreign Policy that has cascaded in and without the country throughout what has been termed the post-post Cold War years. Fortuitously, the Martin government itself underscored the immediacy and salience of the debate by the lengthy buildup and eventual release of its much-anticipated *International Policy Statement* (IPS) in April 2005. Yet amidst the sharp differences in tone and prognosis the work of our contributors are bound together by a commitment to, and a sense of enthusiasm for, the ongoing work to define a realistic and inspired Canadian Foreign Policy.

As a partnership between Carleton University's Norman Paterson School of International Affairs (NPSIA) and The Centre for International Governance Innovation (CIGI) we profited from the resources each of these institutions possessed. NPSIA has built up a huge pool of experience and expertise in producing the *Canada Among Nations* series. NPSIA Director Fen O. Hampson and Janet Doherty provided support and guidance throughout the endeavour. We would like to thank Katherine Graham, dean of the Faculty of Public Affairs and Management at Carleton University, for continuing to support the *Canada Among Nations* series. CIGI showcased its facilities by hosting the Author's Workshop in the spring of 2005. As with all the activities of CIGI this event could not have been held without the enormous support of Jim Balsillie, the Chairman of CIGI's Board of Directors, together with John English, its Executive Director. We also benefited from the advice of Paul Heinbecker and Daniel Schwanen.

For her skilled and confident management of both the Author's Workshop and the process of obtaining and revising the chapters we would like to express our thanks to Kelly Jackson. With a tight deadline amidst the busy schedules of the contributors she handled the process in flawless fashion. With much of this work she was ably assisted by Andrew Schrumm. The staff at CIGI has also been tremendous in their support of the project on many levels and in countless ways. Special thanks go to Andrew Thompson, a PhD student in History at the University of Waterloo, for his technical editing of this manuscript.

Finally we would like to thank all the people at McGill-Queen's University Press who worked efficiently to turn the manuscript into a book. Of particular note in this regard we acknowledge with gratitude the efforts of Philip Cercone, Joan McGilvray, and Brenda Prince.

Andrew F. Cooper
Dane Rowlands

Waterloo/Ottawa
July 2005

Acronyms

ADF	Australian Defence Force
AIDS	Acquired Immune Deficiency Syndrome
ALP	Australian Labor Party
ANZUS	Australia, New Zealand, United States Security Treaty
APEC	Asia-Pacific Economic Cooperation
APFC	Asia Pacific Foundation of Canada
APMS	anti-personnel mines
ASEAN	Association of Southeast Asian Nations
BBC	British Broadcasting Corporation
BMD	ballistic missile defense
BRICS	Brazil, Russia, India, China
BRICSAM	Brazil, Russia, India, China, South Africa, ASEAN, Mexico
BQ	Bloc Québécois
BSE	Bovine Spongiform Encephalopathy
CAFTA	Central American Free Trade Agreement
CCCE	Canadian Council of Chief Executives
CCIC	Canadian Council for International Cooperation
CCW	certain conventional weapons
CEE	Central and Eastern Europe
CE	Canadian Forces
CFB	Canadian Forces Base
CFIA	Canadian Food Inspection Agency
C-IBC	Canada-India Business Council
CIDA	Canadian International Development Agency

CIGI	Centre for International Governance Innovation
CIS	Commonwealth of Independent States
CME	Canadian Space Agency
CSA	Canadian Manufacturers and Exporters
CSOS	civil society organizations
CUSFTA	Canada-US Free Trade Association
DART	Disaster Assistance Response Team
DFAIT	Department of Foreign Affairs and International Trade
DFID	Department for International Development (UK)
DND	Department of National Defence
EDC	Export Development Canada
EU	European Union
FAC	Foreign Affairs Canada
FDI	Foreign Direct Investment
FIRA	Foreign Investment Review Agency
FTAA	Free Trade Agreement of the Americas
G7	Group of Seven (Industrialized Nations)
G8	Group of Eight (Industrialized Nations)
G10	Group of Ten (Industrialized Nations)
G20	Group of Twenty (Finance)
G20/G22	Group of Twenty (WTO Alliance-Doha Round)
GATT	General Agreement on Tariffs and Trade
GDP	gross domestic product
GDP(W)	global domestic product
GNI	gross national income
GNP	gross national product
GROS	grass-roots organizations
GST	Goods and Services Tax
HIV	Human Immunodeficiency Virus
IAEA	International Atomic Energy Agency
ICAO	International Civil Aviation Organisation
ICBL	International Convention to Ban Landmines
ICC	International Criminal Court
ICCC	Indo-Canada Chamber of Commerce
ICRC	International Committee of the Red Cross
IDRC	International Development Research Centre
IFIS	International Financial Institutions
IGOS	intergovernmental organizations
IHA	international humanitarian assistance
IMF	International Monetary Fund
INTERFET	International Force for East Timor
IPR	International Policy Review
IPS	International Policy Statement

ISAF	International Security Assistance Force
IT	Information Technology
ITCan	International Trade Canada
ITU	International Telecommunications Union
JTF2	Joint Task Forces Two
L20	Leaders' Twenty (Summit)
MAI	Multilateral Agreement on Investment
MarCom	maritime command
MDGS	Millennium Development Goals
Mercosur	Mercado Común del Sur (Southern Common Market)
MFA	Multi Fibre Arrangement
MIF	Multinational Interim Force (Haiti)
MINUSTAH	United Nations Stabilization Mission in Haiti
MNCS	Multinational Corporations
MOD	Ministry of Defence (UK)
MP	Member of Parliament
MSF	Médecins Sans Frontières
NAFTA	North American Free Trade Agreement
NAM	Non-Aligned Movement
NASA	National Aeronautics and Space Administration
NATO	North Atlantic Treaty Organization
NDP	New Democratic Party
NEP	National Energy Policy
NEPAD	New Partnership for Africa's Development
NGOS	non-governmental organizations
NORAD	North American Aerospace Defence Command
NORTHCOM	Northern Command
NPSIA	Norman Paterson School of International Affairs
OAS	Organization of American States
ODA	Official Development Assistance
OECD	Organisation of Economic Co-operation and Development
OSCE	Organization for Security and Cooperation in Europe
PCO	Privy Council Office
PMO	Prime Minister's Office
PNG	Papua New Guinea
POGG	peace, order and good government
PRT	provincial reconstruction teams (Afghanistan)
PSEPC	Department of Public Safety and Emergency Preparedness Canada
PSO	Peace Support Operations
R&D	Research and Development
RCMP	Royal Canadian Mounted Police

RHOMA	Retired Heads of Missions Association
S&T	Science and Technology
SARS	Severe Acute Respiratory Syndrome
SCFAIT	Standing Committee on Foreign Affairs and International Trade
SITC	Standard International Trade Classification
SMES	small and medium enterprises
SOES	state-owned enterprises (China)
SOUTHCOM	Southern Command
TICAS	Trade and Investment Cooperation Agreements
TNOS	transnational organizations
TRIPS	trade-related aspects of intellectual property rights
U of T	University of Toronto
UNAMA	United Nations Assistance Mission in Afghanistan
UNDP	United Nations Development Programme
UNICEF	United Nations International Children's Emergency Fund /United Nations Children's Fund
UNHCR	United Nations High Commission for Refugees
USCG	United States Coast Guard
WMD	weapons of mass destruction
WHO	World Meteorological Society
WHO	World Health Organization
WSSD	World Summit on Sustainable Development
WTO	World Trade Organization

Canada Among Nations 2005

1 A State of Disconnects – The Fracturing of Canadian Foreign Policy

ANDREW F. COOPER and
DANE ROWLANDS

Canadian foreign policy is going through a period of profound anxiety, critique, and reconsideration. All of the accepted images of why and how Canada should play an international role have been eroded if not completely shattered. Having been built up as one of the major sources of national unity and collective pride there is now a pervasive sense of disconnect as well as fragility about Canada's role in the world.

To capture the essence of this dissonance we have chosen the title *Split Images*, an allusion both to the glaring divide between different visions of foreign policy, and to photography. In his chapter, Paul Evans presents the camera metaphor: "Users of Single Lens Reflex cameras are familiar with a focusing device that contains a small circle separated by a median bar. The object to be photographed is in focus when the images on both sides of the bar are clear" (Evans, this volume). At this time of foreign policy fracturing, both sides of the bar remain decidedly unclear.

For many observers, the lack of focus is the result of a long-term slippage of will, capacity and status in the location of Canada among nations (Cohen, 2004). Canada has rested on its myths and sense of comfort while actors, rules and events around it have been transformed. For others, the essential debate that must be engaged in is deciding between the main game that lies at the core of Canadian foreign policy and the alternative choices of activity that can be pursued on a voluntary and potentially a re-invigorated basis. Embracing this main game is grounded on an explicit recognition of the United States as the central pivot of Canadian foreign policy. All else beyond this US-centric approach is simply embellishment. Allowing space for alternative options points in the direction of a discretionary approach in which Canada puts an onus on selective issue-areas to differentiate it on the international stage. This first image is geographically limited but deep in terms of its salience for Canada's economic and strategic interests. It focuses on what is deemed necessary to ensure the prosperity for Canadians and the security of North America (Stairs, 2005). The second image encompasses a wider range of visions and voices but is often only loosely attached to Canada's core priorities. There is a strong normative dimension concerning what is judged to be right with respect to policy options.

The underlying structural conditions shaping the image of disconnect between the established self-image of Canada and a sense of anxiety about what Canada should and can be doing today relates to the split between the order established under the post-1945 system (however problematic) or even the post-1989 world, and the unsettled state of the post-post-Cold War or post-9/11 era. The post-9/11 world order – unlike the post-World War II system – is not one in which the Canadian state and a number of selected Canadians hold a privileged place. For all of its imposed discipline, the post-1945 order held obvious attractions for a Canada eager to come of age. We could project our national image by joining a host of multilateral institutions, and release the abundance of Canadian energy and talent that was exemplified by Lester B. Pearson's Nobel Prize and the "invention" of Peacekeeping. The resulting image was of a "Golden Age" of foreign policy. Despite the failure to meet the lofty expectations associated with the fall of the Berlin Wall, the collapse of the Soviet Union, and the end of the system of East/West bipolarity, the post-Cold War period was still largely characterized by optimism, with the (admittedly uneven) spread of democracy and the possibility that self-identified middle powers such as Canada could creatively re-position themselves for the benefit of all.

The unanticipated inception of the post-post-Cold War era has brought with it new waves of discomfort. Multilateralism in many forms has been subordinated to the primacy of the hyper-power. Empire and regime change through the use of force has come back in vogue amidst distant memories in Canada of a troubled era in terms of national unity. Talk of civilizational divides clashes with the promotion of pluralism and diversity. Instead of democracy brought about in an incremental and sustained fashion from the ground up – long the favoured Canadian approach – the big bang approach has assumed at least temporary dominance. Terrorists are seen not only without, but within. The safety of states is placed above the benefits associated with human rights and even economic liberalism. Borders act as barriers, and not as zones of confidence (Cooper, 2004).

Put together, many of the key self-images built up in Canada – either through a long historical process or through their association with the recent orders – have been challenged and overturned. No longer was it deemed a positive attribute in the post-9/11 context to talk about the longest undefended border with the United States. Nor, in the post-post-Cold War era could Canada depict itself as possessing a special relationship with the US. The concept of "coalitions of the willing" – as championed by Canada on land mines and the International Criminal Court (ICC) – as a bottom up, voluntary vehicle has been turned on its head. As witnessed by the Iraq war, coalitions of the willing have been transformed into a top down model with strong elements of coercion. Ambiguity offered no protection against the psychology of "with us or against us."

These split images at the global level have been mirrored by a serious fracturing of style in Canadian foreign policy at the domestic level. Jean Chrétien, through his ten-year tenure as prime minister, stands out in foreign policy terms as a minimalist. Guided by an instrumental view of Canadian foreign policy, he was prepared to embrace only a few initiatives, most notably the Team Canada trade missions. Chrétien's emotional attachment was reserved almost exclusively for Africa. This connection was featured both in his burst of enthusiasm on the 1996 Zaire initiative to rescue refugees and his determination to put NEPAD (New Partnership for Africa's Development) along side terrorism on the agenda at the 2002 Kananaskis G7/8 Summit.

In sharp contrast Prime Minister Paul Martin can be classified as a maximalist, at least with regard to his aspirations. His keen interest in ideas and impatience with organizational constraints has motivated him to focus on a number of issues at the same time despite, or even arguably because of, the minority status of his government. Although these traits come out in regard to high-profile domestic dossiers as well – on health, cities/communities, aboriginal, and education/learning issues – they have become exaggerated on the international front. There is hardly a functional or geographic issue on the global radar that has not received some attention or been made a priority at the Prime Ministerial level and reflected in some Canadian initiative or effort: Darfur in tandem with the *Responsibility to Protect*, the new global distribution of power and institutional reform, climate change, pandemics – the list is an extended one (Martin, 2004a; Martin, 2005a).

To its credit the Martin government tried to impose order on decision-making through the imposition of a number of organizing practices and principles. Procedurally, the Martin government made a "whole of government" approach its priority. Departing from the Chrétien model, the Martin government also re-established a system of cabinet committees that placed some considerable attention on international issues. Initially the Prime Minister chaired the committee dealing with Global Affairs. On a more sustained basis he has chaired the committee on Canada-US relations. Most dramatically, the Martin government set out to define its priorities through an International Policy Review/*International Policy Statement* (IPR/IPS) – with an engagement of all the bureaucratic actors with a major stake in foreign policy.[1]

Substantively, the Martin government made a concerted attempt to systemize Canadian foreign policy by enmeshing it in a thematically linking construct. One expression of this orientation came out in the emphasis placed on the so-called 3D model – encompassing diplomacy, development and defence. This approach was designed to provide a comprehensive and integrative blueprint for reconstruction and nation-building activities in high profile cases of intervention, most notably Haiti and Afghanistan (Martin, 2004b).

VALUES AND INTERESTS

Yet despite the energy driving all of these activities, this approach generated as much friction as enthusiasm. One paramount point of contention concerns the split image of what priorities have, and should guide Canadian foreign policy. As rehearsed throughout this book, in principle interests and values are not mutually exclusive as determinants for the making of foreign policy by any state. In practice, however, there is some considerable temptation in the post-post-Cold War era to see values and interests as competing perspectives and avenues for foreign policy. This sense of divergence comes to the fore with Robert Kagan's compelling – but simplified – rendition of the US and the European Union being pulled apart as distinct *and* separate planets (Mars and Venus).[2]

A similar tendency to view foreign policy choices through a polarized lens – with values and interests at either end of a sharp and differentiated continuum – has taken hold in Canada. For some observers the key attribute of the post-post-Cold War era is how distinctive Canada has become from the US in cultural terms. Taking Michael Adam's *Fire and Ice* as the prime text of reference, this assessment of a North American disconnect highlights not the logic of convergence but the apparently increasing divergence between Canada and the US in respect to social values and modes of citizenship (Adams, 2003). This split is revealed not only by many of the familiar markers of difference

– contrasting attitudes to health care, capital punishment, gun control – but also by new measures of departure such as sharply diverging attitudes to racial profiling, dual nationality, and other forms of social inclusion. The implications, both in cause and effect, of this Canadian-American disconnect have given rise to a far more robust interpretation of Canadian foreign policy than commonly rendered in the past. Rather than couching the prospects of Canada's role in the world in terms of vulnerability, opportunities based on what Richard Gwyn has termed "a new inner strength" (2004: 3–5) have become privileged.

A good deal of this positive thinking about Canadian foreign policy has been informed and promoted by Jennifer Welsh's book *At Home in the World* (2004). Although it provides a far more balanced prognosis than both her champions and critics contend, this book has caught the wave of imagination about the future prospects of Canadian foreign policy and pushed her into the spotlight as an external consultant to the IPR/IPS. Departing from the limitationalist stance of many advocates of an interest-oriented foreign policy, Welsh brings in vision and values as central components to a new debate about Canadian foreign policy. Instead of being a receptor of change, Canada should raise its sights and be an active agent for change.

Jennifer Welsh builds and refines on her argument in the lead off chapter in this 2005 volume of *Canada Among Nations*. She points to a future in which Canada can break free of its reactive state to be more fully engaged on the global stage. Far from framing this vision in terms of a strictly normative prescription, she carefully uses as her guide a revised reality check on what Canada can do in the post-post-Cold War. Instead of continuing to cast the two components at odds with each other, values are meshed with a strategic definition of interests.

For others on the front lines of the debate, the key lesson learnt from the shocks of the post-post-Cold War world has been the need to strip foreign policy down to its bare essentials. The foundation of this approach is the view that interests are everything.[3] One sign of this type of thinking has been the adoption of the position within the Canadian business establishment that "everything has changed" in the post 9/11 context. Rather than the incremental approach still favoured by Canadian state officials to managing the Canada-US relationship (with an emphasis on refining the "smart border" to balance security and commercial concerns), business groups have subordinated all other objectives to the need to swiftly reassure the US concerning a Canadian buy-in to the priorities of homeland security.

All of the so-called "big ideas" about North America put on the agenda in the aftermath of 9/11 share this mindset. Associated with a number of key opinion leaders – such as Allan Gotlieb (2002), and

Wendy Dobson (2002) – these proposals are marked by ambition and certitude about the requisite policy path to be followed. To coin a phrase from Margaret Thatcher, the TINA principle (There Is No Alternative) is invoked. Everything else is romanticism.

As with Jennifer Welsh's contribution, Derek H. Burney's chapter is highly nuanced. Burney's sense of reality though, is one in which a concern with interests trumps values. Whereas Welsh offers an expansionary approach based on the expectation that Canada can stand tall as a global model citizen, Burney's approach subordinates all else to the management of the Canada-US relationship. A strong onus is placed on a combination of political hard-headedness (standing up to the US on issues such as soft-wood lumber, beef imports, and the Byrd Amendment) and diplomatic acumen (fostering coalition-building and promotional activities). The fundamental ingredients for Canada's success are an appreciation and ability to gain access to the numerous loci of power within the US, a consistent pattern of signalling at the leadership level, and the skill of disagreeing with the US on specific issues without contaminating the wider relationship between the two countries.

THE STRATEGIC CHALLENGE POST-9/11

This split image between values and interests is reinforced when the debate is extended to take into account a second contentious policy question: should Canada complement or distinguish itself from the US in the external domain, and by what means? The Martin government has maintained an ambiguous attitude about its connections with the US. On the one hand it has recognized that well-managed relations with its close and predominant neighbour are salient to the management of a number of trade irritants that have refused to disappear, as well as for the entrenched realities of the post-9/11 security agenda. On the other hand, and at odds with the logic of its geographic setting and web of complex interdependence, it seems to retain serious reservations about becoming too isolated on a continental basis. Entrapment is feared as much as estrangement.

This ambiguity has accentuated the security and defence debate with reference to with whom and with what assets Canada should position itself. Joseph T. Jockel and Joel J. Sokolsky contend that for Canada the global "War on Terror," led by the US is the primary security and defence concern and that the Canadian government should support this war both in North America and overseas. Not only would Canada's interests be enhanced by adherence to this approach, so too would its values in terms of promoting democracy. Where the Canadian government has gone wrong is in its sending out of mixed messages. Whatever benefits could have been gained for the Martin government vis-à-vis the Bush Administration through an increase of defence expenditures by $12.8 billion in the 23 February 2005 Budget, its supportive role in Afghanistan, and its extension of the Smart Border initiative, have been undermined by its abrupt decision not to go along on Ballistic Missile Defence (BMD). However, Jockel and Sokolsky argue that, contrary to much of the accepted wisdom in Canada, Ottawa is still in a very favourable position with regard to the future of defence ties with Washington. Notwithstanding the fall-out from the BMD decision in their view it is still possible to restore trust in the bilateral defence and security relationship and fashion a new continental consensus.[4]

Kim Richard Nossal builds on this theme of the willingness and capability of Ottawa to make necessary strategic choices by examining Canadian foreign and defence policy through the lens of the Australian model. As Nossal points out there is a strong temptation to contrast the ambiguous response of the Canadian government to the robust approach in support of the US adopted by the Howard government. That is to say, by following the Bush administration on the "War on Terror" and Iraq, Australia got it right. Yet, after digging deeper into the Australian case, Nossal questions the relevance of this comparative model as an operational guide for Canada. The geostrategic locations of the two countries – and their security cultures – are simply too divergent.

W. Andy Knight situates Canada's anxiety as stemming from wider global trends, most notably a shift from the universal multilateralism associated with the United Nations to various forms of plurilateralism. At times of extraordinary crisis – as in the lead-up to the Iraq War – Canada is pulled back to its multilateral traditions and is itself at odds with the United States. But as the Martin government has gone to great pains to emphasize, multilateralism should not be viewed as an end in itself. This bias towards problem solving reinforces the trend towards global plurilateralism, as featured by Prime Minister Martin's push for a Leaders' 20 (L20) forum on a model (in concert with the US) similar to the G20 of Finance Ministers to deal with the 1997/8 Asian financial crisis.

WORDS AND DEEDS

A third source of dissonance concerns policy delivery, specifically the purported gap between the Martin government's declaratory statements and its operations. Through this critical lens, there was a sizeable disconnect between what the Martin government promised to do and what was actually delivered. As Daniel Drache puts it in his chapter, the Martin government is frequently "unable to add substance to its declarations." Many of the dominant traits of the Martin government played to this negative image. The government had a tendency to oversell its initiatives. Ideas that were promoted enthusiastically raised hackles by raising the level of expectation too high. Another problem was associated with a short attention span, reflected in part by the dissipation of purpose across a burgeoning spectrum of initiatives. Like a photographer taking too many pictures in rapid succession, the government seems unable to focus.

One area where this disconnect stands out has been in the domain of North American integration. Prime Minister Martin had an opportunity in the minds of many opinion leaders to advance a bolder agenda on a trilateral basis with the US and Mexico. In political terms such a move would have allowed him to distinguish himself from his predecessor, given that Prime Minister Chrétien was notoriously unreceptive to overtures of this nature. It would allow the Liberal Party to advance a proposal that played well within the Canadian business community generally and the Canadian Council of Chief Executives (CCCE) more specifically (groupings that were still displeased with the reluctance of the Canadian government to embrace the US position on Iraq). Diplomatically, the dictum of the best defence being a good offence seems apropos, as Canada could push for modifications in the way that the US did business by mooting changes in the regulatory regime of the North American Free Trade Agreement (NAFTA).

The Security and Prosperity Partnership of North America, signed by Prime Minister Martin with Presidents Bush and Fox, lent some weight to these aforementioned claims that things would be done differently (PMO, 2005). Advocates, most notably the CCCE, announced that the arrangement served as "a quantum leap for the continent" (CCCE, 2005). Opponents labelled the "partnership" a sell-out (Dobbin, 2005).

As highlighted by a more sophisticated school of critics, however, the deal was far less a big bang than an incremental shift in design. What was novel was the level of ministerial/bureaucratic engagement that the work plan entailed. Where the Martin government drew the line came in any shift in vision towards either the concept of a single economic and security space or even more controversially a security perimeter. In terms of the detailed plan, the statement lacked any strategic mechanism to establish new or improved institutions. Most tellingly, the overall process lacked any compelling timeframe nor did it identify any responsibility to deliver results (Gotlieb, 2005).

Drache argues alternatively that we must accept the post-NAFTA reality. Instead of acting as a platform for extended innovation through a system of continental governance the NAFTA status quo has been overtaken by the shift following 9/11 to define North America in security rather than in commercial terms. In re-thinking border issues and the Canada-US relationships more generally, the requisite strategy according to Drache is one that blends the management of North American divergence with scepticism towards North American integration, a greater focus on diplomatic self-interest and economic restructuring, and the building of selective alternative alliances primarily in the "Global South."

Another area in which words and deeds continue to not match is in Canada's commitment to peacekeeping and peace enhancement (Ljunggren, 2005). As Nossal pronounces in his chapter there continues to be tremendous difficulties in establishing a hierarchy of priorities. Where among the multiple crises – Afghanistan, Haiti, Darfur – should Canada concentrate its activities? Is there a Canadian niche concerning "failing states" and post-war reconstruction?

The on-going problems of commitment fatigue and capability lag weigh heavily as a source of anxiety. Equipment failures and embarrassments take a psychological, as well as reputational, toll in personnel terms – as illustrated by the fiascos in sending Hercules transport planes to East Timor, the delivery of purchased submarines to Canada and even with the issues related to the cost of utilizing the Disaster Assistance Response Team (DART) in Haiti and South Asia.

A final area where there is a disjunction between image and reality is in Official Development Assistance (ODA). Although ODA received a small boost in the last budget (up 8 percent) and there has been a determination – reinforced by the IPS – to target selective countries/areas for assistance these advances have been pushed and pulled by conflicting pressures (Francoli, 2004).[5] The rationale for choices to be made in terms of aid recipients – and to move away from what Drache calls the "scatter-gun" approach – is contested by political and diplomatic motivations. Need alone has never been the sole criterion for the dispensing of ODA. Domestic considerations continue to dominate as seen by the concern to balance Anglophone and Francophone African recipient countries. There is also a sturdy diplomatic resistance to ODA concentration, in that Canadian ambassadors (and visiting politicians) to developing countries gain considerable leverage by their association with aid projects.

Unexpected events shake up the familiar patterns of assistance as well. Who would have expected prior to 9/11 and its aftermath that

Afghanistan would have become Canada's largest recipient of bilateral aid over traditional countries such as Bangladesh and Tanzania? Who would have expected only a short time ago that Canada would have pledged a huge humanitarian and reconstruction assistance package to Iraq? This is a commitment ten times the amount promised to Haiti – a country that has gone through a serious crisis of its own, that has a large immigrant population in Canada, and is located in Canada's more immediate neighbourhood. Who would have expected the results of the 2004 Tsunami, both in terms of the extent of its regional devastation, and its counter-wave of generosity? Despite this burst of enthusiasm the IPS confirmed that Canada would not meet the ambitious goal of raising ODA to 0.7 percent of Gross Domestic Product (GDP) by 2015, a decision confirmed by the prime minister even amidst the pressure to meet this goal in the lead-up to the 2005 G8 in Gleneagles, Scotland (Cowan, 2005).

THE BRICSAM CHALLENGERS

The theme of split images is reinforced by signs of a new appetite for economic diversification away from the domination of the US market and towards China, India, Brazil and other rising powers. As John Whalley and Agata Antkiewicz detail in their chapter, the targeting of the so-called BRICS (Brazil, Russia, India, China) (Wilson and Purushothaman, 2003; *The Economist*, 2003) – or as they label them the BRICSAM states with South Africa, the Association of South East Asian Nations (ASEAN) countries, and Mexico being added to the mix – may be far more mutually advantageous than the earlier targets in this type of counterweight strategy via the UK (under Prime Minister John G. Diefenbaker) and the European Community (Prime Minister Pierre Trudeau's 'third option'). The prospect of a natural resources boom fuelled by a massive and competing demand in these states for fuel and non-fuel minerals is of major significance to Canada. Another involves the network possibilities facilitated by the large and prosperous immigrant communities from these countries.[6]

Feeding into this revived model of diversification is a strong element of situational expediency relating to a global power shift. The US economy is weighed down by many burdens, most dramatically through its enormous levels of debt and flagging consumer confidence. However, as illustrated by Prime Minister Martin's embrace of the L20 initiative, there are signs of a firm commitment to share responsibilities with this cluster of states in top tier multilateral institutions. This proposal is an important signal that the architecture of international governance needs to be revamped to accommodate the emerging world as we know it at the beginning of the twenty-first century, rather than leave it as a relic of 1945 or the mid- to late-1970s (Martin, 2005b; English et al, 2005).

This generalized appeal of a BRICS or BRICSAM option and its primarily economic foundations can be juxtaposed with the complexity and political reality of Canada's relations with these countries on an individual basis. The subsequent cluster of chapters does this by highlighting the individual differences among the core member of BRICS – Brazil, Russia, India and China. Paul Evans argues in his chapter that there are enormous political and economic stakes involved in the Canada-China relationship. China's arrival as a force on the global stage has brought with it the tremendous economic allure. The connection is made more delicate, however, by China's human rights record, its diplomatic rivalry with Japan, and the potential for geostrategic conflict in the Taiwan Straits. Nor does Canada enjoy any special status as a supplier of raw materials, a position accentuated by the Canadian backlash against the purchase of Noranda by a state-owned Chinese enterprise. As concluded by Evans, the Canada-China relationship will need constant nurturing through diverse contacts, public diplomacy, and creative institutional links.

Canada has similarly been unable to sustain a coherent vision or policy framework for engaging India. The chapter by Ramesh C. Kumar and Nigmendra Narain describe relations between Canada and India as a "bazaar," one built on short-term opportunism and a propensity for reaction rather than premeditation. Canada's policies seem to be unable to catch up to the realities of an emerging market and nuclear power, leading to a relationship distinguished by missed opportunities. The failure to penetrate Indian markets, and to mobilize the sizeable, influential and innovative Indo-Canadian population to strengthen economic, social and political links are illustrative. While there are signs of a more constructive engagement (Janigan, 2005) and ample opportunities to build on mutual interests, there is little concrete evidence to indicate that Canada's relations with India will rapidly expand beyond their current unimpressive levels.

Russia's connection to Canada is more enigmatic. Canada does not miss the era of Communism and bi-polarity but as Bogdan Buduru and Dragoş Popa note there is much about President Putin's Russia that makes Canadian observers nervous. Russia lacks a system of good governance and the proper enforcement of laws. Numerous commercial deals have turned sour on Canadian investors as they have been abandoned or turned on by their partners and the Russian authorities. Canada has also been stung by the sharp end of Russian diplomatic and military engagement both in terms of unease about human rights abuses in Chechnya and Russian attempts at political interference in Ukraine (where members of the Canada Corps took part in the impressive election observation mission). Hope continues that a cooperative relationship can be built up on other issues, most notably the Arctic, global warming, technical cooperation, and the removal and secure disposal of nuclear waste. Nonetheless, the chapter by Buduru and Popa suggests that positive assessments must be treated with caution if not outright scepticism.

Canada and Brazil, as Annette Hester recounts, have had a remarkably troublesome record of dealing with each other, with tensions on a wide spectrum of issues ranging from the Lamont-Spencer prisoner exchange case to the negotiations on the Free Trade Area of the Americas (FTAA). The issue that has come to define the relationship though, is the ongoing and apparently intractable conflict with respect to Bombardier and Embraer. The shallowness of Brazilian-Canadian relations means that otherwise inconsequential matters become blown out of proportion by indifference and incompetence. So while Canada and Brazil do have parallel interests such as the UN mission in Haiti, they seem destined for now to remain captured by issues such as the aerospace dispute (a lightening rod of animosity), that tend to derail real opportunities for meaningful engagement.

CENTRALIZATION AND FRAGMENTATION

A fourth and final point of controversy relates to the machinery of government, particularly in reference to the competing claims of centralization and fragmentation. The media have focused an inordinate amount of attention on the dynamic of centralization and the tightness of the inner circle around both the Chrétien and Martin administrations. In the case of the Martin government, this focus can be misleading. The core central agencies (the Prime Minister's Office/Privy Council Office (PMO/PCO)) remain relatively small in size. In any case, these central agencies cannot be on top of every dossier. As in the past the role of the central agencies is for the most part reactive; making sense of complex situations, getting ideas into circulation, nudging and supporting other administrative activity, and imposing forms of discipline when mistakes are made.

That being said, there is no doubt that what Donald Savoie (1999) has termed "Court Government," remains as entrenched as it was during the time of Chrétien. In part, this structure is a natural consequence of the establishment of a tight web of personal loyalties and trust developed over many years of political/governmental life. It is also in part, the natural consequence of events and timing. That is to say, when crunch time comes, issues move to the centre as key actors become increasingly involved. The Smart Border initiative moved along this trajectory after 9/11, with a unit of the PCO doing most of the heavy lifting on this dossier. So did the formulation and projection of the National Security Policy up to December 2003. Faced with the reality that it was the only major country without a comprehensive security policy the Martin government rushed to catch up. Without much consultation or publicity, Anne McClellan as deputy prime minister and minister of Public Safety and Emergency Preparedness took charge of this file and delivered a major reorganization of federal government activities on 12 December 2003.

Contradicting this image of centralization is the counter-view of fragmentation. Contrary to the image of a concentrated form of management, this view depicts diversity as privileged with almost every political and bureaucratic actor being involved to some extent in at least one area of foreign policy. Members of Parliament make their sensibilities known on a wide array of issues and with a great range of styles. Not surprisingly, it is usually the maverick or idiosyncratic approach that garners the most attention – a bias amply illustrated by the media focus on Carolyn Parrish and her anti-Bush statements. In a minority Parliament rogue members of the House can hold the government hostage while attracting attention for their own causes.

In terms of the federal government's own administrative constellation, a number of departments (and ministers) have moved to make a mark on the international stage. The Department of National Defence (DND) entered into the IPR with an ambitious list of what it wanted in terms of deliverables. Although not getting everything it desired (destroyers/fighter bombers), DND achieved its objective of getting more boots on the ground through the establishment of a new 5000-strong battalion that could be deployed in complex emergencies. The Canadian International Development Agency (CIDA) also strengthened its bureaucratic stature and resource base (with the additional funding of $5 million in the 2005 fiscal year and another $10 million in 2006).

Where does the Foreign Ministry, the traditional focus for international affairs, fit into this schema? At first glance the foreign ministry would appear to be well placed to shine in a period defined so vividly by such a renewal of interest (and by the high stakes) in the global dimension of policy-making. Led by Peter Harder as deputy minister the department showed a determination to respond to the criticism that it had lost its way (Harder, 2004).

In terms of process, the department revealed that it could still emerge as the bureaucratic winner in international policy matters. With the proverbial pen in hand, it had the potential to project its long-held aspirations and to be the "lead" agent right across the span of inter-national-oriented responsibilities. Its status also received some bounce by the establishment of the two Cabinet committees with responsibil-ity for global issues and Canada-US relations.

Nonetheless, even with these advantages in hand, the foreign min-istry has not been able to maximize its leverage in terms of its organi-zational position. On the contrary, it has slipped back into a condition of malaise. To some extent the cause of this outcome has been self-inflicted. Instead of honing its prowess in playing "the Ottawa game," the department wasted some of its opportunities. For whatever reason, the department was not able to deliver either swiftly or substantially what its political masters – and the central machinery of government – expected (Goar, 2004).

On top of this handicap (or perhaps because of it) the foreign min-istry was caught off guard by the impact of the sudden institutional divorce imposed over the spring and summer of 2004. For over two decades the Department of Foreign Affairs and International Trade (DFAIT) has been out in front as an integrated model of management with respect to the political/diplomatic and commercial faces of Canada abroad.

In cause and effect this manifestation of the split image stands out as a classic divorce Canadian-style, as there was no immediate public row, only a lingering atmosphere of sourness. It was not even transparent why the divorce took place. One strong rationale from the trade side as laid out by Louis Bélanger focuses on the need to respond to a new wave of priorities that shifted attention in terms of trade policy away from foreign policy per se to "commerce" policy with an emphasis on economic competitiveness. But as Bélanger makes clear many gaps can be found in this approach. The inner political/bureaucratic ingredients in the divorce are arguably even harder to get a handle on. Did the cul-tural differences prove to be unsustainable? Did personal rivalries play a decisive part?

What has been notable is the build up in sentiment that the decision was a poor one. This bias might represent to some degree the media beginning to sniff out an interesting (or messy) story. Indeed, as elabo-rated by Gerald Schmitz and James Lee, this story became more inter-esting as it progressed with the proposed split running up against the parliamentary committee system in the context of a minority govern-ment.

In an interesting twist to the story many of the leading campaigners for an interest-based foreign policy also stand out as the main defend-ers of the old department. Allan Gotlieb, as one of the architects of the original integration model, exemplifies this sentiment in his pithy comment about: "the destructive splitting off of international trade from the foreign ministry. The reversal of the generation–long reform that amalgamated the two branches comes at great potential cost to our nation" (McGregor, 2005; Burney, 2005).

WHAT ABOUT THE FUTURE?

What is clear is that there will be no return to the past – with a Golden Age of a foreign ministry, full of confident mandarins – ready and willing to manage Canadian international relations. What is less clear is whether there is an opportunity or an appetite for Canada to restore its 'pride and influence' in the world as the IPS has advocated.

In principle, an extended reengagement would be very attractive. But in practice such a prospect seems a stretch. Different actors that participate in, and hold stakes in Canadian foreign policy live increasingly in a construct of specialized worlds with only semi-detached connections between them. On some dossiers of course, some elements of this mix – particularly if it is seen as reflecting a prescient and skilled form of leadership – can race out in front in terms of mobilizing support for selective initiatives.

On most issues, however, a struggle continues not only between those who push for what they believe is right and those that struggle with what seems possible but also between those who see foreign policy through a national or territorial lens and those who prefer to work through a cosmopolitan or global governance framework. Given this set of fractures, the key challenge, as Thomas S. Axworthy notes, in his concluding chapter is one of adapting to disaggregation.

What the Canadian foreign policy of 2005 lacks in coherence with respect to the memories of the Pearsonian era, it compensates for in respect to energy and diffuseness. Amidst the complexity of Canadian foreign policy, an array of actors, agenda items, and forums seek not only attention, but access and deliverables. The push to do something – and to be seen to be doing it – in a world described by Axworthy as "summitry, a twenty-four hour media clock, a total blurring between domestic and foreign policy, engaged mass publics" (this volume) among other forces is insatiable.

With such a patchwork of voices and visions, the machinery and delivery of Canadian foreign policy will always struggle to fulfill what has become a heightened sense of purpose. The attractions of raising its game will continue to be prevalent both as a constructive attempt to deal with an unsettled world and as a symbolic means of therapy to reduce Canadian anxieties. But caught between multiple sources of pressure to act and uncertainty about why, how, when and where it should do so, Canada's foreign policy will perhaps inevitably struggle to achieve clarity and cohesion, and experience as many disappointments as successes in trying to bring competing visions into focus.

NOTES

1 For the long-delayed document, which appeared in April 2005, see Canada (2005a).
2 On this putative Hobbesian-Kantian (or Mars/Venus) divide in global context, see Kagan (2002); for one Canadian adaptation, see Simpson (2003).
3 The clearest statement on the need to privilege the national interest remains Stairs et al. (2003).
4 For critiques of this decision, see Winsor (2005); and, Ignatieff (2005).
5 The IPS targeted 25 countries out of the current 150 to receive 2/3s of ODA by 2010.
6 For the importance of these themes in Prime Minister Martin's thinking, see Martin (2005c).

REFERENCES

Adams, Michael. 2003. *Fire and Ice: The United States, Canada and the Myth of Converging Values*. Toronto: Penguin Canada.

Burney, Derek. 2005. Testimony. House of Commons, Standing Committee on Foreign Affairs and International Trade (SCFAIT). *Evidence*. Ottawa, 12 May. Available at: <http://www.parl.gc.ca/faae>.

Canada. 2005a. *Canada's International Policy Statement: A Role of Pride and Influence in the World*. Ottawa: Department of Foreign Affairs and International Trade (DFAIT). Available at: <http://www.international.gc.ca>.

– 2005b. "Security and Prosperity Partnership of North America Established." Ottawa: Office of the Prime Minister (PMO), 23 March. Available at: <http://pm.gc.ca/eng/news.asp?id=443>.

Canadian Council of Chief Executives (CCCE). 2005. "Trilateral Security and Prosperity Partnership will Boost Jobs and Investment, Say Canada's CEOs," Press Release. Ottawa: CCCE, 23 March.

Cooper, Andrew F. 2004. Contributions to "Most Safely on the Fence? A Round Table on the possibility of a Canadian Foreign Policy after 9/11," Moderated by Robert Wolfe, *Canadian Foreign Policy*, vol. 11, no. 1 (Fall).

Cohen, Andrew. 2004. *While Canada Slept: How We Lost Our Place in the World*. Toronto: McClelland & Stewart.

Cowan, James. 2005. "'I am not going to make a commitment,' Martin says," *National Post*, 22 June.

Dobbin, Murray. 2005. "What's Behind the 'Security and Prosperity Partnership of North America,'" Comment. Centre for Research on Globalisation, 8 April. Available at: <http://globalresearch.ca/articles/DOB504A.html>.

Dobson, Wendy. 2002. "Shaping the Future of the North American Economic Space: A Framework for Action," *Commentary*, C.D. Howe Institute, no. 162 (April).

The Economist. 2003. "Follow the Yellow Bric road," 11 October.

English, John, Ramesh Thakur, and Andrew F. Cooper, eds. 2005. *Reforming from the Top: The Leaders 20 Summit*. Tokyo: United Nations University Press.

Francoli, Paco. 2004. "'We need to do aid in a more focused way': Minister Carroll," *Hill Times*, Policy Briefing, 27 September, 8–9.

Goar, Carol. 2004. "Fresh thinking in foreign affairs," *Toronto Star*, 2 November.

Gotlieb, Allan. 2002. "Why not a grand bargain with the US?" *National Post*, 11 September.

– 2005. "Baby steps towards a partnership," *Globe and Mail*, 13 April.

Gwyn, Richard. 2004. "Surviving Survivalism," *Literary Review of Canada*, vol. 12, no. 10 (December): 3–5.

Harder, V. Peter. 2004. "'While Cohen Slept': Canadian Diplomacy in the 21st Century," Address to the Retired Heads of Missions Associations (RHOMA). Ottawa, 17 March. Available at: <http://www.fac-aec.gc.ca/department/deputy-minister-speeches-2004–03–17–en.asp>.

Ignatieff, Michael. 2005. "Liberal Values in the 21st century," Address to the Biennial Liberal Party Convention. Ottawa, 3 March. Available at: <http://www.liberal.ca/news_e.aspx?type=news&news=934>.

Janigan, Mary. 2005. "Martin: I don't like it," *Maclean's*, 25 April, 18.

Kagan, Robert. 2002. "Power and Weakness: Why the United States and Europe see the World differently," *Policy Review*, no. 113 (June-July). Available at: <http://www.policyreview.org/jun02/kagan.html>.

Ljunggren, David. 2005. "Canada talks a good talk, but the walk is gone," *Ottawa Citizen*, 26 May.

Martin, Paul. 2004a. Address by the prime minister to the Woodrow Wilson Center, Washington, 29 April. Available at: <http://pm.gc.ca/eng/news.asp?category=2&id=192>.

– 2004b. Address by the prime minister at CFB Gagetown, NB, 14 April. Available at: <http://pm.gc.ca/eng/news.asp?id=172>.

– 2005a. "A Global Answer to Global Problems," *Foreign Affairs*, vol. 84, no. 3 (May-June): 2–6.

– 2005b. Address by the prime minister to the CORIM, the CERIUM, the Institut d'études internationales de Montréal à l'UQAM, and the Montreal International organization, Montreal, 10 May. Available at: <http://pm.gc.ca/eng/news.asp?id=201>.

– 2005c. "Questions and Answers, Canada's Role in the World," Release of *Canada's International Policy Statement*, Museum of Civilization, Gatineau, QC, 18 April.

McGregor, Sarah. 2005. "Trade split causes sparks: Allan Gotlieb predicts the DFAIT split won't be permanent," *Embassy*, 16 February, 8.

Savoie, Donald J. 1999. "The Rise of Court Government in Canada," *Canadian Journal of Political Science*, vol. 32, no. 4 (December): 1–30.

Simpson, Jeffrey. 2003. "They're Mars, we're Venus," *Globe and Mail*, 21 March.

Stairs, Denis. 2005. "The Making of Hard Choices in Canadian Foreign Policy," in David Carment, Fen Osler Hampson and Norman Hillmer, eds, *Canada Among Nations 2004: Setting Priorities Straight*. Montreal & Kingston: McGill-Queen's University Press, 21–41.

– et al. 2003. *In the National Interest: Canadian Foreign Policy in an Insecure World*. Calgary: Canadian Defence and Foreign Affairs Institute. Available at: <http://www.cdfai.org/PDF/In%20The%20 National%20Interest%20 English.pdf>.

Welsh, Jennifer. 2004. *At Home in the World: Canada's Global Vision for the 21st Century*. Toronto: Harper Collins.

Whittington, Les. 2005. "The PMO still the Ottawa power source," *Toronto Star*, 11 December.

Wilson, Dominic, and Roopa Purushothaman. 2003 "Dreaming with Bric's: The Path to 2050 Goldman Sachs Report," Global Economics Paper No. 99, *Goldman Sachs*, 1 October. Available at: <http://www.gs.com/insight/research/reports/99.pdf>.

PART ONE
The Way Forward

2 Reality and Canadian Foreign Policy

JENNIFER M. WELSH

Putting the two notions of reality and Canadian foreign policy into the same sentence is a controversial move. For many who study and write about Canada's role in the world, the relationship is best characterized through an "or" and not an "and." Reality and Canadian foreign policy stand in opposition, rather than in harmony.

I will argue that this perception can and must be overcome. Doing so demands a more robust analysis of changes in the global context – and what they mean for Canada – as well as a greater willingness to articulate a strategic vision and a set of supporting policy priorities. Continued drift, and "long-term slippage of will" (to cite the editors of this volume), is not inevitable. Indeed, the current environment offers Canada a unique chance to reinvigorate its global role – for the next decade and beyond. This opportunity transcends the fortunes of any particular prime minister or political party. A series of positive developments, both internationally and domestically, have coalesced to provide Canada with a strategic moment.

At home, Canadians are thriving thanks to a growing economy and sound public finances. After a decade of economic cutbacks and pain, the federal government can reap the rewards and invest wisely in a set of priorities. In addition, the Canadian population has shown itself to be keenly interested in international affairs and strongly oriented toward taking an active role on the world stage.[1] Younger Canadians – the most ethnically diverse generation in Canadian history – aren't just talking about how to live in a globalized world, *they are doing it*. As I have illustrated, they are extremely at home in the world, and are having a remarkable impact within it as entrepreneurs, key players in global organizations such as the United Nations and the World Trade Organization (WTO), leaders of non-governmental organizations, journalists, and documentary film-makers (Welsh, 2004). What is particularly noteworthy about these new global citizens is their confidence and cosmopolitanism: they rarely feel the need to identify themselves consciously as *Canadian*.[2] As participants in a networked world, with a set of daunting and interconnected challenges, it doesn't matter to them *who* is doing the 'good' work – only that the work gets done.

Internationally, there are additional positive forces to build upon. The overwhelming response to the tsunami catastrophe in South Asia has exposed a pool of global solidarity that could, potentially, be directed in the service of other global causes. The United Nations secretary-general, recognizing the need for this post-war institution to respond to its growing legitimacy challenge and adapt to the new context for collective security in the twenty-first century, has laid out an ambitious program of reform. This agenda has met with a remarkably positive reception in capitols around the world – even within the beltway of Washington. The year 2005 is also pivotal in the international community's response to the gap between rich and poor, particularly in Africa. For both the G8 and the United Nations, poverty reduction and development in this tragedy-stricken continent has been and will continue to be a major priority. Britain, for example, is witnessing the spectacle of a prime minister and a chancellor of the Exchequer competing over who can do *more* to support progressive change in African countries.

How will Canada take advantage of this favourable geometry of forces? Many are giving us unsolicited advice. Bob Geldof – the rock singer turned advocate for Africa – proclaimed recently on the BBC that Canada, as one of the only G8 countries with a budget surplus, can and should be a key part of the campaign to bring the peoples of Africa into the twenty-first century. The writer Jeremy Rifkin (2004, and 2005: 36–41) believes Canada's role is to be the bridge between Europe and the US, encapsulating the best of the European and American dreams. Alternatively, the outgoing US ambassador to Canada, Paul Cellucci, has counselled us to reinvest in our military – particularly in the area of strategic lift – so that we can deploy our troops in combat and peacekeeping missions that complement the objectives of US foreign policy.

In any re-evaluation of Canada's role in the world, the country's relationship with the United States will continue to loom large. The prominence of Canada-US relations stems not only from the undeniable facts of economic interdependence, but also from the central role which Washington occupies in many of the international institutions that matter to Canada: the United Nations, NATO, the WTO, and the G8. Moreover, Canada and the United States have worked collaboratively in a series of 'hot spots' during the post-9/11 period, whether it be Afghanistan, Haiti, or the Ukraine. Nevertheless, the Government of Canada's gaze must extend beyond the landscape of North America if it is to fulfil its responsibilities for the protection and welfare of Canadians. As John Holmes (1976: 107), the respected scholar of Canadian foreign policy, wrote: "No country survives ... by limiting its associations to the one power with which it does the most business."

I share the view, expressed most elegantly by Andrew Cohen (2003), that Canada is not playing the global role it once did. Part of this decline is due to changes beyond our control, most obviously the fact that we now live in a world of over 190 states, far more than existed during the heyday of our middle power years. But part of this stems from decisions that our political leaders and elites have made, allowing our core assets to atrophy. We are still resting on our past laurels, but only just. The cracks are beginning to show – whether literally, in the condition of our military equipment, or figuratively, in terms of our diplomatic influence. More troubling, those outside of Canada are starting to notice. When Canadian political leaders emphasize (rightly) the responsibilities of Western countries to protect civilians from violence and mass violations of their human rights,[3] they also face questions about what Canada will *do*, beyond words, to meet that responsibility. In the words of one external observer: "Canada will continue to be irrelevant unless there is a political will to change. Today it adopts high moral standards from a safe distance" (cited in Greenhill, 2005: 17).

Canada's current economic and political standing still gives it the freedom to make choices about how it will contribute globally. But the landscape is shifting before our very eyes. There are new threats to our security, new competition for markets, new challenges facing the international institutions that have governed us for the past half a century, and a changing configuration of power. If we stand idle while our world changes, our voice in international affairs will (continue to) diminish. As Allan Gotlieb (2004: 24) has put it so forcefully, our foreign policy is in danger of becoming solely about rhetoric and "the feel good" factor.

What will we do? In asking this question, I refer not only to the federal government, but to each and every Canadian. Globally, our country is embodied not just by Canada with a capital 'C' – the corporate entity represented by government officials – but also by *Canadians*. In short, foreign policy is no longer something others do, "out there." Many private actors, whether individuals or organizations, make a vital contribution to it.

For the remainder of this chapter, however, I focus on foreign policy in its more traditional sense, as the policies set out by our federal government.[4] In particular, I address the 'two V's' that so often form part of the debate about foreign policy in Canada: Vision and Values. In so doing, I challenge the prevailing wisdom – expressed by a number of distinguished Canadians – that our foreign policy needs to steer away from squishy concepts such as values or ideals and get back to what some have called our "practical interests." I also make the case that foreign policy can be *strategic*; it is not merely the sum total of what a country has done in any given year. A country's foreign policy is a reflection of who its people are: what they value, what they seek to change, and what they are willing to stand up for.

THAT "VISION THING"

This brings me squarely to the first V – vision. Why have it? Many of my critics have contended that foreign policy should avoid broad objectives that inevitably bring with them inconsistency and poor implementation. How can a country as diverse as Canada come together around a common purpose with respect to its international role? The goal, according to this logic, should be much more modest: "good policy on a case-by-case basis" (Scowen, 2004: 23).

Good policy is most certainly the goal. The question is whether reactive and incremental decision-making is the way to achieve it. Witness the United States and the European Union in the wake of 9/11: both engaged in a process of analysis and priority setting which resulted in a strategic vision for responding to a changed global landscape.[5] I hasten to add that I am not advocating that Canada adopt the substance of either the US or EU strategic document – only the discipline of identifying challenges and opportunities, assessing our strengths, and elevating a particular set of objectives.[6]

Good strategies emerge from hard-headed diagnoses of the contexts within which an organization, or a country, is operating. And while there will always be a need to respond to unforeseen developments (who, for example, could have predicted the December 2004 tsunami?), there remains a sphere of activity which can be driven by conscious and long-term planning. Without an overarching objective, and a set of specific priorities to support it, policy-making becomes fragmented and ineffective. Indeed, this has been Canada's problem.

Take one example: Canada's international development policy. Canada's current bilateral development programs are more widely dispersed around the world than those of any other donor. Of the 155 countries that currently receive development assistance from Canada, only 18 receive assistance valued at more than $10 million annually and 54 receive *less than* $1 million annually. Is this a recipe for impact? The wide dispersion of Canada's aid program is problematic for a number of reasons. To begin, it makes it more difficult to develop the local knowledge and contacts that can ensure that Canadian aid dollars are used effectively. In addition, the proliferation of small-scale programming on the part of donors like the Canadian government places a heavy coordination and cost burden on those we are trying to help – the recipient countries. Finally, and most obviously, the fragmentation of the aid programs increases the management and costs for the Government of Canada itself.

To achieve greater impact, Canada must set priorities and make tough choices. In other words, it must be more strategic. By refocusing Canada's strategy for bilateral assistance, and moving away from a thin but global presence, our financial commitment could make a much greater difference – even if in fewer places. The political pressures on members of Parliament to continue "doing a little bit everywhere" are no doubt fierce. But they must be resisted. A more focused development strategy would further everyone's interests: our development partners, the international community at large, and Canada itself.

What, in this instance, would be the strategic vision driving Canadian policy? Quite simply, to bring a core set of development partners up to the health and education targets set out in the Millennium Development Goals (MDGs). The targets have already been identified and have garnered a high degree of consensus in both the developed and developing world (UNDP, 2005). The question now is whether donor countries such as Canada can assist developing countries as they seek to implement their own national strategies for poverty reduction and economic growth. To be sure, there remain significant obstacles to success. There is a long and checkered history of failed attempts to use foreign aid dollars to bring about progress in the developing world.[7] It is also true that non-aid policies, such as further trade liberalization and debt relief, have an equally important part to play (some would say the greater part) in improving developing country prospects. But the fact remains that a more strategic approach to Canadian development assistance is both possible and necessary.

A strategic vision serves many purposes. It provides direction to a disparate set of actors, giving them a sense of what matters most. It also informs the choice of specific spending priorities. Taking the development example again, I would argue that "country concentration" – to use the current buzzword – is only the first step to greater impact for Canadian development policy. Where more focus needs to occur, and where the potential for greater payoff lies, is in the particular sectors that Canada chooses to support. As set out in the 2005 *International Policy Statement*, sector focus should be informed by an assessment of three things: what our development partners tell us they need most; which sectors are likely to facilitate achievement of the largest number of MDGs; and what Canada is best placed to provide, drawing on its skills and expertise (Canada, 2005: 24). Finally, a strategic vision provides a touchstone for Canadians. It helps them to interpret the global changes occurring around them. It is also a statement of where their government intends to lead them, and how it intends to spend their tax dollars. Since the end of the Cold War, Canada has spent over $240 billion on diplomacy, defence, and development. This alone requires a rationale, and a statement of what kind of impact our resources are seeking to have. Above all, a strategic vision for Canada's role in the world can serve as a reference point for Canadian citizens as they engage in their own day-to-day lives – lives which in so many cases involve a significant global component.

VALUES OR INTERESTS?

Let me now turn to my second V– values. In the contemporary debate about Canada's role in the world, there is a chorus of voices proclaiming we have paid too much attention to cosmopolitan values (the "other") in our foreign policy, and not enough to the national interest (the "self").

It is true that the word "interest" doesn't roll off the Canadian tongue very easily. Our foreign policy statements often give the impression that Canada floats above the grubby and corrupt world of power politics. While *other* countries have interests, *we* have values. There are echoes here of Woodrow Wilson's disdain for the "old diplomacy" of the European great powers. It is also true that the moralistic streak in Canadian foreign policy has irritated our southern neighbour, leading one former US secretary of state to refer to Canada as the "Stern Daughter of the Voice of God" (see Cohen, 2003: 158). Canada's policy differences with the US, whether over Vietnam or the International Criminal Court, has been described, at best, as self-righteous and insufficiently appreciative of the complexities and burdens faced by a great military power, and, at worse, as armchair criticism by a country that can afford a values-based foreign agenda because the US effectively underwrites Canadian security.

A number of commentators have recently called for a softening of this stern voice. Thomas Axworthy argues that Canada is damaging its all-important relationship with the United States through its "all talk no action" approach to foreign policy. We might feel virtuous, Axworthy (2004) claims, but – in a nice twist on Ralph Emerson – "virtue is not reward enough." We need to get back to basics, and reinvest in the things that serve Canadian interests. Allan Gotlieb, in his riveting historical overview of Canadian foreign policy since 1945, decries the tendency of Canadian foreign policy to oscillate between realism and romanticism. In Gotlieb's view, Canadian policymakers must break away from the romantic utopianism that puts the United Nations, rule-making, and the promotion of the country's values at the top of the foreign policy agenda. In today's world of uncertainty and turmoil, he argues, "Canada must adopt a reality-based foreign policy by responding to the imperatives of geography, history and economics" (Gotlieb, 2004: 4). Jack Granatstein's line is even tougher. His target is the Lloyd Axworthy era in Canadian foreign policy, which was marked by its pursuit of a human security agenda. During this period, Granatstein suggests, we allowed our 'hard' foreign policy assets, particularly the Canadian military, to decline. According to Granatstein, Canada must not mistake "its loudly professed values" for its national interests. "Moral earnestness and the loud preaching of our values ... will not suffice to protect us in this new century" (Granatstein, 2003: 27).

Add to this one of the contributors to this volume, Derek Burney, and you have a powerful caucus of national interest promoters. In his 2005 Simon Reisman Lecture, Burney warns that if we indulge fancifully about bringing our values to the world, Canadians will be "confined more permanently to the periphery as a dilettante, not to be taken seriously" (Burney, 2005: 5). We must deal with the world as it is, he opines, not as we may wish it to be.

These are tough words, coming from some of the most respected names in Canadian public policy. But let's consider them a little more closely.

The debate between realism and romanticism is in many ways reminiscent of the interwar period, when the discipline of International Relations itself developed. At that time, the "realist school" of international relations appeared – largely in contrast to the "idealists," such as Woodrow Wilson, who dared to believe that the world needed more law and institutions if it was to avoid the kind of carnage wreaked upon Europe between 1914 and 1918. E.H. Carr, the most eloquent of the opponents of inter-war utopianism, penned a masterful critique of the illusions of that age in his book *The Twenty Years Crisis*. But he also wisely reminded us to be wary of so-called realism. "In politics," he wrote, "the belief that certain facts are unalterable or certain trends irresistible commonly reflects a lack of desire or lack of interest to change or resist them ..." (Carr, 1984: 89). For Carr, it was always dangerous to assume that whatever succeeds is necessarily right.

There are four main points I want to make about the call for greater realism and attention to the national interest in Canadian foreign policy. The first involves a closer inspection of what we mean by "reality." The second and third challenge the juxtaposition of values and interests, and call for a new and more expansive notion of the "national interest." Finally, I suggest that a key driver of a strategic foreign policy is identity: who, and what, Canada is, and will become, in the twenty-first century.

WHOSE REALITY?

To begin, let me state my agreement with the "wisemen": we need a reality-based foreign policy. But does acknowledgement of this premise require us to accept the version of reality being offered? Realism, Carr argues, turns out in practice to be just as influenced by particular views and preferences as any other mode of analysis: "even if it uses realist weapons to dissolve other values, it still believes in the absolute character of its own" (Carr, 1984: 92). We must remember that we live in a *social* world. While there are certain unalterable facts, the "rubber hits the road" when we begin to interpret them and tease out the implications for foreign policy. So what, exactly, is the global reality of the twenty-first century?

There is first, and foremost, the reality of power. Call the United States whatever you like – a hyperpower, a hegemon, an empire – but there is little doubt that we are living in a unipolar world, particularly when measured in military terms. Yet, it is also clear that there are other emerging powers, such as China, India, and Brazil, who are already exerting their influence in ways that affect Canadians. This, too, is *reality*. Countries like China and India aren't just markets to tap into; they are the potential leaders of a future multilateral system. As such, we have an interest in ensuring that in the decades ahead, they are embedded into a global governance structure that continues to reflect Canadian interests.

In addition, there are significant limits to American power. Financially, the size of the US economy still allows it to dominate global investment flows and to sustain a large current account deficit. But the degree of freedom the US has enjoyed is shrinking, thanks to its excessive spending. Each day, the US needs to attract approximately US$2 billion in capital to finance its current account deficit; its sources are private investors and foreign governments. To put it another way, it is foreign debt holders, primarily in Asia, who are bankrolling the robust "Jacksonian" moment in US foreign policy.[8] It is the decisions of key central bankers in Japan, China, Taiwan, South Korea, Hong Kong, and India about their US reserve holdings – perhaps even more than the statements of Alan Greenspan – that have the greatest effect on US interest rates. In November 2004, when the Federal Reserve Chairman intimated that the US trade deficit was looking "increasingly less tenable," the Dow Jones fell 115 points and the dollar lost 0.4 percent of its value against the Euro. In February 2005, when a Bank of Korea spokesman hinted that his country might want to diversify its exchange reserves away from dollars, the effect on markets was much more dramatic: a 174 point plunge for the Dow and a 1.4 percent decrease in the dollar's value against the Euro. This is a vivid illustration of how the balance of power in the global economy has shifted.[9]

Politically, the same point can be made. The 9/11 attacks were swiftly followed by an awesome display of American military power against the Taliban regime in Afghanistan. While the US military had held back some of its war-fighting potential in the 1999 Kosovo War, in December 2001 it left nothing to chance. But did the application of military prowess translate into a political solution that the US preferred? According to the first finance minister of post-Taliban Afghanistan, Ashraf Ghani, US power proved necessary but insufficient. A much more intangible phenomenon, legitimacy, was needed to bring about a political settlement. It was only the United Nations – in the form of the secretary-general's special representative – that could create the conditions for a political stability. This, too, is *reality*.

Even in the realm where the US seems unrivalled, military power, there are small but significant signs of weakness. As of April 2005, the US had approximately 135,000 troops in Iraq, but almost half of these were drawn from the reserves or National Guard. As Niall Ferguson has argued, today the United States "suffers from a personnel deficit": the 500,000 troops that it can deploy overseas are not enough to win all of the conflicts the US has to, or might in future have to, fight (Ferguson, 2005: 73). More significantly, the military resources of the US cannot be used in a vacuum: they often require the support, or at least tacit consent, of others. During the recent military action against Iraq, the Turkish parliament's refusal to allow the US to transport ground troops across its soil, and Saudi Arabia's reluctance to give Washington permission to use its air bases, greatly affected the conduct and cost of the war to the United States. This is an interesting example of where "soft balancing can have real effects on hard power" (Nye, 2004: 27).

The second reality to explore is the US-Canada relationship. The proponents of realism, as suggested above, believe that Canada must put the United States front and centre in its foreign policy. For both Gotlieb and Burney, Canada's best foreign policy years were those in which our officials enjoyed a close relationship with government officials in Washington. Yet what is the state of that relationship today? Looking at the facts, it's hard to argue for a "special relationship" – at least in the way the discipline of international relations conceives of the term.[10]

It is also debatable whether Canada could restore to itself the role of bridge to, or interpreter of, the United States for the rest of the world. This is a vocation the British prime minister, Tony Blair, tried to appropriate to himself, with limited success, during the first term of the George W. Bush presidency. But the competition for the part of bridge builder goes even further. In this first decade of the twenty-first century, when the US stands as the world's only superpower, countries *everywhere* are scrambling to understand and influence what is happening in Washington. One need only consider the foreign coverage of the 2004 US Presidential election: foreign journalists traveled to every nook and cranny of the American heartland. Such an important task – understanding the United States – cannot be left to an interlocutor, like Canada. Foreign governments are intent upon establishing their own channels of knowledge and influence.

Let me be clear: Canada and the United States have a deep partnership, built on more than two centuries of close economic, political, and personal ties. Canadians and Americans intermingle constantly, both professionally and personally, and we have together built a regional economy that has outstripped all expectations in terms of trade expansion and economic growth. This is a substantial achievement, and something Canadians can take great pride in. Moreover, Canada and the US can and should continue to pursue economic, security, and political cooperation where it enhances the safety and well-being of citizens in both countries. Canada should also continue to collaborate with the US globally on issues of joint concern. The use of the word "continue" is deliberate: too many Canadians overlook the reality of our past collaboration with the US (whether historically, in the building of post-1945 international institutions or, more recently, in missions to countries such as Haiti and Afghanistan). There is also a tendency to deny that many of the values that Canada promotes internationally are values that we *share* with the United States; democracy, the rule of law, human rights, and an enhanced role for the private sector in development. The values and priorities of the US and Canada are not identical; nor are our means of pursuing them. But why is it considered heresy to admit some overlap?[11] While Michael Adams' research shows that the socio-cultural values of Canadians and Americans are diverging (see Adams, 2003), the same cannot be said for *political* values – such as the commitment to individual freedom, the degree of confidence in government institutions, and levels of national pride (Boucher, 2004).

Yet, does any of this mean that Canada and the United States have a "special relationship" or that Canada is America's *best* friend? I would suggest not. This isn't a normative statement; it says nothing about what kind of relationship Canada might *want* to have with its southern neighbour. I'm only questioning whether "best friend" is the phrase that Americans would use to describe Canada (and Canadians) today.

In a post-9/11 world, in which the US feels under siege, its greatest priority is to secure the American people and the American way of life. The al-Qaeda attacks, in the words of Secretary of State Condoleezza Rice, "crystallized America's vulnerability" (Rice, 2004) and put the idea of threat – even more than power – at the forefront of the Bush Administration's foreign policy. The strategies to secure America are new; they are in many ways departing from the traditional alliances that defined our world in the past. On the eve of his first official trip to Europe, in the summer of 2001, newly elected George W. Bush dared to ask his foreign policy advisors: "Do we want the European Union to succeed?" (cited in Ash, 2004: 102). Such a question looks remarkable when compared with the substantial US commitment to Europe during the Cold War. But the sentiment revealed a shift in America's conception of its strategic priorities – a shift that intensified after the terrorist attacks of 11 September 2001. The Bush Administration's so-called war on terror is reaching out to new 'friends' around the world, who share the same assessment of the threat and have particular assets at a particularly opportune moment. And what does the US need from others to further its security agenda? Intelligence. Airports. Transport routes. Political support. Many states can and will offer these things. Canada will not always be among them.

Today, the US is working through ad hoc coalitions rather than long-term partnerships. As Defense Secretary Donald Rumsfeld (2001) once put it: "the mission determines the coalition, rather than the other way around." One example of this trend is the co-operation between the US and two states of "new Europe," Romania and Poland. Given its strategically important location close to the Middle East and Central Asia, and its willingness to provide the US with bases, Romania has quickly become one of Washington's new friends and has been rewarded with US support for its entry into NATO. Similarly, Poland's commitment of troops to the war against Iraq was rewarded with a zone of occupation in northern Iraq once military hostilities ended. In contrast, some of America's longest-standing supporters throughout the Cold War, such as Germany, were left outside the tent and certainly off the list of countries whose businesses received lucrative contracts to re-build Iraq. The US has also been reluctant to support Germany's push to acquire a permanent seat on an enlarged Security Council.

Rejecting the mantra of America's *best* friend is not to deny the very real links that exist between the US and Canada. As I argued above, our interdependence is substantial, and growing. But it does mean that Canada should stop trying to claim, or to prove, that it has a special relationship. The very idea is unhelpful. In the words of John Herd Thompson, head of Duke University's Canadian Studies Program: "There isn't any special relationship between the United States and anybody, much less Canada. American policy toward Canada pretty much conforms to American policy towards other countries. It serves what the US perceives is in its national interests at any particular time."[12] The Bush administration's preference is to "cherry pick" its allies, according to specific issues and challenges. We must also remember that our status will largely be a function of "what we have done for the US lately." When asked in June 2003 who was their best friend, the American public chose Britain, due to the substantial diplomatic and military commitment shown by Prime Minister Blair during the campaign to unseat Saddam Hussein (Pew, 2003). But new challenges, and new "coalitions of the willing," may change this assessment.

The third reality to consider is the different ways of affecting change, and spreading democracy, in contemporary international relations. The US is demonstrating one, very bold strategy, in its use of force to promote regime change in the Middle East. But the European Union has shown us another. I would argue that Europe's greatest foreign policy success (despite the challenges of referring to a coherent European foreign policy) is EU enlargement. The success began with Spain and Portugal, who joined the community in the 1980s, but it has continued with the latest round of new EU member states. Europe has engaged in peaceful and progressive democratization through the shrewd use of diplomacy and accession criteria. This, too, is *reality*. Before we accept the all-too-easy generalizations about Europe, let's look more carefully at the "zone of peace" they have maintained, and extended, on a continent that only 60 years ago was wracked by a conflict that took the lives of so many young men, including Canadians. The process could even end up with Turkey as part of the EU – which would mean that Europe would border Iraq.

Finally, the reality of contemporary international relations includes institutions. These are not only 'bricks and mortar' organizations, such as the UN and WTO, but also looser rules and forms of collaboration, such as the G20 meeting of finance ministers. To be sure, these institutions exist alongside power, and particular relationships, but they continue to serve functions and purposes that are vital to state interests. However much of the traditional institutions (such as the UN) require reform, their capacity to confer legitimacy on state action matters even to the most powerful members of the international community. We need only consider the challenges faced by the US and the UK, as occupying powers, in reconstructing Iraq after the conclusion of military hostilities.

Canadians are often accused of "fetishizing" the United Nations. While there is some validity in this criticism, there is a strong *pragmatic* case for multilateralism that Canada (alongside other states) can and should be making. First, as the US found in both Afghanistan and Iraq, multilateralism can be an excellent way of sharing financial and military burdens and risks. Second, multilateral fora like the UN Security Council provide a means for legitimising action through collective deliberation, justification, and substantive assessment. These processes help to ensure that narrow interests or particular ideological concerns are filtered out of an action. And states will continue to value that legitimacy as a way of improving the way their actions are perceived (both by those affected and by the broader international community). Finally, multilateralism is actually the *only* means for tackling some of the global problems we face in this new century: infectious disease, global finance, the environment, and global terrorism. These kinds of issues do not yield easily to national action alone, or narrow coalitions of the willing. Arguably, this is the most significant reality that Canadian foreign policymakers must face.

VALUES AND INTERESTS:
A FALSE DICHOTOMY

My second main point concerns the tendency of many recent critics of Canadian foreign policy to champion interests over values. As tempting as the interests-before-values mantra is, it is futile to think we can abandon a values-based agenda. We live in a democratic society, where the values and principles we stand for will inevitably form part of our activities on the international stage. To return to Carr's insights: "It is noteworthy that the attempt to deny the relevance of ethical standards to international relations has been made almost exclusively by the philosopher, not by the statesman or the man in the street" (Carr, 1984: 154).

Values help to forge cohesion across a huge territorial mass and diverse population. They help to make both collective action, and collective judgment, possible. Furthermore, the values Canada projects globally help to define who we are. Foreign policy is partly an exercise in forging national identity. Rather than trying to deny or hide this fact, we should recognize this as part and parcel of our contemporary world. Consider the United States, which portrays itself as the leader of the free world, or China, which defines itself as the guardian of the developing world. It is artificial to juxtapose interests and values, as if the former were selfish and narrow, and the latter ethical and internationalist. In reality, values and interests work much more in tandem.

It is curious that commentators such as Gotlieb think that Canada is unique in swinging between realism and idealism, or that the concern with values is somehow a peculiarly Canadian problem. Countless books and articles have been written over the course of the last century on precisely the same oscillation in US foreign policy. And there are well-known commentators, such as Henry Kissinger, who continue to lament the American proclivity for moralism. In a recent article, he complains that "the United States is probably the only country in which the term 'realist' can be used as a pejorative epithet" (Kissinger, 2005). Continuing on, in the vein of Carr, Kissinger argues that the debate between realism and idealism often misses the point: "The real issue is to establish a sense of proportion between these two essential elements of foreign policy" (ibid).

The nexus between values and interests is something that the United States instinctively understands and employs in its *own* foreign policy. Despite the widely held view that President George W. Bush's 2002 *National Security Strategy* was a defence of "realism" and unilateralism, the document actually lacked any careful and coherent articulation of US national interests. Instead, it is dominated by the notions of freedom and democracy, and links these historical themes of US foreign policy with a new willingness to use power to project them. The inaugural speech of Bush's second term was even more lyrical in its freedom agenda. Indeed, Canada is living next to a colossus which has today – perhaps more so than in three decades – a profoundly values-based foreign policy. Is this the time to become silent about values? Or do we too have something to say about freedom, democracy, pluralism, and equity? Is the agenda for change in international relations to be left entirely to George W. Bush and his advisers?

Far from being an irritant to Washington, as those like Granatstein suggest, values-based perspectives can make an impact, even in the Canada-US relationship. The defining factor will be whether such views are merely rhetorical jibes, or whether they are backed up by concrete ideas and policy commitments. During Canada's latest term on the UN Security Council, in 1999–2000, our representatives pursued policies that were grounded in Canadian values, such as the creation of the International Criminal Court and the Kimberley Process on conflict diamonds. While our perspective sometimes clashed with that of the US, our two governments 'agreed to disagree' and did not allow these differences to overshadow the larger set of issues on which Canada and the US do agree.

THE WIDENING OF THE NATIONAL INTEREST

My third point probes deeper into what we mean by the "national interest." The arguments of those such as Granatstein and Burney tend to assume that national interests are obvious and objective: if only we would recognize them, we would have a coherent foreign policy. But just as values can conflict, so too can interests: for example, protecting Canadian farmers versus lowering tariff barriers globally to bring about greater prosperity. We need only look at French President Jacques Chirac's statement after the referendum on the EU Constitutional Treaty to understand the challenges of articulating one, single national interest.

National interests don't fall from the sky. They are constructed by particular processes, people, and institutions.[13] It is analytically problematic to assume that this is a neutral and straightforward exercise. The "realists" may believe that Canada's national interests are practical and self-evident. But beyond the dictum to pursue prosperity and security – which seems pretty uncontroversial – what are the particular interests of Canada in an interdependent world? Those who dare to suggest that Canada might have an interest in pursuing trade and investment opportunities outside of the United States are instantly branded as promoters of the Trudeau-era "third option." But aren't such considerations also part of a prudent calculation of the long-term national interest? We are, after all, no longer the number one supplier of goods and services to the United States (the European Union and China have surpassed us). Nor is it clear that the *marginal* benefit of increased efforts to promote trade and investment in the US is greater than it would be for similar efforts in a major developing-country market.

The other reality to acknowledge is that countries find themselves sharing mutual interests more often than ever before. A key strength of Tony Blair's tenure as prime minister has been his ability to communicate to the British people about the challenges and opportunities of an interdependent world. One of his strategies has been to expand and deepen the traditional notion of the "national interest," and to demonstrate how values and interests work together. For example, during the Kosovo crisis in 1999, Blair contended that a response to ethnic cleansing could be compatible with the national interest once the notion of "nation" was widened to include the principles for which Britain stood. Britain, as a "civilised nation," had an obligation to respond and demonstrate horror in the face of "uncivilised" action. In a similar way, Blair's New Labour Government has argued that changes in the international system, driven by the forces of globalisation, have necessitated a wider conception of the national interest. As Blair proclaimed in his famous speech to the Labour Party Conference soon after the terrorist attacks of 11 September 2001: The critics will say: but how can the world be a community? Nations act in their own self-interest. Of course they do. But what is the lesson of the financial markets, climate change, international terrorism, nuclear proliferation or world trade? It is that our self-interest and our mutual interests are today inextricably woven together (Blair, 2001).

There are two implications of this logic: first, transnational forces (such as crime, the drugs trade, or weapons proliferation) become part of the national security agenda; and second, pursuit of the national interest requires steps to minimise the causes and effects of political and economic instability around the globe. This is why, for example, providing assistance to failed or failing states should not be seen as a squishy foreign policy ideal. It is firmly in the Canadian national interest to contribute to the creation of stronger and more capable states. As 9/11 showed us, weak states have as great a capacity to hurt us as strong states.

In the end, old parochial conceptions of the national interest are difficult to maintain when the challenges we face are interrelated, and when no one state – acting on its own – can make itself invulnerable. This also rings true for our commercial interests. As the scholar of international relations, Stanley Hoffmann (1987: 407), has put it: "We live in a world economy made of boomerangs, in which states are tied both by their mutual needs – or fears – and by the unforeseen effects of their own domestic decisions or external entanglements." In such an environment, purely national solutions become impossible.

IDENTITY FIRST

The final point I want to make about the values-interests debate is that it starts the discussion about Canadian foreign policy in the wrong place. Before interests and values comes identity: who we are. For many decades, the notion of "middle power" served as the shorthand for our global role and potential. But as I have argued, there are serious limits, both conceptual and practical, to the continuation of the middle power mantra.[14] Instead, three facets of the Canadian identity have become particularly salient for shaping foreign policy.

First, Canada is (relatively speaking), a highly successful liberal democracy. But it is also a liberal democracy of a special kind. In the words of the 2005 *International Policy Statement*:

Canada's continued success depends on the joint pursuit of democracy, human rights, and the rule of law. Though many countries share these values, we have moulded them into a particular constellation that reflects our historical experience and our current aspirations. Our overarching vision is an inclusive society, where the will of the majority is balanced by a commitment to minority rights. That vision unifies Canadians but also celebrates difference manifest in our official policy of bilingualism, our two legal systems, and our open immigration and refugee policy. Above all, it is a distinctly federal model, incorporating vast differences in size, population and resources between our provinces and territories ... This experience also underpins Canada's economic model. By wedding free market principles to a commitment to shared risk and equality of opportunity, we have produced both prosperity and equity. (Canada, 2005: 4)

While managing the partnership that is Canada has been a complex task, it has also developed the country's capacity to accommodate power and inequality – the very realities that we confront today in the international system. The features of the Canadian liberal democratic experiment also help to determine our objectives with respect to the promotion of global prosperity and security.

Second, Canada is a *North American* country. No matter how strong the affiliation with some aspects of Europe's economic model, or foreign policy, it is vital to remember our distinctiveness as part of a "new world." The spectre of the EU referendum campaign, and its scape-goating of immigrants, is a vivid reminder that diversity on this side of the Atlantic is much more deep-seated than in other parts of industrialized world. Our North American destiny is shared with the United States *and* Mexico: it is not in Canada's long term interests to ring-fence the Canada-US relationship and minimize opportunities for trilateral cooperation. The future agenda for that collaboration is not a mystery. It is laid out in the November 2004 *Joint Statement on Common Security, Common Prosperity: A New Partnership in North America*, which was issued by the prime minister of Canada and the president of the United States during George Bush's official visit to Canada.[15] In the domain of security, key initiatives include: enhanced critical infrastructure protection, increased collaboration on aviation and maritime surveillance, and implementation of new border security and bioprotection measures. In the economic sphere, the core priorities are: increased regulatory cooperation; the development of new sectoral strategies for energy, transportation, and financial services; the removal of "rules of origin;" costs on key categories of goods; and freer movement of highly skilled labour across the continent.

Despite the ambitious nature of the North American agenda, there is a third feature of Canada's identity that cannot be denied: our global concerns and responsibilities. Proximity to the US is a huge advantage to Canada, and one source of our national power (Rice, 2004: 124–5). But it is not – contra Gotlieb – Canada's *greatest* asset. And while the relationship with the US is Canada's most important foreign relationship, it is not and should not be the sole focus of our foreign policy. In short, Canada cannot choose between the United States and the rest of the world.[16] To do so would be to deny the kind of country we have become. Our country's commitment to the shape of today's world, as Canadian historians remind us, was not a mere token. It was real.

Thus, while Gotlieb argues that our geography, history, and economic context all point in the direction of a foreign policy defined as Canada-US relations, I think they point us to something slightly different. There are a series of factors compelling us to look beyond North America – not instead of pursuing a productive relationship with the US, but in addition to it.[17]

The first is geography. Because of its location, and massive coastline, Canada is both isolated and exposed. When you combine these facts with the existence of only one – and one very powerful – neighbour, you have an argument for developing a wide set of international relationships. The second factor relates to the size and nature of our economy. Canada's impressive rates of growth and budget surpluses during these first years of the twenty-first century have made us a valued member of the G8 and an obvious place to look for financial leadership on issues like global poverty and infectious disease. Membership in the international community carries with it responsibilities as well as benefits. There are two more significant reasons that Canada has aspired – and should continue to aspire – to act beyond the North American continent. Our immigration and refugee policy, combined with our changing ethnic make-up, constitutes one of these key drivers. Canada has quite literally opened itself to the world, and many parts of the world live within our borders. Hence, Canada's net migration rate is 6.0 migrants/1,000 population, compared with 1.37 migrants/ 1,000 population for Switzerland. A gap also exists between Canada's rate and that of the US (3.5 migrants/1,000 population). Thus, while 10 percent of the US population is foreign born, that figure is 18 percent for Canada.

A final factor pushing Canada to have a robust foreign policy is the nature of our twenty-first century world. Focusing only on the United States might have made some sense during the 1990s, when the West had won the Cold War and was enjoying an unprecedented level of security. But the post-Cold War era presents a host of new threats to international peace and security (such as transnational organized crime, poverty, environmental degradation, and terrorism), and to the safety and prosperity of Canadians. According to the recent report of the UN's High Level Panel addressing collective security, today's threats know no boundaries and must be addressed at the global and regional levels – not only at the national level.[18] Canadian foreign policy must actively address these threats, in collaboration with other actors on the international stage. It must contribute to the reform of existing institutions, and to the creation of new rules and structures to manage global problems. Canadian foreign policy must also build capacity in other members of the international community so that they too can contribute, both economically and politically.

In so doing, Canadian policy-makers must dare to entertain the notion that the United States will not be the world's only superpower forever. This is not to invite decline or ruin for the US. Rather, it is to do some prudent long-term planning. Canada's interests are best served if future superpower(s) are firmly embedded in international institutions and have been 'socialized' to cooperate with others in the management of common problems. This will require us to remain engaged in the world beyond North America's shores and to engage politically and diplomatically – not just commercially – with rising giants in other parts of the world.

CONCLUSION

A foreign policy that engages with vision and values will not doom Canada to irrelevance, or lead it into a utopian sunset. The world of international relations is not, and cannot be, devoid of power considerations. In fact, many commentators on the Iraq crisis seemed to forget that the United Nations Security Council itself, though an important normative feature of international society, is rooted in power politics. The vision of the Founding Fathers of the UN in 1945 was to bring together the world's greatest powers to manage threats to the international system – by making the prospect of their collective response a deterrent to those who sought to destabilize the post-war order. So, in proclaiming that "the international system must be ruled by law not power," the drafters of the 1995 foreign policy review, *Canada in the World,* were painting a false picture. Norms and values work together with power and interests in the world of 2005, just as they have done in the past.

Second, Canada does need a vision for its role in the world. Why? Because Canada must think more strategically about its role internationally. And a strategy, as I've defined it, requires choice. It also requires wise investment. A strategic vision will languish on the desktops of politicians and civil servants unless the resources to implement it are mobilized. This is the challenge now facing Canada – to stop talking about foreign policy, and to start doing it.

Let me conclude by returning to E.H. Carr. His wisdom, it seems to me, was in setting up a dialectic between realism and idealism – not championing one against the other. "All healthy human action, and therefore all healthy thought," he wrote, "must establish a balance between utopia and reality ... The characteristic vice of the utopian is naivety; of the realist, sterility" (Carr, 1984: 89). What Carr suggests, then, is that a split personality is not necessarily bad. Indeed, it might be healthy, as long as it doesn't mean violent swings between one and the other, but rather a way of thinking and acting that integrates both. In the end, the categories of realism and idealism have greater rhetorical value than they do analytical value. They allow us to condemn or applaud, but they rarely help us to understand or to move forward.

NOTES

The author thanks the Master of Massey College, John Fraser, along with the Fellows and students of the College, for the opportunity to present an earlier version of this chapter.

1 See, for example, the public opinion research report "Visions of Canadian Foreign Policy," conducted by Innovative Research Group for the Dominion Institute and the Canadian Defence and Foreign Affairs Institute, October 2004. Available at: <http://www.cdfai.org/PDF/DCI_CDFAI_report_formatted_V5.pdf>

2 These two traits are explored by the non-governmental organization, Canada25, in their 2004 report *From Middle to Model Power: Recharging Canada's Role in the World*. Available at <http://www.canada25.com>.

3 See, for example, Prime Minister Paul Martin's first speech to the United Nations General Assembly, 22 Sept. 2004. Available at: <http://www.pm.gc.ca/eng/news.asp?id=266>.

4 This is not to deny the increasingly important role being played by provinces and municipalities in Canadian diplomacy and commercial policy.

5 See *The National Security Strategy of the United States of America* (Washington, September 2002), available at: <http://www.whitehouse. gov/nsc/nss.pdf>; and *A Secure Europe in a Better World: European Security Strategy* (Brussels, December 2003), available at: <http://www. iss-eu.org/solana/solanae.pdf>.

6 The Government of Canada did issue its first *National Security Policy* on 27 April 2004, which was the first major initiative of the Department of Public Safety and Emergency Preparedness (PSEP), established on 12 December 2003. But while international security is one of six areas covered in the document, the main focus is on transportation, border security, and emergency management. See *Securing an Open Society: Canada's National Security Policy* (Ottawa: PSEP, April 2004). Available at: <http://www.pco-bcp.gc.ca/docs/publications/NatSecurnat/natsecurnat_e.pdf>.

7 For an overview of donor efforts to strengthen public institutions in developing countries, and the lessons learned, see Unsworth (2005).

8 I am referring to one of the four traditions of US foreign policy set out by Mead (2001). The "Jacksonians" are the most "muscular" of Mead's traditions, and argue for a more activist, and less isolationist, US foreign policy.

9 In the short term, Asian central banks have an incentive not to engage in dramatic action (given the effect a significant revaluation would have on

their countries' public finances), but many analysts agree that the current relationship between the Asian lender and American borrower is unsustainable. See Chris Giles, "Why George Bush should heed Asia's central bankers," *Financial Times*, 26–27 February, 2005.

10 See David Reynolds, "'A Special Relationship?' America, Britain and the International Order since the Second World War," *International Affairs*, vol. 62, no. 1 (Winter 1985–86): 1–20.

11 I would like to thank Richard Gwyn for drawing me out on this point.

12 Cited in Sheldon Alberts, "US losing faith in northern neighbour," *National Post*, 8 Feb 2003, A1.

13 For more on the process of defining the national interest, see Martha Finnemore, *National Interests in International Society* (Cornell University Press, 1996).

14 For an elaboration of this argument, see Welsh (2004: ch. 6).

15 In March 2005, at their meeting in Waco, Texas, Paul Martin, George W. Bush, and Vicente Fox expanded the partnership into a trilateral arrangement.

16 For more on the argument that Canada – particularly post-9/11 – no longer has the luxury of having a foreign policy with global reach, see Richard Gwyn, "Our foreign policy is making us invisible," *Toronto Star*, 23 Feb 2003.

17 For a more detailed version of this argument, see Jennifer M. Welsh, "Fulfilling Canada's Global Promise," *Policy Options*, vol. 26, no. 2 (Feb 2005): 56–59.

18 The full report is available at: <http://www.un.org/secureworld>.

REFERENCES

Adams, Michael. 2003. *Fire and Ice: The US, Canada, and the Myth of Converging Values*. Toronto: Penguin.

Ash, Timothy Garton. 2004. *Free World: Why a Crisis in the West Reveals the Opportunity of Our Time*. London: Penguin, UK.

Axworthy, Thomas S. 2004. "On Being An Ally: Why Virtue Is Not Reward Enough," Address to the Institute for Research on Public Policy, Ottawa, 1 April.

Blair, Tony. 2001. Address to the Labour Party Conference, Brighton, UK, 3 October. Available at: <http://politics.guardian.co.uk/labour2001/story/0,1414,562006,00.html>

Boucher, Christian. 2004. "Economic Integration Without Value Convergence," Paper presented to the Policy Research Initiative Conference, North American Integration: The Emergence of Cross Border Regions, Ottawa, 21–22 June.

Burney, Derek. 2005. "Foreign Policy: More Coherence, Less Pretence." Simon Reisman Lecture in International Trade Policy, Centre for Trade Policy and Law, Carleton University, Ottawa, 14 March.

Canada. 2005. "Overview," in *Canada's International Policy Statement: A Role of Pride and Influence in the World*. Ottawa: Department of Foreign Affairs and International Trade (DFAIT), 19 April.

Carr, E.H. 1984. *The Twenty Years Crisis: 1919–1939*, 2nd ed. London: Macmillan, 89.

Cohen, Andrew. 2003. *While Canada Slept: How We Lost Our Place in the World*. Toronto: McLelland and Stuart.

Ferguson, Niall. 2005. "Sinking Globalization," *Foreign Affairs*, vol. 84, no. 2. (March/April): 64–77.

Gotlieb, Allan. 2004. "Romanticism and Realism in Canada's Foreign Policy." C.D. Howe Institute Benefactors Lecture, Toronto, 3 November.

Granatstein, J.L. 2003. "The Importance of Being Less Earnest." C.D. Howe Institute Benefactors Lecture, Toronto, 21 October.

Greenhill, Robert. 2005. *Making a Difference? External Views on Canada's International Impact*. Toronto: Canadian Institute for International Affairs.

Hoffmann, Stanley. 1987. *Janus and Minerva: Essays in the Theory and Practice of International Politics*. Boulder: Westview Press.

Holmes, John. 1976. "Shadow and Substance: Diplomatic Relations Between Britain and Canada," in Peter Lyon, ed, *Britain and Canada: Survey of a Changing Relationship*. London: Frank Cass.

Kissinger, Henry A. 2005. "Realists vs. Idealists," *International Herald Tribune*, 12 May.

Mead, Walter Russell. 2001. *Special Providence: American Foreign Policy and How It Changed the World*. New York: Alfred Knopf, 231–50.

Nye, Joseph S., Jr. 2004. *Soft Power: The Means to Success in World Politics*. New York: Public Affairs.

Pew Global Attitudes Project. 2003. *Views of a Changing World 2003*. Washington, DC: The Pew Research Center, 3 June.

Rice, Condoleeza. 2002. "A Balance of Power that Favours Freedom." Sixteenth Annual Wriston Lecture, 1 October, Manhattan Institute, New York.

Rice, Susan E. 2004. "Canada's Relationship with the US: Turning Proximity into Power – An American Perspective," in Graham F. Walker, ed., *Independence in an Age of Empire: Assessing Unilateralism and Multilateralism*. Halifax, NS: Centre for Foreign Policy Studies.

Rifkin, Jeremy. 2004. *The European Dream: How Europe's Vision of the Future is Quietly Eclipsing the American Dream*. New York: Tarcher/Penguin.

– 2005. "Canada and the Blue States: A New Romance," *The Walrus*, vol. 2, no. 2 (March): 36–41.

Rumsfeld, Donald. 2001. Remarks on Face the Nation, CBS, 23 September.

Scowen, Reed. 2004. "Re-inventing Foreign Policy: A 'Model Citizen' Concept for Canada May Not Work," *Literary Review of Canada*, vol. 12, no. 10 (December): 23.

United Nations Development Program (UNDP). 2005. *Investing in Development: A Practical Plan to Achieve the Millennium Development Goals, The Millennium Project Report to the UN Secretary-General*. New York: UNDP.

Unsworth, Sue. 2005. "Focusing Aid on Good Governance: Can Foreign Aid Instruments Be Used to Enhance 'Good Governance' in Recipient Countries?" Working Paper, *Global Economic Governance Program* (February). Available at: <http://www.globaleconomicgovernance.org>.

Welsh, Jennifer. 2004. *At Home in the World: Canada's Global Vision for the 21st Century*. Toronto: HarperCollins.

3 The Perennial Challenge: Managing Canada-US Relations

DEREK H. BURNEY

In managing relations with the United States, the perennial challenge for any Canadian political leader is to find the right balance between a level of trust and engagement with Washington that anchors our substantial economic and security interests and a global role that accentuates distinct Canadian aspirations. The two are not incompatible but, over the years, various approaches have been attempted with equally varying degrees of consistency and achievement.

Under Pierre Trudeau, Canada identified the "Third Option" as a middle course between getting closer to or further from the United States. His government sought counter-weights to temper the growing economic dependence of Canada on the US market. That was triggered, in part, by the Nixon shock (10 percent withholding tax) and led, among other things, to the Foreign Investment Review Agency (FIRA), the National Energy Policy (NEP), the Contractual Link with Europe and a Framework Agreement with Japan. The latter two were reminiscent of John Diefenbaker's attempts to divert 15 percent of Canada's exports to the United Kingdom in the late 1950s just as the UK was turning more towards the continent and away from commercial preferences for the Commonwealth. Neither the Third Option nor the 15 percent diversion had the desired effect but both underscored what might be called the "Canadian conundrum" on foreign policy, trying to reconcile the notion that, as Robert Thompson once observed, "the Americans are our best friends whether we like it or not," with the recurring desire of Canadians (and Canadian leaders) to be perceived as distinct from America in world affairs.[1]

It is a difficult task because attitudes in Canada (and more recently in the United States as well), complicate what might be normal behaviour between neighbours whose linkages are as extensive as those between Canada and the United States. Many Canadians may in fact want to have a "good" relationship with the US but the definition of "good" can be open to lively debate and affected by the issues or personalities of the day. Some may prefer the geographic separation of Australia, or even the policy distinction of France. Many recognize the importance of the US to Canada in virtually all fields of endeavour but some resent it even though they understand it.

There are definitely streaks of anti-Americanism – latent and blatant – in Canada reflecting the wariness, the discomfort and the distaste of living along side the one and only global superpower.[2] These sentiments are stimulated not just by what Americans and their governments do but by the pervasive influence of America in the life of most Canadians, notably English Canadians – from books and magazines to television, from films and popular music to sports; from what Canadians eat to what they watch, read and hear; from where they shop to where they travel. It is not surprising, therefore, that Canadians see difference or distinction as an end in itself. Nor is it surprising that Canadian governments of all stripes strive rhetorically and sometimes quixotically, if not realistically, for a role in the world dissimilar to that of the United States.[3]

There is a penchant in Canada for more "independence" in foreign policy and great sensitivity to "sovereignty," labels that tend to confuse attitudes about how our interests can best be served and compound the challenge of efficient management of the bilateral relationship. For one thing, independence is not a legitimate objective for foreign policy. It is an illusion, especially in an increasingly inter-dependent world (North Korea enjoys a kind of "independence"). If by independent what is really intended is "something different from the United States," it may be easy to achieve but it is less likely to promote or protect tangible national interests and may well require major increases in government spending, e.g., on security, to be credible. International agreements of any kind – bilateral or multilateral – can be misconstrued as compromises of sovereignty even though they often reflect a level of consensus and commitment that improves prosperity and security, thereby strengthening the capacity for independent action.[4]

Very few Americans spend much time concerning themselves with Canada. Many tend to see Canadians benignly as being "just like Americans." Canadians can also be perceived as prickly or, at times, sanctimonious in their desire to proclaim distinctions in a manner once described by Dean Acheson as being like the "stern voice of the daughter of God."[5] More recently however, and reflecting heightened US concerns about security, there have been atypical streaks of anti-Canadianism in America, including from some influential, as opposed to fringe, elements (Senator Hillary Rodham Clinton comes to mind, as do Pat Buchanan and Fox News), and concern in some quarters about Canada's reliability on issues of greatest importance to Americans. When the apprehension or ambivalence of Canadians combines with indifference or, worse, annoyance among Americans, the management challenge can be formidable. By becoming more peripheral in Washington, Canadians may see themselves as more independent. In reality, we are simply less relevant.

The enormous power difference between the two countries compounds the difficulty of constructive engagement and concepts of closer bilateral cooperation. The Americans are singularly powerful, number one in many ways. They know it and act accordingly. Canadians know they are not number one and, in that sense alone, are much unlike Americans. Indeed, some celebrate their "not-American" status as the most distinct Canadian attribute! But Canadians also seem less certain about what or who they are other than "not-American." Being genuinely concerned about what the US may do with its awesome military power contributes not only to the unease but also to outbursts of moral superiority or high-mindedness, from time to time, by Canadians – what Michael Ignatieff described as the "besetting sin" of Canadian foreign policy.[6]

Canadians tend to forget that our systems of government are very different.[7] The locus of power in Washington can be elusive, depending on the issue. The president does have an awesome amount of military power at his disposal but the unique system of checks and balances helps fragment or separate many vestiges of day-to-day political power. Even if the White House wants to help resolve a particular bilateral problem, it cannot always get its way. It does help, however, when the Administration is inclined more to resolve rather than to prolong disputes and that is probably the best that can be expected from a positive tone between leaders. Nonetheless, Americans can be tough to deal with, whether in Congress, the Administration or at the State level. They play hardball, serving their own priorities, their own electoral constituencies and, increasingly these days, their own view of the world.[8] For Canada, this trend is accentuated by what some also suggest is a growing divergence in shared values, notably on social policy.

A Canadian prime minister has real power, day in day out, even with a minority government and without much military prowess. He can make decisions and set directions for domestic or foreign policy if and as he chooses to exercise this power. The prime minister can also lead and set the tone for managing our most vital foreign relationship. But, it is never easy to find "the right balance" with the United States and seldom rewarding in popularity terms, which also helps explain the quest for counterweights or diversions.

It can be tough, too, because the Americans no longer need as much in the way of alliance solidarity – a trump card many lesser powers, including Canada, used with effect during the Cold War. In a unipolar world, global issues like the Gulf War or the Iraq War become "defining moments" in Washington when others are seen to be either "with us or against us." And the more powerful the US becomes, the less tolerant it is likely to be to the sensitivities or nuances of others. The 9/11 attack and the war against terrorism simply heightened this tendency. The real choices and room for manoeuvre by US allies are therefore now more limited than ever. The tolerance for policy differentiation, especially poorly articulated differences, is smaller as well.[9]

Some contend that Canada could do more in world affairs by choosing multilateralism as a means to distance itself from the US and US positions. But distance and differentiation are not ends in themselves, nor are they substitutes for influence flowing from systematic engagement. A longstanding objective of Canadian foreign policy has been to try to keep the United States engaged constructively in supporting the multilateral system in order to temper unilateralism on the one hand, isolationism on the other. Canadians may pretend that multilateralism will, by itself, offset excessive dependence on the US but history demonstrates that, without American commitment and involvement, multilateralism has limited effect. It is difficult to imagine progress in global trade negotiations without consistent US leadership and commitment just as a more assertive "out of theatre" role by NATO depends in the first instance on the will and contribution of the United States. But, no matter how powerful American military capability has become, the US still values support and cooperation from its friends and allies. The need and the benefit can be mutual.

It is simplistic to suggest that Canada needs to "go along in order to get along." By building respect and trust through serious dialogue and by showing some sensitivity to fundamental US concerns, Canada can actually establish a credible platform from which contrary views will receive a fair hearing. This is especially the case when our contrary view is related to a distinct national interest (South Africa, Star Wars and Haiti are examples where this happened more than a decade ago). However, when a clear Canadian interest is not articulated as the reason for a "different" Canadian position, it can be difficult for Canadians, let alone Americans, to comprehend.

Canadians have every right and good reason to be apprehensive about what the United States will do, unilaterally or otherwise, with its massive military power. But, in order to influence decisions of that kind, we need to have something sensible to say and be ready to make a tangible commitment of our own. That may not be popular on the home front, which is probably why it is often avoided, but popularity should not be the best measure of influence or effectiveness in foreign or security policy.

Foreign policy practitioners must deal with what is real rather than what is desired. The fundamental objective of foreign policy should be to serve Canadian interests – promoting prosperity and security in a stable, more humane world – and the extensive economic, social, security and environmental interests we share on this continent with the United States are vital in that context – whether we like it or not.

We can seek to counter our proximity and extensive linkages to the United States with "weights," however calibrated, and with policy positions that differentiate or distance us from the United States. It is not an either/or, zero sum game but the implications of some differentiation can extend well beyond the fabric of our bilateral relations.

Virtually all aspects of Canadian public policy are affected by the relationship with the United States; when Canadians act as if the US factor is not consequential, we inevitably pay a heavy price. Two examples bear this out – the GST and the Kyoto Protocol. One can argue that Canada's action in each case was sound and in its own best interests but, by failing to take into account the very different position of the United States on each, Canada created additional burdens for itself. The fact that the same is not the case for the United States only compounds the challenge for Canadians involved in managing this relationship.

With the GST, and despite thorough analyses by the department of Finance, the government underestimated or ignored what Canadians would do initially to avoid paying the new tax. They shopped in droves across the border, spending billions of retail dollars in the United States rather than Canada and making the 1990–1991 economic downturn more severe in Canada than in the United States. They were saved, if that is the right term, from prolonged negative effects only by the fact that their dollar eroded in value to the point where cross-border shopping, even without the tax, was no longer advantageous (incidentally, American seniors are doing much the same in reverse, albeit on a much smaller scale, in purchasing less expensive Canadian pharmaceuticals).

The GST was an excellent tax initiative for Canada. It was consumption-based, the fairest form of taxation, replacing a hidden sales tax that had discriminated against Canadian manufacturers and exporters. It greatly enhanced the subsequent government's effort to transform the deficit into a surplus. The fact that Canadians rebelled against the tax initially by shopping in the United States simply proved that Canadian policies do not operate in a vacuum and that sovereignty has its limitations, even for Canadians! With the Canadian dollar again on the rise and the American dollar weakening, cross-border buying may once again intensify.

The difference on the Kyoto protocol has a potentially more damaging effect. Canada chose to ratify with the best of intentions, wanting to be in the vanguard of countries supporting action against global warming, even if its contribution will be marginal at best and even though the government has no real idea of the costs of implementation. More ominously, the Americans (and the Mexicans) have chosen not to ratify thereby giving them an automatic, perceived advantage over Canada with decisions on investment and expansion for our individual economies (among other things investors prefer certainty). Every advantage given the Americans has to find an offset somewhere – in productivity, tax rates or exchange rates – and it is a competition Canada is not winning.

What would have been a more practical and more effective course of action for Canada on climate change, in my view, would have been a call for a North American accord, challenging and engaging the United States (and Mexico) in the spirit of Kyoto to negotiate commitments to a mutually agreed amount of reductions in greenhouse gas emissions for our shared environment, much as we did in the early 1990s to combat Acid Rain. Tougher certainly than solemn declarations relatively free of substance, but unquestionably better in the long term for our economy and our environment. Better overall, but less compelling politically, which is probably why it was not contemplated.[10]

The American objection to Kyoto is based essentially on their view that the obligations would have been more onerous for them (and for Canada incidentally) than those negotiated by the Europeans. There is a sound basis for this concern, which only makes the notion of a North American solution as a step towards Kyoto more practical all around. But, as committed multilateralists, Canada chose the "high road" before we knew the price or the means to meet our obligation.

The impact of almost any domestic policy initiative by the United States can have a direct if not decisive impact on Canada. Changes to tax laws can affect not just American economic prospects but the relative competitiveness of Canadian firms, notably in terms of investment and productivity. This is particularly the case when so much bilateral trade is on an intra-firm basis. Canada can also be side-swiped, wittingly or unwittingly, by American actions directed at others, whether on trade or other issues. Although we may still share "the longest undefended border in the world," the border itself is increasingly becoming a topic for greater scrutiny and concern in Washington, reinforced by actions or attitudes on security issues that are perceived as reflecting a lack of priority in Canada for what Americans see as their uppermost priority.

I had the rare, if not unique, experience of day-to-day management responsibilities for the bilateral relationship from Ottawa and Washington respectively over a ten-year period – from 1983 to 1993. I experienced different trends of management, tone and achievement and spent a good deal of time analyzing factors influencing Canadian approaches and the results. My preferences reflect that experience. It is not difficult to play the differentiation game. In fact, assertions of difference almost certainly ignite warm headlines ... in Canada. But we should not confuse difference for the sake of being different with significance, influence, or even independence. It would have been much easer to sit on the sidelines and chirp against positions taken by the United States. However, if we choose to criticize or oppose the Americans from the sidelines, in high moral tones, as we did on Iraq or on Ballistic Missile Defence, we should not be unduly surprised if expressions of Canadian concern about bilateral issues – mad cow disease, or lumber, etc. – fall on deaf ears in Washington. A level of mutual trust is essential to smooth management and disproportionately more important to Canada than to the United States.

Over the years, various techniques have been used to manage relations, often determined by the mood of the moment. During a period of serious controversy in the early 1980s (prompted primarily by disputes over the National Energy Policy, FIRA, acid rain, and Canadian defence spending) quarterly meetings between the US secretary of state and Canada's secretary of state for External Affairs were instituted to try to contain the differences. These meetings may have helped temper the tone at the time but they achieved little in terms of resolving disputes. Mr. Trudeau's 'peace crusade' did not help, notably because his premise seemed to position the US and the USSR as being morally equivalent.

For the 1984 election we, as officials, prepared a memorandum offering a blueprint of ideas to refurbish the relationship and, essentially, harness our proximity more to Canada's advantage. When the Mulroney government was elected it proceeded to implement many of these ideas. The quarterly meetings between ministers were sustained but, significantly, annual Summits involving the prime minister and the president were initiated and became the dominant mechanism to shape and drive the agenda. These summits and the strong commitment by the two leaders improved the tone generally and inspired success in the negotiation of the Free Trade Agreement (FTA) (in 1987), an Agreement on transit through the Northwest Passage (1988) and an Acid Rain accord (1991). Special envoys were appointed to contain differences and propose solutions on the latter two. In this period, the manner for handling differences was best described by Joe Clark who declared that "we should be able to disagree without being disagreeable." George

Shultz's attitude was more graphic, "if you want to kick us in the shins, do it in private, we get the message just as well."[11]

Despite the positive chemistry at the top between Prime Minister Mulroney and President Bush, the management of bilateral disputes, especially on trade and environmental issues, was at the centre of Embassy activity during my tenure (1989–93). There was no magic formula for success. No longer was the State Department the exclusive channel of influence for Canada or other countries in the Washington "power game." Diplomats were obliged to play in all courts, asserting openly and vigorously positions to defend or promote their national interests.

Each bilateral dispute required different tactics and we did not always win. It can be frustrating when you are pressing for solutions in a system where the scope for restrictions is broader than the avenues for redress. The general objective for the embassy in my time was to debate forcefully with our opponents while trying to build coalitions of support wherever possible from those constituents who would suffer from US restrictions on specific Canadian products. On softwood lumber, for instance, this meant rallying the US Homebuilders Association, namely those consumers who would pay higher prices if duties were applied to Canadian imports. On wheat, we turned – more successfully – to processed food, e.g., pasta manufacturers.

Retaliation is always tempting in theory but, when you are only one-tenth the size of your adversary, retaliation has to be very selective, exercised prudently and, preferably, in good company. Linkage was another temptation. "You hit our softwood; we will curtail energy exports." Very appealing perhaps on the surface, but never seriously contemplated because of the spiral of unintended consequences such action could provoke. The embassy's basic objective on trade disputes was to try to curtail or at least contain damage, preferably before action against Canada became legislated, and prevent matters from escalating into an all-out trade war. For effective redress, we held firmly to the rule of law and the dispute settlement mechanisms of the FTA and NAFTA.

No one should assume that a positive chemistry between the prime minister and the president, along with the provisions of the FTA, made the challenge of managing day-to-day trade relations easy. Invoking the tone of relations at the top did help open doors and generally prompted constructive efforts by some in the Administration, but Congress was and is a force unto itself. Some examples will illustrate the challenge. No trade dispute has been as frustrating, costly and, inconclusive, as the long running battle over softwood lumber. All the goodwill and positive tone from the leaders of our respective governments could not temper the fierce protectionist phalanx of US lumber producers, namely those in the Pacific Northwest and Southeastern United States. They have an enormous war chest that can sustain endless legal wrangling. They also have substantial political clout from key regions and senior personalities in Congress. Because the issue under dispute is a provincial responsibility, and the practice differs from province to province, the Americans also tended to use a crude, but effective, divide and conquer strategy to weaken Canada's resolve and eventually oblige our government to adopt, with provincial and even industry blessing, a managed trade solution at variance with the principles of free trade. (We seem headed in that direction once again in 2005.)

Canada came very close to not participating in NAFTA. The Mexicans wanted very much to learn from our Free Trade negotiating experience but, at least initially, were not sure about having us at their table. Mexico's minister of Commerce, Jaime Serra Puche, did make some preliminary soundings with Canadian ministers, as did some of his officials, but concluded that Canada was not keen to participate and might in any event constitute a drag on the negotiations.

The Americans, possibly because of the FTA experience, did not really want us either. Each had a bilateral agenda and neither saw the need or advantage of a role for Canada. In Canada, there was little enthusiasm for involvement, including at the Cabinet table. The country was in the throes of an economic slump. Support for the FTA had waned sharply and there was little appetite for more free trade. Besides, and despite the FTA, we still had a host of trade irritants with the United States.

Views in Canada were, in fact, more negative than positive. There was free-trade fatigue at the political level and little enthusiasm at the bureaucratic level. Nonetheless, some of us were convinced that Canada had to be at the table primarily to preserve what we had negotiated in the FTA and to prevent the United States from implementing a hub and spoke approach of different preferential agreements throughout the hemisphere. That could undercut our desire to maintain a competitive platform for investment in Canada as well as an open environment for trade. The prime minister and his key economic ministers – Mike Wilson and, eventually, John Crosbie – were of the same view but we had to lobby hard in Washington to secure a seat and an equal voice in the negotiations.[12]

I had several sessions with senior Administration officials, including the secretary of state and several White House aides, to make our case as firmly as I could. The prime minister raised our desire to participate both with the then President Bush and the Mexican President Salinas. That made it difficult for either to resist. But the American Administration was under pressure from key senators, like Lloyd Bentsen of Texas, who wanted a negotiation exclusively with Mexico for political as well as economic reasons and did not want matters "complicated" by Canada. I met Bentsen and other concerned senators as well as key congressmen to reinforce our wish to participate.

The Administration was concerned that we would not only complicate the negotiations by reopening issues left over from the FTA but also that we would delay ratification beyond the point of no return. They were mindful, belatedly, of the enormous political challenge the FTA had posed for Canada and may have been worried that we would face more of the same. By then the polls were not favourable to the Canadian government and the Opposition Liberals were openly opposed to NAFTA.

In the event, Mr Mulroney's intervention at the top proved decisive and, after giving solemn pledges that we would neither complicate nor delay proceedings, Canada was invited to join the negotiations. In due course, according to both Mexican and American negotiators, Canada played a constructive role throughout under the able leadership of our chief negotiator, John Weekes and our trade minister, Mike Wilson. It was, in fact, the Americans who ultimately delayed ratification. Additionally, it is interesting to note that despite campaigning fiercely against NAFTA during the negotiations, the Liberal government of Jean Chrétien approved it quietly shortly after the 1993 election.

In a lighter vein, there was one potential trade problem that did get resolved in a timely, if unusual, manner. A Manitoba printer of lottery tickets had won a significant order in Mexico and planned to ship the tickets by truck through the United States. Unfortunately, this shipment would have run counter to a nineteenth century piece of US legislation prohibiting the shipment of "gambling devices" through the United States. The company had appealed to the embassy for help and I was advised that we might try to enlist the support of a friendly senator to request a waiver of the restriction from the Senate. This, in turn, would work but only if there was no dissent.

A few weeks earlier, my wife, Joan, and I had accompanied Senator Bob Dole and his wife on a semi-official visit to Ottawa. That acquaintance was sufficient for me to call the senator – the minority leader at the time – to see whether he might help get the necessary waiver. After all, the sale was not jeopardizing any US economic interest. Senator Dole was more than happy to oblige and asked me to fax him the particulars. I did so and, shortly after, watched on TV as Senator Dole read the request on the Senate floor. He then handed it to a Senate page. To my surprise, a Democrat in the Senate at the time casually scanned the resolution and rose on a point of order declaring that the top of the page said clearly "Fax Canadian Embassy." "Exactly who is the honorable gentleman from Kansas representing in making this request?"

he asked. A somewhat sheepish Senator Dole acknowledged quickly that he was indeed making the request on behalf of "our friends and neighbors to the north."[13] And the waiver went through unopposed. I often thought, however, that if something similar had happened in the Canadian Parliament – a government minister acting on the basis of a fax from the US embassy – there would have been cries of interference galore and some genuine fireworks. I also used this incident to illustrate the intrinsic value of goodwill in diplomacy (and from senatorial visits).

On balance, and despite the difficulties of a soft economy in 1990–91, I believe we made progress on the trade agenda. Some disputes will never die but the FTA, and subsequently NAFTA, are serving Canadian interests well. As both the United States and Canadian economies recovered in the mid-1990s, the benefits of greater, more secure market access generated unprecedented growth in bilateral trade, so much so that some of the fiercest opponents of the trade agreements became their strongest champions. It also became clear to me from my stint in Washington, however, that Canada needed more than a positive tone at the top to ensure efficient management and to help contain the shock of unexpected events.

When the Liberals returned to office in 1993 there was less inclination in either capital for regular summits or quarterly ministerial sessions, let alone anything new. Instead, a task force was established in the Privy Council Office (PCO) to help manage relations, signalling the desire for a coherent approach from Ottawa to the management of our key relationship. During this period, it is important to note that President Bill Clinton did inject himself into Canada's national unity debate in a manner that went well beyond the traditional US position but undoubtedly reflected his personal friendship with Prime Minister Chrétien as well as more basic concern in the United States about the stability of its northern neighbour. In this instance, Canada's national unity transcended the normal constraints of American foreign policy.

A period of general somnolence in bilateral relations came to an abrupt end with the 9/11 attack and immediate actions by the US to close its borders. The impact on Canada was profound as was (and is) the longer-term threat. Under the lead of Deputy Prime Minister John Manley and his counterpart, Homeland Security Director Tom Ridge, the governments quickly scrambled to put in place Smart Border measures, intended primarily to ensure greater security while at the same time facilitating relatively efficient movement of goods and people across our shared border.[14] However, Canada's open opposition to the Iraq war and some intemperate remarks by government officials undermined this effort and added new strain to the relationship.

In late 2003, Prime Minister Martin came to office determined to place relations with the United States on a more positive footing. He strengthened the role of the PCO for day-to-day management (at the expense of the Department of Foreign Affairs and International Trade), created a special Cabinet Committee on Canada-US relations under his lead and appointed a parliamentary secretary for Canada-US relations reporting directly to him. While the intent to upgrade management was clear from these structural initiatives, as well as from the press release issued during President Bush's visit to Canada in November 2004, tangible results have been less evident. Nor has there been much indication that Washington is reciprocating with management upgrades of any kind for Canada. In any event, these attempts to project a more positive tone from Ottawa were hobbled by Canada's abrupt and unexpected decision to "stand down" on Ballistic Missile Defence after the prime minister and several of his cabinet colleagues had given the impression that Canada would participate. The Americans (as well as many Canadians), were at a loss trying to understand how this decision on missile defence served Canada's interests. What it will do is reduce sharply whatever potential influence Canada might have had with the US on the anti-missile project or on security issues more generally in North America and at a time when security concerns continue to be paramount in Washington. Canada may have the advantage of geographic proximity but this also tends to give us the luxury of vacillation (or the pretence of independence) on matters related to our own security.[15]

In March 2005 the three leaders of Canada, Mexico, and the US met in Texas and announced a "Partnership for Prosperity and Security" but the sentiment and rhetoric for greater cooperation among the three North American entities seemed stronger than the will.[16] For one thing, neither the Mexican president nor the Canadian prime minister was in a strong political position on the home front. Each also has had sharp disagreements with the US on issues pertaining to security and both are embroiled in seemingly intractable trade disputes with the United States (on cement and lumber, respectively). Furthermore, the common ground for new arrangements among the three is pragmatically much less than what might be possible for Canada or Mexico individually on a bilateral basis with the United States. At best, any concept of trilateralism would have to proceed at two speeds and on two distinct tracks. The "Partnership" announced stopped well short of the "North American Community" concept that had been proposed a few days earlier by a private trilateral group sponsored by the Council on Foreign Relations in association with its Mexican counterpart and the Canadian Council of Chief Executives.[17] Instead, the political trio chose a workmanlike, incremental line of least resistance – to harmonize wasteful, inefficient regulations and standards and to bolster border security cooperation. Whether these announcements will be sufficient to paper over larger disagreements or to attenuate the wariness in Canada and Mexico about US unilateralism remains to be seen. What was most evident from this Texas summit was a general reluctance at the top political level for a deeper commitment to continental integration.

Access is the lifeblood of diplomacy. It is determined by relevance, trust and a capability to deliver when and where it counts. The personal qualities and the interpersonal chemistry between leaders can make a difference even if it is limited. They affect the tone and can help set the basic direction for bilateral relations but they cannot override the system of governance on issues. When leaders get along – as Mulroney did with Reagan and Bush – they converse frankly and frequently. Their priorities become priorities for others in each government. Officials try harder to forge solutions rather than stimulate complications. When the relationship is sour or cool, as it was for Trudeau with Nixon and Reagan or for Chrétien and Martin with George W. Bush, the opposite is true. Access and influence is by the book; nothing more, nothing less. And, when Prime Minister Martin has difficulty getting an answer to his phone calls, there is a fundamental problem with access.

The long delayed *International Policy Statement*, issued in April 2005, offered some sensible analyses on the challenges ahead and called for a revitalization of security and prosperity objectives with the United States, but the prescriptions proposed cannot be construed as a strategy and are not likely to elicit stronger political leadership or commitment in either capital.[18]

Looking forward, pressures arising from the huge fiscal imbalance and the burgeoning trade deficit in the United States pose significant threats to Canada's well-being as well as to the global economy more generally. These, together with the prospect of a serious security breach or lapse along our border, represent the most serious future challenges to efficient management of our bilateral relationship. Whether we like it or not, the onus will be primarily on Canada to ensure that these security risks do not become reality.

Genuine efforts to improve both the tone and the substance of our relationship need first a clear injection of political will from the top, along with the stamina and fortitude to override emotional impulses of the day that can otherwise frustrate actions to bolster our mutual self-interest. Complacency or a lack of consistent political oversight will inevitably have more serious cost implications for Canada just as mismanagement and miscommunications carry disproportionately higher risks for Canada. We should not rely exclusively on the goodwill of individual leaders to sustain mutual benefit anymore than we should be distracted from what is in our best interest by negative attitudes about individual leaders. Therefore, in addition to systematic engagement at the top political level, the complexity and importance of relations with the United States warrant clearer commitments, more efficient dispute resolution procedures, and some creative institution-building. Canada should initiate early negotiations to renew NORAD and signal clearly our willingness to assume a larger role both for continental security and counter-terrorism. This by itself may facilitate a more positive response to ideas for new institutional underpinnings that would help make our border part of the solution not part of the problem between us. Border security, trade, energy and the environment are all sectors that would benefit from more mature and concerted institutional approaches. Attention to each would help diffuse political atmospherics (and personalities) of the moment and provide a more pragmatic basis for mutual benefit. New institutions should be considered that would enable both countries to use innovative technologies and procedures to underpin our growing interdependence and stimulate greater security and prosperity on our shared continent.

It may be frustrating to contemplate new agreements or institutions or deeper economic integration in the face of capricious, if not abusive, actions by the United States that undermine the efficacy of existing agreements. No matter how vexing this behaviour, Canada should continue to initiate and advocate new approaches and procedures to govern the relationship. Because, for Canada, better rules and better institutions, operating under clear commitments to contain and resolve differences and increase cooperation are not only sensible in their own right but are, ultimately, the best means of attenuating the huge power imbalance that otherwise bedevils the bilateral relationship. Furthermore, by establishing a more confident relationship with the United States, Canada would also be better positioned to play a more constructive role on global issues, especially where we have relevant capabilities, and in strengthening relations with countries whose significance is certain to expand during the balance of this century.

NOTES

This chapter is adapted from the author's 2005 Simon Reisman lecture, "Foreign Policy: More Coherence, Less Pretence," available at

<http://www.carleton.ca/ctpl> – and his memoir, *Getting It Done* (Montreal and Kingston: McGill-Queen's University Press, 2005).

1 Thomson quote cited in Bruce Little, "Domestic politics shows U.S. view of fair trade," *Globe and Mail*, 28 March 2002, B15. For a general history of the bilateral relationship, see J.L. Granatstein and Norman Hillmer, *For Better or For Worse: Canada and the United States to the 1990s* (Toronto: Copp Clark Pitman, 1991). Allan Gotlieb frames the challenge in "Foremost Partner: The Conduct of Canada-US Relations," in David Carment, Fen Osler Hampson, and Norman Hillmer, eds., *Canada Among Nations 2003: Coping with the American Colossus* (Toronto: Oxford University Press, 2003), 25.
2 For a thorough assessment of anti-American themes in Canadian history, see J.L. Granatstein, *Yankee Go Home? Canadians and Anti-Americanism* (Toronto: HarperCollins, 1996).
3 For an analysis of the trends of anti-Americanism in Canadian foreign policy attitudes, see Denis Stairs, "Challenges and Opportunities," *International Journal*, vol. 58, no. 4 (Autumn 2003): 503.
4 For a selection of articles which espouse foreign policy independence for its own sake, see Stephen Clarkson, ed., *An Independent Foreign Policy for Canada?* (Toronto: McClelland & Stewart, 1968). Although published almost 40 years ago, its irrelevance as a practical guide to foreign policy making has stood the test of time.
5 Margaret McMillan, "A new foreign policy? Not necessarily." *National Post*, 11 September 2003, A18.
6 See Michael Ignatieff, "Peace, Order and Good Government: A Foreign Policy Agenda for Canada," O.D. Skelton Lecture 2004, Department of Foreign Affairs and International Trade (DFAIT). Ottawa, 12 March, 2004. Available at <http://www.dfait-aeci.gc.ca/skelton/lecture-2004–en.asp>.
7 It is instructive, for example, to contrast the making of Canadian trade policy, as described by Michael Hart, *A Trading Nation: From Colonialism to Globalization* (Vancouver: University of British Columbia Press, 2002), with the making of US trade policy, as described by I.M. Destler, *American Trade Politics*, 4th ed. (Washington: Institute for International Economics, 2005).
8 A good, historical overview of US foreign policy can be found in Walter Russell Meade, *Special Providence: American Foreign Policy and How It Changed the World* (New York: Knopf, 2001). For a good description of the foreign policy of President George W. Bush, see Ivo H. Daalder and James M. Lindsay, *America Unbound: The Bush Revolution in Foreign Policy* (Washington: Brookings Institution, 2003).
9 Bill Dymond and Michael Hart provide a cogent analysis of the realities

for Canada of the hyper power world in "Canada and the Global Challenge: Finding a Place to Stand," *C.D. Howe Institute Commentary*, no. 180, (Toronto: C.D. Howe Institute, March 2003). Available at: <http://www.cdhowe.org/pdf/commentary_180.pdf>.

10 Warwick J. McKibbin and Peter J. Wilcoxen explore what such an approach would entail in *Climate Change after Kyoto: Blueprint for a Realistic Approach* (Washington: Brookings Institution, 2002).

11 This dialogue between Clark and Shultz is also described by John J. Noble, Remarks on Canada-US Defence Relations to the 21st Annual Conference of Defence Associations Institute's Seminar, Ottawa, 3 March 2005, 4. Available at: <http://www.cda-cdai.ca/seminars/2005/Noble05. pdf>.

12 For an account of how the Canadian decision to participate in NAFTA was reached, see Maxwell Cameron and Brain Tomlin, *The Making of NAFTA: How the Deal Was Done* (Ithaca, NY: Cornell University Press, 2000), 63–8. See also Michael Hart, *A North American Free Trade Agreement: The Strategic Implications for Canada* (Ottawa: Centre for Trade Policy and Law and Institute for Research on Public Policy, 1990).

13 For further elaboration on this event, see Burney, *Getting It Done*, 157.

14 The text of the Smart Border Accord is available at: <http://www.dfait-maeci.gc.ca/can-am/menu-en.asp?act=v&mid=1&cat=10&did=1668>. This site also provides convenient access to reports on the accord's implementation.

15 For a useful prescription see Thomas Axworthy, "On Being an Ally: Why Virtue Is Not Reward Enough," *Policy Options,* vol. 25, no. 6 (June-July 2004): 79–82. Available at: <http://www.irpp.org/po/archive/jun04/axworthy.pdf>.

16 The Crawford Declaration is available at: <http://www.pm.gc.ca/eng/news.asp?id=443>.

17 The Task Force's final report, *Building a North American Community,* is available at: <http://www.cfr.org/pub8102/cfr/building_a_north_american_comm unity.php>.

18 See *Canada's International Policy Statement: A Role of Pride and Influence in the World.* Ottawa: Department of Foreign Affairs and International Trade (DFAIT). Available at: <http://www.dfait-maeci.gc.ca/cip-pic/ips/ips-home-en.asp>.

4 A New Continental Consensus? The Bush Doctrine, the War on Terrorism and the Future of US-Canada Security Relations

JOSEPH T. JOCKEL and
JOEL J. SOKOLSKY

So, George W. Bush was right about Iraq. As a result, a new foreign policy consensus is emerging in the United States. Where does that leave Canada in terms of the future of its defence and security relations with the US? In a pretty good position. A consensus between both countries is quite possible, about both the pursuit of the Global War on Terrorism abroad and continental defence at home.

The very suggestion that Canada's situation with regard to security relations with the US might be favourable is likely to prompt scepticism from both the left and the right. For the anti-Bush, (and unfortunately) increasingly anti-American Canadian left, US foreign and defence policies have placed the country between a rock and hard place. If Canada does not buy into the American neo-conservative agenda, they say, the US will simply take matters into its own hand and increasingly apply its unilateralist defence policies, and perhaps its economic policies as well, toward Canada thereby compromising the country's security and prosperity. But if Ottawa does accept the Bush agenda, it will have compromised its multilateralist traditions, sovereignty and values (Sokolsky, 2005a: 324).

For the pro-US, and generally pro-defence right, any idea that Canada might be in an advantageous position in terms of security relations with the United States is dismissed as fanciful given the sorry state of the Canadian Forces (CF). How can Ottawa hope to cooperate fully with, and influence Washington, when the Canadian military is on the verge of disappearing? Doesn't Canada have to buy its influence back? And doesn't the Martin government's decision not to participate in the

US Ballistic Missile Defense (BMD) program fatally damage Canada's standing in Colorado Springs headquarters of the North American Aerospace Defence Command (NORAD)?

In reality though, and contrary to the left, there is no inconsistency between Canadian security and values and the policies undertaken by the Bush administration when it comes to the most vital issue in international security for both countries, the Global War on Terrorism. Moreover, the security and stability that American policies afford Canada and other allies actually makes it possible for Canada to pursue active internationalist foreign policies which include multilateral activity.

And although the CF has indeed become smaller and less capable of overseas operations, the Canadian military can still play a role in the American-led war on terrorism and in contributing to US homeland security by collaborating in the defence of North America. But Canada's modest capabilities will be of value only if they are matched with an overall approach to Canadian foreign and defence policy, which places Ottawa firmly and openly on the side of the United States in the war on terrorism – not just in North America, but overseas as well.

If the right decisions are made, despite the fall-out from Ottawa's mishandling of the Iraq War and BMD, then it may well be possible to fashion a new continental consensus on bilateral security relations to help win the war on terrorism, just as the Cold War consensus between Washington and Ottawa helped win that "long twilight struggle."

BUSH WAS RIGHT: THE US, CANADA AND THE GLOBAL WAR ON TERRORISM

The courage of the Iraqi electors has dispelled the notion that democracy was being externally imposed on an unwilling or unready people and has put an end to the obnoxious claim that the insurgent terrorists expressed the popular will. The Iraqi insurgency is being beaten, although it will remain able, in desperation, to exact a high cost in lives, both Iraqi and foreign. Up until the very eve of the Iraqi election the many congressional Democrats, including Senator Edward M. Kennedy, were still warning of the new, Vietnam-like quagmire. Now the US is contemplating an orderly and measured draw-down of its forces as the Iraqis gradually take control of their own country's security. As Fouad Ajami observed after a visit to Iraq, "The insurgents will do what they are good at. But no one [in Iraq] really believes that those dispensers of death can turn back the clock ... By a twist of fate, the one Arab country that had seemed ever marked for brutality and sorrow now stands on the frontier of a new political world" (cited in Krauthammer, 2005: A16).

Indeed, the overall, long-term approach Washington has taken to the Global War on Terror is now showing distinct signs of being vindicated. The Bush administration realized soon after 9/11 that in essence, the struggle was neither a law enforcement matter nor a Samuel Huntington-style clash of civilizations. Nor were the terrorists driven by any Third World set of economic grievances against wealthier countries, embodied especially by the US.

No, the struggle was to be yet another stage, as the American critic Paul Berman put it, in "the war between liberalism and the apocalyptic and phantasmagorical movements that have risen up against liberal civilization ever since the calamities of the First World War" (2004: 183). It would, in fact, *be* the Fourth World War, Norman Podhoretz concluded (2004: 17). Safety for the US was to be found not in the search for stability, but rather in its opposite: the promotion of fundamental change, starting with regime change in the Middle East. The Bushites saw that liberal democracy itself confronted Middle Eastern authoritarianism, be it in the form of Islamist theocracy, Baathist Arab nationalist thuggery, or Arafatist kleptocracy. Washington, in conjunction with many other countries, used force to topple the theocrats in Afghanistan and the thugs in Baghdad. And it cut off ties with the Arafat-led Palestinian Authority until the day he died.

The notion of regime change in Iraq did not begin with the Bush Administration. The Iraq Liberation Act of 1998, signed by President Bill Clinton made it US policy "to support efforts to remove the regime headed by Saddam Hussein from power in Iraq and to promote the emergence of a democratic government to replace that regime." The more active promotion of democracy has been a part of the US struggle against terror since the attack on Afghanistan; it was also among the reasons the US Congress listed in its authorization for the attack. But in the case of Iraq, it was overshadowed by the issue of weapons of mass destruction. The focus and scope of US efforts since have become clearer, especially after President Bush's second inaugural address in January 2005. Seeking to marry realism to idealism, he said, "the survival of liberty in our land increasingly depends on the success of liberty in other lands ... America's vital interests and our deepest beliefs are now one" (Bush, 2005). This profession of modern Wilsonianism was met around the world with enormous scepticism, until the Iraqis lined up to vote and showed their purple-stained fingers.

In sum, the early results have been encouraging. Democracy has come to both Afghanistan and Iraq in the form of participatory elections. The Lebanese demanded that the Syrian dictator end his occupation of their country. Elsewhere in the Arab world and broader Muslim world people are following intently what has been occurring in Iraq and there are some signs of liberalization in both Egypt and Saudi Arabia.

Yes, yes, the trends are not yet irreversible. We do well to remind ourselves that liberal movements can falter or be successfully repressed, as they were in Europe in 1848 and China in 1989. Things might still go wrong in Iraq and elsewhere. But as Eliot Cohen has noted, even as he called upon Americans to exercise "humility" and caution in the face of the undoubted success of the Iraqi election,

The election indubitably demonstrates the power of freedom, and the courage that love of it can elicit even in a terrorized population. Surely, even those so-called realists who disparaged the project of building civil society in Iraq share Lincoln's wish, expressed about another group, also believed incapable of self-rule, "that all men every where could be free." ... Most of the Arab world may hate America, but a disjointed yet palpable movement for reform has gathered strength. This movement has broken through in a few countries, it has sympathizers in the rest, who note the irony of free elections as a by product of American occupation. (Cohen, 2005: A18)

Abroad, even in Canada, the reassessments of the Bush foreign policy have begun. In Canada, Richard Gwyn led the way in his widely noted *Toronto Star* column. "Admit it," he wrote, "Bush was right on Iraq ... [but] wasn't right to invade Iraq" (2005: A13). Gwyn further argued,

But on the defining, fundamental question, Bush was right. He understood that to defeat an idea, no matter how perverse and brutal it might be, it was necessary to have an opposite and superior idea. He understood, in other words – instinctively, rather than intellectually – that the only way to win a war against terrorism was to turn it into a war for democracy. This is now happening. Against the quest of ordinary Iraqis for dignity and self-respect and freedom, the terrorists in Iraq had nothing ultimately to offer, except blood and hatred. Already, Palestinians and Afghans have made the same choice. Inevitably, many others elsewhere in the Arab and Islamic worlds are going to start to wonder why those choices are still denied to them.

The position that the Democratic Party takes in the US may now be critical. Many commentators have drawn parallels between the early years of the Cold War, 1947–1952, and these early years of the Global War on Terror, albeit with the positions of the two US political parties reversed. Then, the Democratic Party and the resolute Democratic president, Harry S. Truman, led the country, under the banner of containment into resisting Soviet expansionism, while the Republican Party, divided between its isolationist and internationalist wings, hesitated. The nomination of Dwight D. Eisenhower as its presidential candidate in 1952 was decisive. As David Halberstam wrote in his history of the 1950s, "Isolationism as an end in itself was finished. The Republican party had put on its international face and had chosen the man most identified with collective security and involvement with Europe as its leader" (1993: 312).

When the 2004 US election campaign had just gotten underway, Norman Podhoretz asked himself if the 1952 parallel was not immediately applicable. Would the Democrats "do unto the Bush Doctrine as the Republicans of 1952 did unto the Truman Doctrine? ... Will they resolve to go on fighting that war with the strategy adumbrated by the Bush Doctrine, and for as long as it may take to win it?" He concluded that under Senator John Kerry, they would not (2004: 17).

But in 2005 with even Senator Kerry calling recent developments in Iraq promising, a reassessment clearly is underway within the Democratic Party that while still divided, also knows that it has suffered very badly from its image of being weak on terrorism. So the chances are very good that the 2008 presidential election will be the 1952 of the Global War on Terror with perhaps Senator Hillary Rodham Clinton, whose foreign policy views have been decidedly hawkish, playing the role of Dwight D. Eisenhower. The role of Richard M. Nixon, Eisenhower's vice-presidential running mate in 1952, will be especially hard for the Democrats to cast.

Should a new foreign policy consensus continue to coalesce in the US, Canada will soon find itself roughly where it did in 1947: faced with the question whether it wants to join the US and like-minded states in the shaping of peace and the search for world order in the face of threats posed to them by authoritarianism (Holmes, 1982). This time the threat originates mainly in the Middle East and the strategy will not be long-term containment of the threat, but its reversal through the muscular, but still at times patient, promotion of liberal democracy.

Joining in again is compatible with Canada's values and interests, and it is within its military capabilities. As Jennifer Welsh notes in her chapter, "There is ... a tendency to deny that many of the values that Canada promotes internationally are values that we *share* with the United States: democracy, the rule of law, human rights, and an enhanced role for the private sector in development" (see Welsh, this volume). Could it not easily have been a Canadian prime minister who said that his country's vital interests and deepest beliefs were one? In other words, hasn't the promotion of Canadian values become central to Canadian foreign policy recently, and isn't one of those core values the promotion of liberal democracy? Isn't the robust Wilsonianism being preached and practiced by George W. Bush, a close American cousin to the "human security" doctrine that Lloyd Axworthy sought to make the driving principle of Canadian foreign policy? Many Canadians obviously would agree. A comprehensive survey of Canadian attitudes towards foreign and defence policy conducted in the fall of 2004 for the Canadian Defence & Foreign Affairs Institute (CDFAI) and the Dominion Institute revealed that 75 percent of Canadians preferred "engagement with the world rather than staying out of world affairs" a figure slighter than in the United States (Innovative, 2004: 14).

Additional Canadian values beyond liberal democracy are, of course, also at stake as Canada contemplates how far to follow US leadership in the Global War on Terror. Prominent among these is the multilateralism upon which Canadian participation in the toppling of the Iraqi dictatorship nominally stranded in the absence of a mandate from the UN Security Council. There can be no doubt that Canada's commitment to multilateralism and to international institutions runs very deep. But as the Chrétien government's 1999 decision to participate in the Kosovo War, which was launched without UN blessing, so clearly demonstrated, Canada can also be flexible in its implementation when required. It is easy to imagine the Canadian decision on Iraq having gone the other way. Indeed the Chrétien government seemed to have been seriously considering such a decision until the very last moment. In his November 2004 visit to Canada, President Bush, bowing to Canadian sensitivities said, that he was "determined to work as far as possible within the framework of international organizations." But in no way did he limit the future use of US armed forces to situations where they have been approved by an international organization, implicitly justifying once again his prosecution of the war in Iraq without having obtained reauthorization from the UN Security Council. He pointedly added, the "success of multilateralism is measured not merely by following a process, but by achieving results. For the sake of peace, when those bodies promise serious consequences, serious consequences must follow" (White House, 2004).

Another Canadian value is caution, which may be the very best explanation for the ultimate decision of the Chrétien government not to join the US in the war in Iraq. Provoked, the Americans had set out to change the world. As Margaret Atwood once put it years ago, "Americans think that anything can be changed, torn down and rebuilt. Canadians tend to think that nothing can" (Atwood, 1982: 383).

The deepest conflict may be with the oldest Canadian value, namely anti-Americanism, particularly with regard to future Canadian military support for the US overseas in the struggle against terror. The CDFAI/Dominion Institute poll found last year that when it came to the use of force overseas, that "Canadians are not all that different than Americans in their willingness to use troops." However, there were major differences when it comes to understandings of the purposes for which force is employed (Innovative, 2004: 27).

More importantly, at a time when things seemed to be going badly in Iraq, fully 79 percent of Canadians believed, the "US is behaving like a rogue nation – rushing into conflicts without attempting to first find solutions by working with its friends and allies." As the survey concluded, "The Bush administration doctrine of pre-emptive actions with or without multilateral sanction does not find a receptive audience in Canada" (ibid: 15). This anti-Bush trend that went beyond the Iraq issue and may also help to explain, at least partially, why Ottawa felt it could not accept the US invitation to join the missile defence program. While Martin's BMD decision was generally panned by the media and the business and political elite, polls indicated that it was supported by a large majority of Canadians, in "virtually every constituency in the country … from teenagers to senior citizens, men and women, urban and rural dwellers, and a majority of respondents in every single province" (cited in Whitaker, 2005: A14).

There has been an especially raw anti-American or anti-Bush tenor in much of the Liberal Party of Canada, particularly its parliamentary caucus, first under Prime Minister Chrétien and now his successor. This has been exacerbated by the Martin government's minority status. The CDFAI/Dominion Institute poll found that overall only 51 percent of Canadians "do not believe that the US can be trusted to treat Canadian concerns fairly." In Ontario, 54 percent and in Atlantic Canada, 68 percent said that the United States could be trusted. In Quebec however, two out three or 66 percent said they did not trust the United States "to provide fair treatment of Canadian concerns" (Innovative, 2004: 14). The minority Martin government's dependence in the House of Commons on the Bloc Québécois and the coming struggle between these two parties for votes in Quebec only heighten these anti-American, anti-Bush tendencies. A Conservative or Liberal majority government would have a freer hand to align more closely with the US.

The Canadian preference for multilateralism and suspicion of the Bush agenda now have to contend with the new and encouraging realities in the Middle East. If the wave of democracy continues to roll on, will Canadians really want to sit the changes out because they don't like George Bush? Even before he leaves office in 2009, Bush himself will become less and less available as a punching bag, as Canadians will in all probability be watching first hand the emergence of a new American foreign policy consensus broadly consistent with the Bush approach, especially as the Presidential election approaches.

They will also be watching as attitudes in Europe and elsewhere continue to change. The signs are there already. "Germany loves to criticize US President George W. Bush's Middle East Policies—just like Germany used to criticize former President Ronald Reagan," *Der Spiegel* wrote in February 2005. "But Reagan, when he demanded that Gorbachev remove the Berlin wall, turned out to be right. Could history repeat itself?" (Malzahn, 2005). To be sure, as in the 1980s, there is a measure of unease about Washington's so-called imperialist approach to the spread of democracy. As Michael Ignatieff has argued, "Other democratic leaders may suspect Bush is right, but that does not mean they are joining in his crusade." However, "[t]he problem here," as Ignatieff points out is:

that while no one wants imperialism to win, no one in his right mind can want liberty to fail either. If the American project of encouraging freedom fails, there may be no one else available with the resourcefulness and energy, even the self-deception, necessary for the task. Very few countries can maintain freedom with outside help ... Who else is available to sponsor liberty in the Middle East but America? Certainly the Europeans themselves have not done a very distinguished job defending freedom close to home. (Ignatieff, 2005)

It goes without saying that Canada will be giving its full support in principle to the democratization of the Middle East. As the Martin government's new foreign policy statement proclaimed, "We believe the best weapon against terrorist recruitment is the promotion of accountable, democratic governments that respect human rights, allow for peaceful dissent and fulfill the aspirations of their people" (Canada, 2005: 12). There are also practical steps that it has committed itself to, especially in Afghanistan, but also in Iraq. The crunch will come of course, if the US again wants to use force and calls upon its friends and allies to join it. There is no doubt that it could issue such a call. President Bush expressed a fundamental truth about US defence policy when he told his Halifax audience, that "America always prefers to act with allies at our side" (White House: 2004). It may partially be, as many have argued, that the US needs allies to "legitimize" some of its overseas military interventions to others. But something even more fundamental is also at work. Americans although aware of their power remain more comfortable knowing that they are not alone when they go to war. For all the recent charges of US unilateralism, the Bush administration has been no different in this regard. Even tokens of support count. Hence the substantial coalition that it gathered in Iraq, involving such countries as the UK, Austria, Romania Poland, Japan, and the Netherlands. And even more countries, including those such as Canada who opposed the war, are contributing to the economic reconstruction in Iraq and the establishment of democracy there.

It is no secret to the Bush administration or anyone else that

Canada's ability to deploy armed forces will continue to decline, the victim of years of defence budget cuts, especially those applied by Prime Minister Martin when he was Finance Minister in the 1990s. True, the Martin government surprised just about everyone with the size of the increase to the defence budget that was pledged in February 2005, namely $13 billion over the next five years; it is the biggest cash infusion to the Canadian Forces in over twenty years. Nonetheless this increase, if actually carried out in the coming years, still will not reverse the impending shrinkage of Canada's military capabilities.

This still does not mean that Canada will be completely unable to participate in US-led overseas operations. The Canadian navy for example, will still be able to deploy with US carrier-battle groups, while the army will, as it is doing now in Afghanistan still be able to deploy small units in situations not involving high-intensity combat, supported by a limited theatre airlift capability supplied by the air force's fleet of C-130s and small number of CF-18 fighter aircraft. However, Canada will only be able to sustain even these limited capabilities, if it simultaneously limits the number of overseas missions it undertakes (Lagassé, 2004: 90).

Despite the decline in the country's military standing and utility, Ottawa should be prepared to support and contribute to American-led multilateral operations in the war on terrorism. Canadian participation in US-led operations overseas lets Washington know that Canada's security concerns extend beyond ensuring that the border remains open for trade. Sending forces overseas tells the American people, and just as importantly the Canadian people, that Canada takes America's global security obligations seriously and sympathizes with the problems and dilemmas that the United States faces in seeking to secure its own (and by extension, its allies') interests. While potential Canadian military contributions might not unfairly be described as tokens to the US, they have largely been welcome tokens. Moreover, an overt reluctance on the part of allies and trading partners like Canada to assist the United States may well persuade Washington that it should not even bother trying to secure multilateral support in the future. This could ultimately lead to an even more unilateralist America.

But Canadians cannot expect that dispatching forces to collaborate with the US overseas will yield influence in Washington. Even with the proposed increases in defence spending, Ottawa should be under no illusions about being able to significantly influence American decisions. Since 11 September 2001, the United States is determined to do what it takes to secure the American people, and to do so unilaterally if necessary. As the recently released US *National Defense Strategy* states, "at the direction of the President, we will defeat adversaries at the time, place, and in the manner of our choosing-setting the conditions for future security" (United

States, 2005a). As with other allies, the United States will not alter its policies in order to secure Ottawa's participation. As one senior official has
stressed, "I don't think that there's anything in our Constitution that says
that the president should not protect the country unless he gets some non-
American's participation or approval of that" (Herndon, 2005).

Given the highly symbolic, but not entirely unimportant character of
Canadian contributions to US-led operations overseas, Canada is actually in a very advantageous position. Canada can, as was stated in
Securing an Open Society: Canada's National Security Policy, "be
selective and strategic when it comes to the deployment of our armed
forces ... [asking before hand] which efforts would be of the greatest
relevance to our national interests ... [and whether] we have the capacity to meaningfully contribute to a successful outcome" (Canada,
2004). Combined with the measures Canada is taking to help secure
North America, a selective Canadian approach to overseas operations
will not be problematic for Washington.

Canada remains a major western industrial democracy necessarily
active in international trade and monetary relations. As a wealthy
nation, it has a role (if not an obligation), in assisting poor and developing countries. And while the United Nations will never be the
guardian of either global stability or Canadian security, there will continue to be instances where the UN, with or without the full support of
the United States, will be involved in regional crises and humanitarian
operations. The international strategic stability afforded Canada and
other allies by American military dominance, makes it possible for
Ottawa to focus its attention and resources elsewhere, thus meeting the
public's desire for an internationalist multilateral foreign policy.

THE GLOBAL WAR ON TERROR IN NORTH AMERICA: THE UNITED STATES, HOMELAND SECURITY AND CANADA

Since the onset of the Global War on Terror it has seemed at times as
if, when it came to North America, Canada-US military relations were
back in the Cold War days of the 1950s. Once again, the US is taking
a vivid interest in its own protection. "There is," President Bush said
in July 2002 "an overriding and urgent mission here in America today
and that's to protect our homeland. We have been called into action
and we've got to act" (White House, 2002). Once again, it is deploy-
ing a new strategic defence, this time against ballistic missiles. And
once again, it has created a new military command at Colorado
Springs for its own defence, this time the Northern Command.

As if to complete this nostalgic picture Prime Minister Martin has
been doing a pretty good imitation of John Diefenbaker as he struggles

with continental defence issues, in Martin's case missile defence. Like Diefenbaker, Martin has managed to look indecisive and confused about the details involved and to exasperate the Americans by his backtracking from an implied commitment.

Desmond Morton was undoubtedly right when he observed that,

our priority under Paul Martin, junior, as it was under John Alexander Macdonald or Louis St. Laurent is to do what we must do to make Americans feel secure on their northern frontier. Americans may remember 9/11; we must remember 9/12 when American panic closed the U.S border and shook our prosperity to its very core (2004).

Nonetheless, there are two reasons why Canada is militarily in a far more comfortable position today in its dealings with the US concerning continental defence than it was in the 1950. First, the US sees the improvement of its security at home in the face of terrorist threats as overwhelmingly a civilian matter, to be executed under the leadership of the newly-created Department of Homeland Security. Canada shares that perception. It responded swiftly to the new North American security environment with the creation of its own new and very powerful department, Public Safety and Emergency and Preparedness Canada. Canada's approach to the US has led to a set of new arrangements designed to keep the border open, beginning with the SMART Border Declaration of December 2001.

Second, while Canada became more important to the defence of the US in the 1950s because Soviet bombers, increasing in numbers and capability could be detected and intercepted in Canadian airspace, the post-9/11 terrorist threat has not reversed the long-term decrease in the military importance of Canada to the US – except at sea. The creation of the Northern Command involving all the US armed services, led briefly to some Canadians imagining pitched battles with terrorists spilling over the border into Canada or US generals taking command of Canadian soldiers in Canada to root out jihadi and violating the *Canadian Charter of Rights and Freedoms* and *Official Languages Act* while imposing the death penalty and suppressing homosexuality along the way. In fact though, the focus of the Northern Command's planning involving the US Army, is on how it could provide assistance after a calamity such as a natural disaster or the terrorist use of a weapon of mass destruction. "Aid to the civil power" is what such responsibilities have long been called in Canada. Of course, such calamities could have effects across the border. How to respond effectively in such situations has been one of the subjects under consideration by a Canada-US Binational Planning Group, located at Northern Command and NORAD headquarters. Bilateral cooperation in civil affairs has been highlighted by exercises involving civilian agencies from both sides of the border working with American and Canadian military units.

After the failure to detect and stop the highjacked aircraft on 9/11, continental air defences have been improved. But unlike the 1950s, when a vast air battle over Canada was the plan, air defence today, including defence against the terrorist threat, remains not only very limited in scope but quite local in focus. In other words, outside of American airspace, not much more is required to defend New York or Washington. Conversely, areas in need of more attention include Canada's Atlantic and Pacific coasts and in the St. Lawrence-Great Lakes system. The US is taking understandable interest in vessels approaching the continent. The Canadian Navy is divided between its duties close to Canada and those away in blue waters. Meanwhile, the Canadian Coast Guard remains in home waters, unarmed, unlike its US counterpart. Canada will need to acquire new capabilities, or turn some responsibilities over to the Canadian Navy or the US Navy and US Coast Guard (see Sokolsky, 2005b).

It will be an enormous surprise if Washington and Ottawa do not renew the NORAD agreement when it expires in 2006. At the same time, the joint command's longer-term future is quite uncertain. Canada plays no direct role in the detection and tracking of ballistic missiles. No system for these purposes is currently or planned to either be located in Canada operated by the Canadian military. Canadians have stayed at the very heart of operations at Colorado Springs, though, because of NORAD's most important responsibility, that of warning of and assessing an attack on this continent. Eventually, this may very well change, as a result of the Martin government's 2005 decision not to participate in missile defence. To be sure, the government also took great pains, quietly announced in a summer 2004 decision, to allow Canadians to keep their warning and assessment responsibilities, which means they will be working very closely with the missile defence system. Indeed, as it now stands, NORAD will provide critical information to the missile defence, which will be the responsibility of Northern Command.

But the US may eventually decide not to maintain the status quo with regard to NORAD. It may, within a couple of years, conclude that inasmuch as Canadians make no contribution to the detection and tracking of missiles, and seeing that their government has expressed a distinct aversion to the destruction of hostile missiles, cooperation with Canada through NORAD in the broad range of aerospace defence, no longer makes sense. Warning and assessment responsibilities would be transferred to a US command, presumably Northern Command.

Thus while NORAD renewal in 2006 might seem to be the logical time to make major changes, with the missile defence system just becoming operational and with both countries still figuring out their domestic command arrangements for homeland defence, these decisions will probably come later. The Canadian Forces will be establishing a Canada Command with responsibilities roughly similar to US North- ern Command. For these reasons, in 2006 Ottawa and Washington may decide on simple renewal of NORAD, as it is.

Sooner or later though, NORAD may very well lose what long has been its key function: warning of and assessing an aerospace attack. Strikingly however, this still does not mean that the bi-national command must come to an end (although that would certainly be an option) or that Canada-US defence relations would deteriorate. There is still enough for a bi-national command: a NORAD without the 'A'; that is, a North Amer- ican Defence command. It would combine the command's longstanding, although much shrunken air defence functions with responsibilities for the new post-9/11 areas of aid to the civil power and maritime defence. On the American side, this new NORAD would be directly linked to NORTHCOM and the Department of Homeland Security and through DHS to the US Coast Guard. On the Canadian side it would interface with the new Canada Command and the Department of Public Safety and Emer- gency Preparedness. This would be consistent with the Pentagon's recently released *Strategy for Homeland Defence and Civil Support*, which drew attention to the importance of Canada (and Mexico) in helping to secure the air, land and maritime "approaches" to the US homeland (United States, 2005b: 11) Thus the revised bilateral organiza- tion would be focused precisely where it is needed most, on maritime threats and on military support to the civil authorities on either side of the border. A NORAD without Aerospace could therefore even be legiti- mately celebrated by both countries as a wise and mutually agreed upon response to new strategic realities and as a renewed commitment to defence cooperation.

Nonetheless, the nature of Canada-US defence cooperation would thereby undergo a significant shift, and not just laterally from having aerospace defence at its core to being based on other forms of cooper- ation. In one sense, Canada would be downgraded. It has long seen its membership in the joint aerospace defence command as not only a key source of information on US planning concerning, but as a way to influence such planning. Those expectations about Canadian access and influence though were overblown. Both Ottawa and Washington may be relieved at the prospect of not having to deal with one another on issues of aerospace defence. In other words, despite the disagree- ments over missile defence, a new Canada-US consensus about defence cooperation, focusing on air, land, and sea tasks, should be debated.

CONCLUSION

In general, the April 2005 foreign and defence statements are consistent with the emergence of a new bilateral consensus on North American security. Yet there still may be a problem here. A major theme of the statements is that although Canada recognizes the new importance of maintaining a strong security partnership with the United States, it will not, in Prime Minister Martin's words, become Washington's 'handmaiden.' Thus while Ottawa, on the one hand pledges to enhance security cooperation with the US in North America, it appears on the other hand, to be striving for a more independent Canadian role internationally as part of the restoring of Canada's "role of pride and influence in the world."

Speaking to the Canadian domestic audience, the Martin government appears to be performing a rhetorical balancing act. Confronting the inescapable and unavoidable emphasis upon cooperation with the Americans in the North American sphere and making promises that Canada will not always follow the US lead overseas and may choose to contribute to international security in other ways. Americans have heard this before, and as we argue above, such an approach for the most part, poses no real problems for the US or for the bilateral security relationship.

However in the post-9/11 world, Washington is unlikely to be as patient with traditional Canadian schizophrenia in respect to foreign policy rhetoric and conduct as it was in the immediate post-Cold War era. Although collaborating with the US in overseas military operations and seeking interoperability with American forces, Ottawa also seemed to go out of its way to adopt non-American policies, such as those on land mines and the International Criminal Court, in order to cut a distinct international figure abroad and especially at home by "pulling the eagle's feathers." And when the Iraq war began many Canadians, and some in the previous Liberal Government, adopted what Moisés Naim, editor of *Foreign Policy,* has called "lite anti-Americanism." This is the kind of fashionable, anti-US sentiment which claims that it loves America and the ideals for which it stands, but disagrees with and even despises its policies and which often gives credence to and "disseminates the worst possible assumptions about the malicious nature, dark motivations and hidden agendas of the United States." As Moisés cautions, "[t]hose who partake and spread lite anti-Americanism, even while sharing the principles and values the United States stands for, undermine the country's ability to defend such principles abroad" (Naim, 2003).

Ottawa must avoid these temptations. It needs to recall what being a good ally meant during the Cold War. In the present strategic environment this means recognizing that Washington views homeland security and any collaboration with Canada, as inseparable from what is necessarily a *global* war on terrorism. For the United States, North American security, as the Pentagon's new homeland defence strategy makes clear, is just one part of an "active, layered defense," that is "predicated on seizing the initiative from adversaries" through "forward" overseas military and diplomatic activities as the best way to secure the American homeland (United States, 2005b: 10). Allies are expected to support these efforts. This does not mean that the United States will demand that Canada contributes to all future American overseas military operations in the war on terrorism. But it does mean that some contributions will be expected and that they will be important in terms of bilateral security relations. Above all, Ottawa cannot adopt positions that pander to anti-American sentiment in Canada by openly challenging US policies overseas and expect to maintain Washington's trust and confidence in Canada as a reliable partner in terms of helping to secure the American homeland.

To be sure, recent expressions of anti-Canadianism in the US, though far from the level of anti-Americanism present in Canada, do not serve American interests and Washington owes it to itself to counter them. But a Canadian approach which matches defence and security capabilities with a renewed, public commitment to bilateral security cooperation overseas, as well as in North America, would go some way to encouraging Washington to avoid the kind of rhetoric that can make it difficult for a government in Ottawa to express its support for US policies. In short, Canada is fully capable of maintaining that trust and confidence in a manner that will help to shape a new consensus with the United States, one that meets the national interests and international objectives of both countries.

REFERENCES

Atwood, Margaret. 1982. "Canadian-American Relations: Surviving the Eighties," in *Second Words: Selected Critical Prose 1960–1982*. Toronto: Anansi Press.

Berman, Paul. 2004. *Terror and Liberalism*. New York and London: W.W. Norton.

Bush, George W. 2005. Presidential Inaugural Address. Washington, 20 January. Available at: <http://www.whitehouse.gov/inaugural/>

Canada. 2004. *Securing an Open Society: Canada's National Security Policy*. Ottawa: Department of Public Safety and Emergency Preparedness (PSEP), 27 April.

— 2005. "Diplomacy" in *Canada's International Policy Statement: A Role of Pride and Influence in the World*. Ottawa: Department of Foreign Affairs and International Trade (DFAIT), 19 April.

Cohen, Eliot A. 2005. "A Time for Humility," *The Wall Street Journal*, 31 January, A18

Gwyn, Richard. 2005. "Admit it, Bush was Right on Iraq," *Toronto Star,* 1

February, A13.

Halberstam, David. 1993. *The Fifties*. New York: Fawcett Columbine.

Herndon, John. 2005. "Policy OKs first strike to protect US," *The Los Angeles Times,* 19 March.

Holmes, John W. 1982. *The Shaping of Peace: Canada and the Search for World Order*, vol. 2. Toronto: University of Toronto Press.

Ignatieff, Michael. 2005. "Who are Americans to think that freedom is theirs to spread?" *The New York Times*, 26 June, 6–42.

Innovative Research Group. 2004. "Visions of Canadian Foreign Policy," Conference Report for the Dominion Institute and the Canadian Defence and Foreign Affairs Institute, 4 November.

Iraq Liberation Act of 1998. 1998. (Public Law 105–338, 31 Oct.), *United States Statutes at Large*, 112: 3178–3181.

Krauthammer, Charles. 2005. "High principle won't help Iraq," *National Post*, 4 July, A16.

Lagassé, Philippe. 2004. "Matching Ends and Means in Canadian Defence," in David Carment, Fen Osler Hampson and Norman Hillmer, eds. *Canada Among Nations 2004: Setting Priorities Straight*. Montreal and Kingston: McGill-Queen's University Press.

Malzahn, Claus Christian. 2005. "Could George W. Bush be right?" *Der Spiegel Online,* 23 February. Available at: <http://www.spiegel.de>.

Morton, Desmond. 2004. Keynote Address to the Inter-University Seminar on Armed Forces and Society. Toronto, 1 October.

Naim, Moisés. 2003. "The Perils of Lite Anti-Americanism," *Foreign Policy*, no. 136 (May/June): 96–7.

Podhoretz, Norman. 2004. "World War VI: How It Started, What It Means, and Why We Have to Win," *Commentary*, vol. 118, no. 2 (September).

Sokolsky, Joel J. 2005a. "Between a Rock and a Soft Place: The Geopolitics of Canada-US Security Relations," in Hugh Segal, ed. *Geopolitical Integrity*. Montreal: Institute for Research on Public Policy.

— 2005b. "Guarding the Continental Coasts: US Maritime Homeland Security and Canada." *IRPP Policy Matters*, vol. 6, no. 1 (March).

The White House, Office of the Press Secretary. 2002. "President Bush Thanks Homeland Security Workers," 10 July. Available at: <http://www.whitehouse.gov/news/releases/2002/07/20020710-1.html>

— 2004. "President Discusses Strong Relationship with Canada," 1 December. Available at: <http://www.whitehouse.gov/news/releases/2004/12/2004 1201-4.html>

United States. 2005a. *The National Defence Strategy of the United States*. Washington, D.C.: Department of Defense (DOD), 1 March.

— 2005b, *Strategy for Homeland Defence and Civil Support*. Washington D.C.: Department of Defense (DOD), 30 June.

Whitaker, Reg. 2005. "Out of touch." Letter to the Editor. *The Globe and Mail*. 25 March, A14.

5   Looking Enviously Down Under? The Australian Experience and Canadian Foreign Policy

KIM RICHARD NOSSAL

During the debate over Canada's international policy in 2004, the Australian government of John Howard was often held up as a model for Canadian foreign and defence policy makers. A number of commentators pointed to Australia as an example of a government which had made a number of crucial strategic decisions in global policy. For example, the *National Post* ran a series of feature articles in October 2004 under the title "Australia Rules" that conveyed the clear implication that the Canadian government of Paul Martin should follow the Australian lead (Goodspeed, 2004; Taylor, 2004; Wattie, 2004). In a similar vein, Derek Burney argued that an effective foreign and defence policy depended not only on making "an honest appraisal of what we are, as well as what we may like to be," but also having "the political courage to drive change, reallocate resources and implement identified reforms – in short, to lead" (2005: 31). He explicitly pointed to Australia as a country with a government which had engaged in precisely that strategic decision-making in foreign and defence policy.

   This chapter examines the Australian model in foreign and defence policy more closely. On the one hand, there can be little doubt that after 1996, when the Liberal Party/National Party Coalition defeated the Australian Labor Party (ALP), the government of John Howard took a series of strategic decisions in foreign and defence policy that self-consciously sought to "reposition" Australia in global politics. Of particular importance was the decision to align Australia as closely as possible with the United States, not only in global strategic terms but also in economic terms.

At first glance, this model might indeed seem attractive to Canadians who looked at their country's foreign policy and wished for a government in Ottawa that was capable of making strategic decisions in global policy, that pursued relations with the United States with an eye to maximizing influence in Washington, and that spent strategically on defence. However, when examined more closely, it can be argued that the Australian experience offers few lessons for Canada. While we can see some evidence of what Michaud and Bélanger (1999) have called the "Australisation" of Canadian security policy, the overall conclusion must be that Australia and Canada occupy such very different strategic locations in the contemporary global order that there are few strategic lessons that Canadians can learn from the robust foreign and defence policies pursued by the Howard government.

REPOSITIONING AUSTRALIA, 1996–2004

In the 1996 election campaign, the Liberal Party/National Party Coalition articulated a comprehensive critique of the foreign policy of the Australian Labor Party (ALP), which had focused on Australia's engagement with Asia (Higgott and Nossal, 1997). The Coalition promised that it would not abandon Asia, but would not make it the sole focus of foreign policy. Rather, the Coalition promised that it would focus instead on key bilateral partnerships, and in particular would "reinvigorate" Australia's bilateral security relationship with the United States. The Coalition also targeted the ALP's approach to multilateral diplomacy, arguing that Australia should avoid "inflated expectations or an exaggerated perception of our likely influence which can be seen as meddlesome." Generally, the Coalition argued that insufficient attention had been paid by the ALP to defending Australia's national interests (Liberal Party of Australia/National Party of Australia, 1996).

In power, the new Howard government moved to entrench this new vision of foreign policy in a White Paper, *In the National Interest: Australia's Foreign and Trade Policy White Paper*, which was released in August 1997. Not surprisingly, many of the themes that had been emphasized by the Coalition, both in opposition and in its first year in government, were central to the foreign policy elaborated in the White Paper. This included the theme of the Coalition's election platform in foreign policy – a confident Australia: the unambiguous willingness to engage in "the hard-headed pursuit of the interests which lie at the core of foreign and trade policy: the security of the Australian nation and the jobs and standard of living of the Australian people" (Australia, 1997: iii). A second theme was the importance of bilateral relationships rather than multilateralism as the cornerstone of Australian foreign policy. While multilateral approaches were not dismissed outright, the White Paper described bilateral relationships as the "basic building block" for advancing Australian national interests (Australia, 1997: chap. 4).

Not surprisingly, however, the Howard government's foreign policy also manifested elements of continuity. The engagement with Asia – a cornerstone policy of the ALP government in the 1980s and 1990s – was also embraced by the Coalition. Moreover, like its ALP predecessor, it promised that it would continue to seek the Australian foreign policy grail: trade liberalization, particularly in agricultural products. Indeed, as Shirley Scott (1998: 226) has argued, "to the extent that the White Paper represented substantive change from the previous government's conceptual framework, it was primarily one of emphasis – away from multilateralism and internationalism and towards bilateralism and national sovereignty."

What did this mean in practice? In retrospect, three features of Australian foreign and defence policy can be identified: an increasing effort to enmesh Australia and the United States; a willingness to take a leading role in the maintenance of peace and security in Australia's immediate neighbourhood; and a willingness to make some strategic decisions about Australian defence policy.

"ALL THE WAY WITH THE USA"

In December 1966, Prime Minister Harold Holt fought an election on the slogan "All the way with LBJ" – a catch-cry that because of its association with Australia's participation in the escalation of the Vietnam War initiated by the US administration of Lyndon B. Johnson has acquired a highly negative connotation in Australian politics. While some Australian critics of John Howard in the 2000s have characterized Howard's approach as "All the way with the USA" – forensically invoking the memories of Holt's endorsement of American global policy in the 1960s – the catch-phrase does capture the essence of John Howard's foreign policy, particularly since 11 September 2001.

From the outset in 1996, Howard worked hard to align Australia more explicitly with the United States in global affairs and to reinvigorate the bilateral relationship. This involved overt Australian support for the role of the United States "in balancing and containing potential rivalries" in the Asia-Pacific region, as the Minister for Foreign Affairs Alexander Downer put it in a speech in 2000 (cited in Gurry, 2001: 12). It also involved Australian support for the ballistic missile defence program which began to evolve during the administration of Bill

Clinton. Australia and the United States found themselves on the same side on the issue of the reduction of greenhouse gas emissions at the negotiations at Kyoto, though Australian opposition to the Kyoto Protocol was more pointed (Scott, 1998: 226–8). However, it should be noted that this alignment was not automatic and did not extend to all global issues. For example, the Howard government took a divergent line on the International Criminal Court, playing a leading role in the process that led to the Rome treaty.

Despite these efforts, Canberra's relations with the Clinton administration actually soured in the late 1990s. This was partly because of disputes over protectionist measures adopted by the US Congress against Australian products. It was also partly because of differences over how best to deal with what was happening in East Timor in 1999 (Wheeler and Dunne, 2001: 813–4; Maley, 2000). Perhaps the best indication of the state of the relationship was the fact that when Howard travelled to Washington to meet the president in 1999, Clinton gave Howard precisely 20 minutes for a private meeting and left after a brief working lunch.

Because of this deterioration in Australia-US relations in 1999, the election of George Bush in 2000 was seen as an opportunity to reinvigorate the relationship. Bush's election coincided with a decision by the Howard government to reverse its 1997 rejection of a Clinton proposal for a bilateral trade agreement and to seek a comprehensive bilateral trade agreement with the United States. The initial rationale behind Howard's change of mind was security: an agreement between Australia and the United States would not only benefit Australians as a result of the increases in the volume of trade such an agreement would bring, but would also bind the United States closer to Australia in geostrategic terms.

This security rationale was entrenched after the terrorist attacks of 11 September 2001, and the "War on Terror" that followed. For Howard, who happened to be in the United States on 11 September, this was an opportunity to flesh out the re-orientation of Australian foreign policy he had been embracing since the election campaign of 1996. The Australian government thus not only expressed strong support for the American response but also committed some 1300 troops to the US-led coalition that invaded Afghanistan to overthrow the Taliban regime, including Special Forces, naval vessels in the Persian Gulf, Hercules aircraft for strategic lift, and Boeing 707 air-to-air refuellers.

Australian support for the global policies of the United States became even more pronounced after attacks by Islamist extremists were overtly directed at Australians, with the planned bombing of the Australian High Commission in Singapore in late 2001 that was thwarted by security forces, and the successful bombings of nightclubs in Bali in October 2002, which killed over 200 people, including 88 Australians. Certainly the desire to demonstrate solidarity with the United States led the Howard government to support the United States-led invasion of Iraq in March 2003 by contributing 2000 troops, including Special Forces, F-18 fighters and naval units to the coalition (O'Neil, 2003).

The intensification of Howard's efforts to pursue closer relations with the United States was made clear in a second White Paper on foreign policy, issued merely a month before the Iraq war (Australia, 2003). *Advancing the National Interest* stressed the importance of a hard-headed realist approach to the defence of Australian national interests, including the measures to be taken to combat terrorism and efforts to ensure trade liberalization. And unlike the 1997 White Paper, the 2003 White Paper articulated an explicit connection between Australia's economic relationship with the United States and its security/strategic relations with Washington. Perhaps not surprisingly, therefore, there was considerable willingness to articulate the free trade agreement in security terms – on both sides of the Pacific. In August 2002, Downer argued that a trade agreement would "help engender a broader appreciation – in both countries – of the bilateral security alliance" (cited in Capling, 2005: 53). This view was echoed by the US Trade Representative, Robert Zoellick, who stated that an agreement would "strengthen the foundation of the security alliance" (ibid: 54). The most explicit connection was made by Mark Vaile, the Minister of Trade, when the agreement was eventually signed in 2004. The Australia-US Free Trade Agreement, he said, was to be "the commercial equivalent of the ANZUS treaty" (ibid: 75).[1]

Canberra's robust support for American global policies – and its willingness to go softly on the issue of Australian citizens held by the US at the camp at Guantanamo in Cuba – would lead to a closeness in personal relations between the president and the prime minister. Howard received invitations to the Bush ranch at Crawford and to address a joint session of Congress. Bush administration officials openly praised Australia as a "firm ally" and a friend. And Bush himself went out of his way to heap praise on Howard. For example, Howard's decision to contribute to the Iraq coalition in the face of considerable domestic opposition prompted Bush to laud Howard openly as a "man of steel" (Taylor, 2004).

AUSTRALIA AS "DEPUTY SHERIFF"?

The second feature of Australian "repositioning" itself after 1996 was the embrace of a more robust policy in its immediate neighbourhood, marked by security operations in East Timor in 1999,

Solomon Islands in 2003, and police operations in Papua New Guinea in 2004.

The intervention in East Timor in September 1999 was triggered by the outbreak of widespread violence by Indonesian-backed militias. The Howard government abandoned the long-standing Australian policy of recognizing Indonesian claims to sovereignty over the former Portuguese territory that it had invaded in December 1975, and took the lead in organizing an intervention force to stop the violence and allow the continuation of a UN-backed supervision of Timorese independence. While the operation had the nominal consent of the Indonesian government in Djakarta, the International Force East Timor (INTERFET) had no assurance that the local militias would accept the intervention. In the end, Australia ended up contributing 5000 of the 9500 troops for the mission. The relative success of this multinational mission (Cotton, 1999; see Maley, 2000) would contribute to the image of Australia as a forceful and decisive actor in its immediate neighbourhood, with the military capacity to project its power.

In the aftermath of 9/11, the Howard government's interventions in Australia's immediate neighbourhood would be characterized by Canberra as an effort to bring stability to areas that might otherwise become bases for terrorists. Thus, when violence escalated in Solomon Islands in 2003, Australia organized an intervention force that was deployed to the Solomons to disarm the gangs and restore law and order. The Australian-led Regional Assistance Mission Solomon Islands (RAMSI) was legitimized internationally by support from the Pacific Islands Forum and domestically within Solomon Islands by a vote of the parliament. Of the total force of 2225, Australia contributed 1500 combat troops and 245 police officers (McDougall, 2004).

Likewise, an increase in civil violence in Papua New Guinea (PNG) prompted the Howard government to tie Australia's annual development assistance to the country to the acceptance by the government in Port Moresby of an Enhanced Cooperation Program – a $1.1 billion package that saw more than 150 Australian police officers patrol the streets of PNG cities and Australian civil servants placed in key administrative positions in the PNG government. The program, which began in 2004, came to an abrupt halt in May 2005 when the PNG Supreme Court, ruling on a constitutional challenge launched by the governor of Morobe Province, unanimously found that the legal immunity granted to Australian police was unconstitutional (Forbes, 2005).

There is little doubt that the United States government welcomed such robust initiatives. For example, in a submission to an Australian parliamentary enquiry into the Australia-US defence relationship, the US Embassy in Canberra welcomed Australian leadership in the region:

"The very proximity of Australia to terrorist-threatened nations in Southeast Asia means that a ready first-response neighbour is on hand to help in crisis situations" (Kerin, 2004).

Doing what the Australian government itself called the "heavy lifting in terms of security assistance, foreign aid, humanitarian relief and economic support" (ibid), its involvement in the Southwest Pacific has been characterized by some as the "Howard doctrine," and by others as Australia's new "deputy sheriff" role in the Pacific.

It is widely believed that Howard himself used the term "deputy sheriff" to characterize Australia's new policy orientation in the Asia-Pacific. In fact, Howard never used either word. Fred Brenchley of *The Bulletin*, Australia's leading newsweekly magazine, suggested during an interview with Howard that Australia was acting as a "deputy" for the United States in the region, a characterization that the prime minister did not contest. A subeditor at *The Bulletin* subsequently dropped the word "sheriff" into the story to create a catchier headline (Brenchley, 1999; Henderson, 2003). However, the image of an Australian deputy sheriff keeping order in the Asia-Pacific at the behest of the United States did not sit well with Australia's neighbours, and when the interview generated considerable criticism throughout Southeast Asia, Howard hastily disavowed the characterization.

However, the term stuck and was not only widely used by Howard's critics in Australia to decry his subservience to George Bush and the United States but was also used by his supporters. Indeed, even Bush used the sheriff terminology about Australia. In October 2003, Bush was asked during a photo opportunity whether the US saw Australia as its deputy sheriff in South-East Asia. According the official transcripts, Bush responded, "No, we don't see it as a deputy sheriff. We see it as a sheriff [laughter]. There is a difference. I see you are playing off the Crawford visit to the ranch, the sheriff thing [laughter]. Anyway, no, equal partners and friends and allies. There is nothing deputy about this relationship."[2]

DEFENCE DECISIONS

The third element of the efforts of the Howard government to reorient Australia's location was on defence policy. In 2000, the government published a White Paper on defence, *Defence 2000: Our Future Defence Force*, that outlined an aggressive and comprehensive restructuring of the Australian Defence Force (ADF) and a plan for multi-year guaranteed funding that enabled a substantial increase in capabilities.

Indicative of this orientation was the articulation of a set of wide-ranging strategic objectives that ranged from the most immediate –

protecting Australia from an attack without having to rely on help from other states – to the broad goal of "supporting the international community to uphold global security." In between were goals of a distinctly regional/neighbourhood nature, reflecting the reorientation of foreign policy to pay closer attention to stability in the Australia approach. However, the government made it clear that the forces would be structured for neighbourhood and regional operations only, and not specifically structured for operations beyond the region (Australia, 2000).

To give effect to this, the Howard government announced a dramatic increase in Australian military defence spending – some $24 billion over 10 years that would see the size of the defence force grow from 51,000 to 54,000, with the idea that the ADF would be capable of deploying two brigades overseas simultaneously (Wattie, 2004). The analysis was sound, and immediately drew praise from the Australian Labor Party. However, as Gurry (2001: 17) concludes, the defence White Paper of 2000 was also "good politics." Increased spending was announced for regional defence establishments, for the cadets and the reserve force, and for the defence industrial base.

A MODEL FOR CANADA?

Under John Howard's prime ministership, the Australian government has pursued policies of the kind that many critics in Canada would like to see the government in Ottawa practice. Under Howard, Australia has been a strong ally of the United States, not slavishly following the American lead on all policy matters (as divergences over the International Criminal Court in the late 1990s and over approaches to China in the mid-2000s show), but taking considerable care in selecting which issues on which to challenge the United States. As prime minister, Howard has been meticulous in trying to cultivate good relations with the United States president (though he has had much more success with Bush than with Clinton). The Australian government has been willing to make significant decisions about its geostrategic assets and where and how, to deploy them in a regional context. As a result, the Australian government enjoys an image in Washington of a firm friend and ally upon whom the United States can count and the Australian prime minister enjoys access to the White House.

To be sure, many of these decisions were taken in the face of strong domestic criticism. While the country's role in East Timor was widely celebrated in Australia, the Howard government's participation in the "War on Terror" and its unambiguous support for the global policies of the United States generated considerable opposition. The Australian

Labor Party in particular was unrelenting in its attacks on what it saw as Howard's subservience to the United States, though few were as derisive in their condemnation as Mark Latham, an ALP member of Parliament and leader of the party between December 2003 and January 2005, who called Howard an "arse-licker" (McKew, 2002) and the Howard cabinet "a conga line of suckholes" (Flitton, 2004). However, despite the considerable domestic opposition Howard's foreign policy generated, Howard and the Coalition kept winning majorities – in October 1998, November 2001, and October 2004 – and ALP leaders kept resigning.

But what lessons can the Australian model offer Canada? After all, as numerous observers have noted, the geostrategic locations of the two countries differ dramatically. Canada's geographic location as an immediate neighbour of the United States provides Canadians with such a high level of security that they can afford to be as complacent as they have historically been about national security. In such circumstances, Canadians have spent as little on defence as they could get away with. Moreover, Canadians have been generally indifferent about relations between the political leaders of the two countries, safe in the knowledge that a poor or sour relationship between president and prime minister not only has little effect on the massive trade between the two countries, but more importantly, that in a crunch, the United States would always defend Canada from any external threat.

Australia's geostrategic location, by contrast, has always generated considerable insecurity within Australian political culture. Canada experienced its last full-scale invasion in the War of 1812 and its last small-scale incursions during the Fenian Raids between 1866 and 1871. For Australians, by contrast, the historical experience of almost being invaded by Japan in 1942 as a result of the collapse of British power in Asia – and being 'rescued' by the United States – still features heavily in Australian political culture. The search for a "great and powerful friend" (to cite the phrase commonly used in Australian national security discourse) to protect the thinly populated continent has been a persistent feature of Australian defence policy.

This sense of insecurity has had an important impact on Australian political discourse and practice. First, the fact that there is no great power which will automatically come to Australia's aid breeds a certain solicitousness towards the one power who did in the past – and who many Australians hope would do so again if circumstances demanded. While one finds in Australia similar strains of anti-Americanism found in many other countries, it is less accepted in elite circles than, for example, in Canada. Thus, when Latham was selected as leader of the ALP, his colourful anti-American derision stopped immediately. In addition, to demonstrate his *bona fides* to both the Australian electorate (if not to the United States government), he appointed Kim Beazley as his shadow minister of defence. Beazley had been ALP leader from 1996 to 2001, and had consistently expressed support for the alliance with the United States. In Canada, by contrast, anti-Americanism is widely tolerated in the governing Liberal party. To be sure, Jean Chrétien took that toleration to unprecedented limits in his soft responses to those within his caucus, his cabinet, and his personal staff who expressed anti-American sentiments in public. Indeed, as Chrétien himself once openly admitted (albeit when he did not know he was talking into an open microphone), he liked taking anti-American stands because it was popular in Canada.[3]

Likewise, Canada's geostrategic location means that governments in Ottawa can be as careless as they like about relations with the United States without suffering long-term adverse strategic consequences to national security. For example, a Canadian prime minister can sandbag the United States on an issue regarded as of crucial importance in Washington. Chrétien did this in March 2003 over Canadian participation in the invasion of Iraq, by letting Americans think that in the end Canada would join. Then, at the last minute and without telephoning the president, he rose in the House of Commons to announce, to a standing ovation delivered by cheering Liberals, that Canada would not be joining. Or, as Paul Martin did in February 2005, announcing that Canada would not participate in the US Ballistic Missile Defense program, without offering either a public explanation for the decision or any prior, private indication to Bush that Canada was about to deny the United States the legitimacy of Canadian participation in this scheme.

A second difference is that the opportunities for regional activism differ. While Australia has a number of potential areas of instability on its margins and approaches designed for these areas, such as instability in Papua New Guinea and Solomon Islands, secessionism in West Papua, ethnic/religious conflict in different parts of Indonesia, Canadians face no comparable "failing state" on their margins. The closest source of political instability is Haiti; but because the Canadian government has neither the will nor the military resources to intervene in a significant way in Haiti, and because the deterioration of the situation there has actually produced relatively few negative externalities that might prompt international action, this 'failing state' is kept firmly off the Canadian agenda.

A third difference is that the military enjoys a much more privileged place in Australian politics and culture than the military enjoys in

Canada. One measure of this is the difference in per capita spending on defence: in 2002, Australia spent US$388 per capita on defence, compared with Canada's US$247 (Wattie, 2004). The Liberal/National Coalition could thus make strategic choices about the Australian military in the late 1990s and early 2000s, and could devote significant resources to defence because they could be sure that such a move would be popular domestically.

The privileged position of the military is in part a function of the continuing recognition within Australian political culture of the role of the armed forces in the development of the Australian nation. This is perhaps best exemplified by the reverent place that the disastrous Gallipoli campaign of 1915 still occupies in Australian popular culture, and the homage that is still paid to the expeditionary force of the First World War, the Australia and New Zealand Army Corps (ANZAC), in the annual celebration of ANZAC Day on 25 April. In part, it is also a recognition of the importance that Australia's military capabilities played in the Second World War and in 'saving' the country from Japanese domination. And finally, it is partially a function of the high visibility of the armed forces, which are stationed in all of Australia's major cities. Popular affection for the military follows naturally. One small example of this was the national celebration held to greet the Australian INTERFET contingent on its return from East Timor in April 2000, during which the central business district of Sydney simply shut down to welcome the returning troops.

By contrast, the Canadian military enjoys no comparable status. For quite logical reasons that are grounded in the contested role of expeditionary wars in Canadian history and the equally contested notion of the "nation" in Canada, there is no 'national' day that celebrates the contribution of war-fighting to the formation of "the nation." Furthermore, the Canadian military is relatively invisible to the vast majority of Canadians who live in large urban areas, since Canadian Forces Bases tend to be situated outside of Canada's large cities. As a result, funding for the military in Canada has always been grudging at best, with the dominant assumption being that increased military spending is a losing proposition both politically and electorally. Instead, as Desmond Morton (1987: 643) reminds us, the perspective of an Ontario MP shortly after Confederation appears to have guided successive generations of Canadians: "In a country situated as we are, not likely to be involved in war, and having a large demand upon our resources for public improvements, it was highly desirable to have our military affairs conducted as cheaply as possible."

In sum, the Australian government under the prime ministership of John Howard offers us an image of a government that was able to develop a strategic vision for foreign and defence policy and to work to achieve that vision by making strategic choices about both policy goals, and the policy tools needed to achieve those objectives. By embracing a robust regional role, the Australian government made itself useful to the United States, increasing Australian visibility in Washington. Howard himself offers us a model of how the leader of a small power can seek to maximize access to decision-makers in Washington in the contemporary era of American hyperpowerism.

At the same time, however, the markedly different geostrategic locations of the two countries mean that it is difficult for Canadians to draw lessons from the Australian experience. Australians have always worried about the implications of their existence in a geostrategic location deemed at different times in Australian history to be lonely, perilous or precarious. Australian attitudes on foreign and defence policy flow naturally from their location. Moreover, it is telling that Australians have sustained Howard in power in three successive elections. While it would be inappropriate to infer from the 1998, 2001 and 2004 election results that Australians therefore support the robustly pro-American foreign policy that Howard has pursued, what we can conclude is that Howard's unambiguous support for Washington's global policies as a means to enmesh the United States in Australian security has not alienated Australian voters sufficiently for them to embrace an alternative vision.

By contrast, Canadians have been increasingly insouciant about their relations with the United States, their proper role in the western hemisphere, and their military assets. But it can be argued that it is an insouciance that flows no less directly and naturally from their country's geostrategic location in the contemporary global order.

NOTES

1 Indeed, the essential geostrategic purpose of the trade agreement with the US can be seen in Howard's refusal to accept the advice of his own trade negotiators to walk away from the table once it was clear that the United States was not going to bend on those issues of importance to Australians. On the contrary: Howard insisted that his trade minister, Mark Vaile, sign the agreement, even though it was widely seen as more in the interests of the US than Australia. See Nossal (2004).

2 White House, Office of the Press Secretary. "Remarks by President Bush and Prime Minister Howard of Australia," Canberra, Australia, 22 October 2003. Available at: <http://www.whitehouse.gov/news/releases/2003/10/20031022–11.html>; also *Sydney Morning Herald*, 17 October 2003.

3 While attending a NATO summit in July 1997, Chrétien and Jean-Luc Dehane, the prime minister of Belgium, were chatting with one another in French – without realizing that their microphones were open. Chrétien confided to Dehane that he had made defying the United States "my policy. The Cuba affair, I was the first to stand up [unintelligible]. People like that." But ever the pragmatist, Chrétien quickly added: "You have to do it carefully, because they're friends." See Anthony Wilson-Smith, "The moral of the microphone," *Maclean's*, 21 July 1997; and, *Globe and Mail*, 10 July 1997.

REFERENCES

Australia. 1997. *In the National Interest: Australia's Foreign and Trade Policy White Paper*. Canberra: Department of Foreign Affairs and Trade, 4 August. Available at: <http://www.dfat.gov.au/ini/>
– 2000. *Defence 2000: Our Future Defence Force*. Canberra: Department of Defence, 6 December. Available at: < http://www.defence.gov.au/whitepaper/>
– 2003. *Advancing the National Interest*. Canberra: Department of Foreign Affairs and Trade, 12 February. Available at: <www.dfat.gov.au/ani/>
Brenchley, Fred. 1999. "The Howard Defence doctrine," *The Bulletin*, 28 September.
Burney, Derek. 2005. "A Time for Courage and Conviction in Foreign Policy," *Policy Options*, vol. 26, no. 2 (February): 28–31.
Capling, Ann. 2005. *All the Way with the USA: Australia, the US and Free Trade*. Sydney: University of New South Wales Press.
Cotton, James. 1999. "'Peacekeeping' in East Timor: An Australian Policy Departure," *Australian Journal of International Affairs*, vol. 53, no. 3 (November): 237–46.
Flitton, Daniel. 2004. "Issues in Australian Foreign Policy, July to December 2003," *Australian Journal of Politics and History*, vol. 50, no. 2 (June): 229–46.
Forbes, Mark. 2005. "Police pullout plunges PNG into aid crisis," *The Age*, 14 May.
Goldsworthy, David. 2001. "Overview," in James Cotton and John Ravenhill, eds., *The National Interest in an Global Era: Australia in World Affairs, 1996–2000*. Melbourne: Oxford University Press.
Goodspeed, Peter. 2004. "Australia rules: National credo – 'We Pull Our Weight,'" *National Post*, 13 October.
Gurry, Meg. 2001. "Perspectives on Australian Foreign Policy 2000," *Australian Journal of International Affairs*, vol. 55, no. 1 (April): 7–20.
Henderson, Gerard. 2003. "Howard should end confusion on foreign policy," *The Age*, 3 June.
Higgott, Richard A. and Kim Richard Nossal. 1997. "The International Poli-

tics of Liminality: Relocating Australia in the Asia Pacific," *Australian Journal of Political Science*, vol. 32, no. 2 (July): 169–85.

Kerin, John. 2004. "You police the Pacific: US," *The Australian*, 5 March.

Liberal Party of Australia/National Party of Australia. 1996. "A Confident Australia: Coalition Foreign Affairs Policy," mimeo. Melbourne, 10 February.

Maley, William. 2000. "Australia and the East Timor Crisis: Some Critical Comments," *Australian Journal of International Affairs*, vol. 54, no. 2 (July): 151–61.

McDougall, Derek. 2004. "Intervention in the Solomon Islands," *The Round Table*, vol. 374 (April): 213–23.

McKew, Maxine. 2002. "Lunch: Mark Latham," *The Bulletin*, 26 June.

Michaud, Nelson and Louis Bélanger. 1999. "Les politiques canadiennes en matière de sécurité: vers une australisation?" *Études internationals*, no. 30 (June): 373–96.

Morton, Desmond. 1987. "Defending the Indefensible: Some Historical Perspectives on Canadian Defence 1867–1987," *International Journal*, vol. 42, no. 4 (Autumn): 627–44.

Nossal, Kim Richard. 2004. "Upper Hand Down Under: American Politics and the Australia-US Free Trade Agreement," Paper presented to the annual meeting of the Australian and New Zealand Studies Association of North America, Toronto, 20 February. Available at <http://post.queensu.ca/~nossalk/papers/nossal_ausfta.pdf>

O'Neil, Andrew. 2003. "Issues in Australian Foreign Policy, January to June 2003," *Australian Journal of Politics and History*, vol. 49, no. 4 (December): 540–57.

Scott, Shirley. 1998. "Issues in Australian Foreign Policy, July-December 1997," *Australian Journal of Politics and History*, vol. 44, no. 2 (June): 225–32.

Taylor, Peter Shawn. 2004. "Australia Rules: A friendship that could prove costly to Canadians," *National Post*, 15 October.

Trood, Russell. 1998. "Perspectives on Australian Foreign Policy-1997," *Australian Journal of International Affairs*, vol. 52, no. 2 (July): 185–99.

Wattie, Chris. 2004. "Australia rules: A land that encourages its military to 'Go For It,'" *National Post*, 14 October.

Wheeler, Nicholas J. and Tim Dunne. 2001. "East Timor and the New Humanitarian Intervention," *International Affairs*, vol. 77, no. 4 (October): 805–27.

White, Hugh J. 2003. "Mr Howard Goes to Washington: The US and Australia in the Age of Terror," *Comparative Connections*, vol. 5, no. 2 (July): 137–49. Available at <http://www.csis.org/pacfor/ccejournal.html>.

Woolcott, Richard. 2005. "Foreign Policy Priorities for the Howard Government's Fourth Term: Australia, Asia and America in the Post-11th September World," *Australian Journal of International Affairs*, vol. 59, no. 2 (June): 141–52.

6 Plurilateral Multilateralism: Canada's Emerging International Policy?

W. ANDY KNIGHT

Derek Burney recently noted that no country "has reviewed, pondered and consulted about its foreign policy more often, and more openly, than Canada" (2005: 1–2). He surmised that this may be an indication of "an undercurrent of self-doubt in Canada about our role and place in the world" (Ibid). If that is true, what a complete about face from the "Golden Age" of Canadian diplomacy under the leadership of Lester B. Pearson who won a Nobel Peace Prize for his bold and confident contributions on the international stage. Like Burney, one is left to wonder whether the more recent perpetual state of consultations, reviews, and self-reflections with respect to Canada's external relations may not have something to do with a lack of leadership in this country on issues of international policy.

Burney criticized the current Canadian government for what he called "an abdication of responsibility" for seeming to prefer an international role that is "long on good intentions but short on substance," for confusing foreign policy activity with results, for putting process ahead of purpose, and for being more concerned with "how we are perceived rather than by what we actually do" (ibid: 2). Whether or not one agrees with Burney's assessment of Canadian international policy, there is a growing sense that, as the editors of this volume starkly state in the introduction, Canadian foreign policy "is going through a period of profound anxiety, critique, and reconsideration."

It would appear indeed, as Andrew Cohen noted back in 2003, that Canada may have in fact already lost its place and role in the world. Canada, once a major international player that punched above its weight on a number of stages and in a plethora of areas, has in recent times been living off the Pearsonian legacy while slowly eroding the pillars that supported its international stature. No longer a world leader in peacekeeping and mediation, the Canadian state is now perceived as being engaged in pinch-penny diplomacy – doing international policy on the cheap – and as being stingy on foreign aid.[1] With a depleted, beleaguered and under-funded foreign service, gone are the days of confident Canadian mandarins. Instead, Canada seems quite content to contract out much of its "foreign policy outputs"[2] and to allow other countries to assume the leadership role it once had within the international community (Cohen, 2003).

This is, at least, the perception. Now, what is the reality? I argue in this chapter that if Canada seems to have lost its way in the world it is because that "world" is in the midst of turbulence and transition (Rosenau, 1997). Shifts in Canada's international policy today are reflective of the uncertainty associated with world order transformation and the concomitant reconceptualization, or reshaping of multilateralism (see Hampson and Maule, 1993). The emerging world order is exhibiting a number of tensions, particularly in the area of governance. Using social network theory, this chapter depicts the complexity of the global governance arena in which Canada operates, and demonstrates that the Canadian government's international policy is one that tries to strike a balance between two tendencies: normative universal multilateralism and pragmatic plurilateralism. In my conclusion, I argue that Canada should engage in plurilateral processes only if those processes contribute to broader multilateralism, and resist such processes if they are only ends in themselves.

WORLD ORDER TRANSFORMATION AND CHANGING VIEWS OF MULTILATERALISM

"World Order" and "multilateralism" are interrelated concepts, although the latter is generally subordinated to the former. But as Robert Cox put it: "Multilateralism can only be understood within the context in which it exists, and that context is the historical structure of world order" (1996: 494).

The historical structure of world order really refers to a specific configuration of power at a given historical moment. In this sense, world order is a neutral concept that can be imbued with different permutations of the entities that constitute the historical structure at the time of observation. Cox views world order through the matrix of ideas, institutions, and material conditions which allow for the establishment of hegemony by a state, set of states, or a civilization at a particular moment in the history of the world.[3]

Ideas can be of two kinds. The first is what can be called "intersubjective meanings" – i.e. "those shared notions of the nature of social relations which tend to perpetuate habits and expectations of behavior" (ibid: 98). For instance, traditionally, there have been shared notions that people are organized and commanded by states which have authority over defined boundaries; that states relate to one another through diplomatic agents; that certain rules apply for the protection of diplomatic agents as being in the common interest of all states; etc. The second form of ideas is the "collective images" of social order held by different groups of people. "Whereas intersubjective meanings are broadly common throughout a particular historical structure and constitute the common ground of social discourse (including conflict), collective images may be several and opposed" (ibid: 99).

As Cox notes, the "clash of rival collective images provides evidence of the potential for alternative paths of development and raises questions as to the possible material and institutional basis for the emergence of an alternative structure" (ibid). During the post-Cold War period, we have witnessed shifts in both the intersubjective meanings and the collective images people have held of social order.

The ideas that are used to support world order at any given point in history are generally embedded in institutions (both formal and informal). According to Cox, the institutionalization process "is the means of stabilizing and perpetuating a particular order. Institutions reflect power relations prevailing at their point of origin and tend, at least initially, to encourage collective images consistent with these power relations." However, over time, institutions can take on a life of their own, becoming sites of battle between "opposing tendencies." Additionally, rival institutions may spring up, reflecting "different tendencies." It is fair to say that multilateral institutions have been experiencing those kinds of tensions particularly during the post-Cold War period. In any event, institutions "are particular amalgams of ideas and material power which in turn influence the development of ideas and material capabilities" (ibid).

Material conditions refer to "technological and organizational capabilities," which appear in "their accumulated forms as natural resources" that can be transformed by technology. Material conditions also include stocks of equipment (for example, industries and armaments), and "the wealth which can command these" (ibid: 98). Shifts in material conditions can result in state actors moving up and down the hierarchy of the international system and can determine which forces are more powerful or dominant within multilateral institutions. Hegemonic states and great powers benefit from having greater material capabilities than say middle powers and underdeveloped states.

In large part, the materially powerful actors within the international system have traditionally shaped the multilateral institutions according to their ideas, which are generally predominantly held and accepted by most of the other actors within the system. When there are upstarts in the system, i.e., formerly subdominant actors that are on the rise materially and ideologically, hegemons and great powers may be challenged, resulting in shifts to world order.

Another shift in world order that has an impact on the nature of multilateralism is the development of regional groupings. According to Björn Hettne, global regionalization has been a major trend since the end of the Cold War. This trend is having a significant impact on the shaping of world order as inter-regional linkages and networks seem to be vying for contention with multilateralism (see Hettne, 2004). If Canada is to carve out successfully a new international role for itself, it will have to understand how the emerging world order is being shaped by the tensions between universal multilateralism and a more limited form of multilateralism – plurilateralism. As ideas, institutions and material capabilities evolve and change, historical structures (i.e. patterns of world order) are altered and sometimes transformed. Canada's international policy will therefore be affected by the vicissitudes that accompany such shifts in world order.

Contemporary scholars like James Rosenau, Yoshikazu Sakamoto, Robert Cox and Jessica Mathews are convinced that our prevalent world order is undergoing a major transformation. As early as 1992 Rosenau was already observing myriad changes that, in his opinion, were transforming global politics. At the time, he suggested that as "the scope of this transformation widens and its pace intensifies," people will begin to ask urgent questions about the nature of global order and governance (Rosenau, 1990: 37). In *Turbulence in World Politics*, Rosenau said this about the world order transformation he was witnessing at the time: "what once seemed conceptually impossible may now be merging as empirical reality." He suggested that if we are to understand the nature and extent of the changes being made to world order, we should alter the "conceptual premises with which we organize and interpret the course of events ..." (ibid).

Rosenau sees the contemporary era as "a historical breakpoint." In his words, "Global life may have entered a period of turbulence the likes of which it has not known for three hundred years and the outcomes of which are still far from clear." He suggests further that today's changes are "so thoroughgoing as to render obsolete the rules and procedures by which politics are conducted, thereby leaving observers without any paradigms or theories that adequately explain the course of events." While some may dismiss these changes as mere anomalies, Rosenau is convinced that these "anomalies" are more pervasive than the recurrent patterns and the discontinuities are more prominent than the continuities (ibid: 5–6).

If Rosenau is correct then this, in part, provides a plausible explanation as to why the Canadian government and policy makers in the Department of Foreign Affairs have found themselves in the difficult bind of not knowing how best to chart Canada's international policy. Indeed, when the ground is shifting under you, it is easy to fall back onto, and to hold on to familiar turf. In the Canadian case, one observes during this current post-Cold War period of uncertainty and transition that the Canadian government has relied to a large extent on old shibboleths about our "multilateralist tradition" and our "Pearsonian legacy," without evaluating the extent to which changing world order is affecting our approach to multilateralism.

Like Rosenau, Sakamoto, a highly regarded Japanese scholar and astute observer of world order changes, suggests as well that global change is underway even though he is quick to add the caution that it is not yet clear "exactly what is changing, how, and into what" (1994: 15). Cox supports Sakamoto's position but went further in a recent book explaining how agency can lead to changes in the structural underpinnings of world order (Cox and Schechter, 2002). In this case, agency refers to social forces at work in the world – from globalization to the agitation of civil society. Rapid improvements in technology and the proliferation of telecommunications and transportation systems world-wide have, for example, been part of the globalization phenomenon causing shrinkage of the globe and increasing complex interdependence amongst states and peoples. These forces have also put pressure on the state system – in some cases undermining that system and in other cases forcing traditional multilateral institutions to accommodate bottom-up multilateralism (see Knight, 2005a; and, Knight, 1996: 43–69).

As is the case with world order, multilateralism is undergoing modification and shifts. The term "multilateralism" is often used with little regard for its actual meaning. John Van Oudenaren suggests, with respect to the use of the term, that political rhetoric tends "to obscure the fact that there is no consensus in either the academic or policy-making communities about how multilateralism should be defined" (Oudenaren, 2003: 34).

The traditional approach to multilateralism stems from a state-centric and hierarchical conception of world order and global governance (see Coate et al, 2005: 15). This approach takes as a given the existing forms of intergovernmental cooperation and usually entertains only incremental and piecemeal changes to those forms. An exemplar of this thinking on multilateralism is demonstrated by Robert Keohane (1990: 731) who defines multilateralism as "the practice of coordinating national policies in groups of three or more states, through ad hoc arrangements or by means of institutions." But, as Ruggie (1992: 567) points out, what is distinctive about multilateralism is not merely that it involves more than a specific number of actors, but rather that it is based on certain principles that order the relationship between those actors.

In concurrence with Ruggie, Van Oudenaren states that there is "an older diplomatic tradition that regards multilateralism more as a matter of norms than of sheer numbers" (2003: 35). For instance, multilateralism in the Concert of Europe referred to the fact that this institution operated in accordance with a set of unwritten rules tacitly observed by the five major powers within the Concert. One of those rules was that none of the great powers would act unilaterally. Another was that under no circumstances would any of the great powers be humiliated or isolated, nor would any of the great powers allow the mobilization of the less powerful members of the international system against one of the big five.

The League of Nations multilateral system also operated in accordance with principles and norms. For instance, the League built in a norm of collective security in its Covenant (Articles 10 and 16) that stipulated that its members would "undertake to respect and preserve as against external aggression the territorial integrity and existing political independence of all Members" of the organization, and that if one of its Members resorted to war without adhering to a number of steps stipulated in the Covenant then this would, *ipso facto*, be considered an act of war against all other Members of the organization (see Armstrong et al, 2004: 19). Similarly, the UN multilateral system has also been governed by both written and unwritten principles and rules (see Knight, 2000: 61–81). John Ruggie (1992: 3) identified three broad norms which guided the post-1945 multilateral system: indivisibility, generalized principles of conduct, and diffuse reciprocity. Along this vein, the Canadian government has stressed the need for global actors to adhere to a "rules-based" global governance system since a "more predictable international system produces better results than one that is dominated by independent and uncoordinated action" (Canada, 2005b: 27). The principles and norms that undergird multilateral cooperation tend to be achieved through consensus-building and the procedural tendency has been to broaden the number of actors and universalize these principles and norms.

However, the universalization of multilateralism has traditionally been limited conceptually and practically to the Westphalian inter-state system. This is so because multilateralism was associated, until recently, with relations that occur among states through traditional diplomatic channels or via inter-governmental organizations (IGOs). However, as we all know, acceleration in the phenomenon of globalization particularly over the past few decades has not only expanded the number of actors operating on the world stage, but also, reconfigured the Westphalian notion of sovereignty (Ilgen, 2003: 6).

For instance, there are several entities today besides states that are engaged in politics at the global level (e.g. grass-roots organizations (GROs), civil society organizations (CSOs), non-governmental organizations (NGOs), transnational organizations (TNOs), regional organizations, trans-regional organizations, intergovernmental organizations (IGOs), Multinational Corporations (MNCs), hybrid organizations, and covert groups such as terrorists, money launderers, drug traffickers, pirates, etc.). Some of these entities compete with states on the global stage. Many of them interact cooperatively with states, while others are in conflict with them. The nature and pattern of this interaction leads to the conclusion that at the historical juncture of the beginning of the twenty-first century, multilateralism has broadened to include the interaction and activity of state and non-state actors.

Some of these actors have actually increased their power vis-à-vis the state. Jessica Mathews, president of the Carnegie Endowment for Peace, has argued that this phenomenon has resulted in "a new redistribution of power among states, markets, and civil society" (1997: 50–66). In some cases, it has forced national governments to share power with non-state actors – a true sign of a profound change to the underpinnings of the Westphalian world order – and has led to the emergence of what some have called "social networks."

SOCIAL NETWORKS, PANARCHY AND THE EMERGENCE OF PLURILATERALISM

Some scholars have used social network theory as a means of grasping some of the changes that have been occurring in this era of accelerated globalization. Social network theory investigates systems of interconnected individuals and can yield important insights about social structure and social agents. Social networks consist of nodal and linkage relationships that combine to make up the network's structure. Paul Hartzog, one of those scholars, has posited that "the emerging complexity of our social and political structures, composed of many interacting agents, combined with the increasing importance of network forms of organization, enabled by technologies that increase connectivity, propels the world system towards a transformation that culminates in a global political environment that is made up of a diversity of spheres of governance, the whole of which is called panarchy" (2005: 14).

Panarchy exhibits "self-organized order, and is therefore distinct from the chaotic implications of the term 'anarchy'." It comprises "a system of overlapping networks of cooperation and legitimacy, or authority," and therefore resembles what is being called in the recent IR literature "new medievalism." Medievalism is characterized by a system of overlapping authority and multiple loyalties, held together by a duality of competing universalistic claims. In the Middle Ages, for example, there was a highly fragmented and decentralized network of sociopolitical relationships that were more or less held together by the competing universalistic claims of the Empire and the Church (see Friedrichs, 2001).

Analogously, our post-Cold War world seems to be exhibiting a characteristic similar to that of the medieval period. Specifically, governance during our contemporary period is best depicted as consisting of a complicated web of overlapping spheres that are held together by the competing claims of universal multilateralism (embodied in the UN system) on the one hand, and plurilateral multilateralism (being pursued by the global hegemonic power – the United States of America) on the other. Needless to say, Canada is caught between these two tendencies.

The overlapping governance networks of panarchy have facilitated a context conducive to the above competing multilateralisms. Björn Hettne, in noting the post-Cold War trend of global regionalization, points out the subtle difference between (universal) multilateralism and plurilateralism (Hettne, 2004: 1). He posits that whereas (universal) multilateral processes are inclusive, plurilateral ones tend to be exclusive. Plurilateralism allows and enables relatively simple negotiations between a small group of actors with common (but narrow) interests. It exhibits all the signs of the nominal definition of multilateralism, except that membership within the plurilateral arrangement is generally limited to a small group of "like-minded" actors.

Usually, plurilateralism is resorted to when multilateral processes are stalled or when multilateral institutions prove ineffective and unable to reach decisions among their many members. As proven time and again, it is not always easy to reach agreement in bodies with large membership. One can point to several examples of this failing in such organizations as the UN, with 191 members, and the World Trade Organization (WTO), with 135 members. Plurilateral arrangements therefore hold out the promise that one can usually get agreement from a relatively small group of likeminded actors, and overtime, if necessary, expand the circle of the membership of that group as other actors are persuaded, cajoled, or otherwise convinced to become part of that arrangement. The ultimate goal of plurilateralism could be universal multilateralism, although plurilateralism may be considered simply a pragmatic way of getting certain things done. Thus, it is also quite conceivable that a plurilateral grouping may choose to remain "exclusive" with respect to its membership and its overall goals. It has been argued by some that plurilateralism can be a method of avoiding the multilateral process whenever that process does not suit one's national interest.

Raimo Vayrynen adds another dimension to our understanding of plurilateralism. He notes that: "In plurilateralism, the international system structure is complex and volatile because it is not stabilized by any hierarchical system ... It takes all kinds of actors seriously – not just states – and explores how they operate across different levels and functional structures" (2002: 110–11). So plurilateral processes can embrace both state and non-state actors in its complex governance network because they rely on diversity and they resist "hierarchy in order to function and adapt" (Hartzog, 2005: 3). Former Canadian Foreign Minister, Lloyd Axworthy, utilized such a process to manufacture agreement, with the help of Jody Williams and the International Campaign to Ban Landmines (ICBL) as well as the International Committee of the Red Cross (ICRC), among several "like-minded" states for a treaty banning anti-personnel landmines during the Ottawa Process. This particular process was hailed as a "model for cooperation" between governments and non-governmental organizations (NGOs). Axworthy called the Ottawa process "a new type of diplomacy suited to a new era" (Short, 1999: 481).

The Ottawa Process was in fact a response to a stalemate of the 1980 multilateral conference to review the Convention on Prohibitions or Restrictions on the Use of Certain Conventional Weapons (CCW) in order to strengthen Protocol II – which regulates anti-personnel mines (APMs). This failed meeting led Pieter Van Rossem of the Netherlands to assemble a coalition of 'good' countries, meaning those countries that favoured an outright ban on this class of weapons,[4] to see how this issue could be moved forward outside of the CCW review process. It was decided to invite NGOs to join the ten states selected at the first plurilateral meeting in January 1995 in Vienna. The second meeting of these states, the Core Group,[5] and NGOs, held in April 1996, was organized largely by David Atwood and the Quaker organization in Geneva. In October 1996, Canada took over the lead and held a strategy conference in Ottawa to push the discussions on the ban of anti-personnel landmines forward.

In December 1997, Lloyd Axworthy and the Canadian government brought back to Ottawa an increased number of states and NGOs to rally further support for the ban. What is significant about this effort is that Canada's international policy and public diplomacy was shifted closer to the plurilateralism, which Vayrynen speaks of, and away from traditional multilateralism through this fast-tracked Ottawa process. Instead of viewing NGOs as adversaries, Axworthy considered them as crucial allies in the effort to convince states to join the ban (see Williams, 2002). After all, many of those NGOs had witnessed firsthand the ravaging effects of mines and had grown impatient with the only treaty (the CCW) that controlled the use of these weapons.

CANADA'S EMERGING INTERNATIONAL POLICY: MULTILATERALISM, PLURILATERALISM, OR BOTH?

With the current world order in flux and transition, Canada's international policy seems tentative and uncertain. Any dispassionate review of Canadian foreign and defence policy rhetoric and practice since the end of the Cold War will show that Canada has been caught between both universal multilateral and plurilateral arrangements. The reasons for this are many. But certainly we ought to consider, as a central explanatory factor, the ideological split between the Canadian government's desire to support utopian and universalizing multilateral arrangements, such as those within the UN system, and its thrust into the vortex of the pragmatics of a *realpolitik* form of plurilateralism practiced by its neighbour, the global hegemon.

Stephen Lewis once claimed that Canadians have "a lasting and visceral commitment to multilateralism which is ingrained, and endemic to the Canadian character" (cited in Keating, 2002: 1). His view is echoed by Tom Keating, who has documented the multilateralist tradition in Canada's foreign policy since the end of the World War II. Keating asserts that multilateralism "has been an article of faith in the practice of Canadian foreign policy for decades" (ibid). In fact, one can trace the beginning of Canada's multilateral tradition back to the post-World War II construction of multilateral institutions. Canada was not only present at the founding of the United Nations, it played a significant role in establishing this most universal of multilateral organizations.

Over the years, Canadian policy makers have relied repeatedly on multilateralism as a vehicle for projecting its image abroad and for pursuing a diverse range of foreign policy objectives. In most cases, for Canada the cornerstone multilateral instrument was the UN system. It was hoped that the UN would provide the kind of stable and peaceful global environment within which Canada, a trading nation, could do its business and prosper. But in other cases, Canada's international policy was carried out within other multilateral bodies such as the Commonwealth and La Francophonie. As Tom Keating rightly points out, however, "One should not assume that support for multilateral processes and institutions is inherently enlightened and reflects an abnegation of national interests, nor that there is an inconsistency between the pursuit of milieu goals and serving national objectives. On the contrary ... in examining Canada's policies and practices, multilateralism has frequently been viewed as the most effective strategy for pursuing national policy objectives" (ibid: 5). This pursuit of national policy objectives would not always be done within broad-membership multilateral organizations. For instance, because of Canada's perception of the Soviet threat during the Cold War period, Canadian policy makers saw the North Atlantic Treaty Organization (NATO) as an obvious alternative to the still-born collective security mechanism of the UN. One can view Canada's entry into NATO as the beginning of its pragmatic flirtation with "plurilateral" bodies. NATO was, and still is, a limited membership security organization, albeit acting within a collectivist "multilateral framework."

It is also clear, as Keating puts it, that Canada's efforts to construct a global, or in the case of NATO, a trans-regional multilateral framework aimed at establishing "a stable structure of peace and prosperity," were also done with a view to offsetting "the dominant and potentially domineering power of the United States" (ibid: 2). Indeed, this multilateralist strategy has in the past been used as a "counterweight to an exclusively continentalist foreign policy" (ibid: 12). With respect to NATO, former prime minister of Canada, Lester B. Pearson had this to say:

under such a treaty the joint planning of the defence of North America fell into place as part of a larger whole and would diminish difficulties arising from fears of invasion of Canadian sovereignty by the US. It would be easier to advocate a policy of Canadian aloofness if the present state of affairs was maintained. An Atlantic pact would go a long way towards curing our split personality in defence matters by bringing the US, the UK and Canada into regular partnership. (Cited in Reid, 1977: 108–9)

Despite the end of the Cold War and the expansion in NATO membership, Canada still considers this plurilateral body as "an essential collective defence structure" that "embodies the transatlantic link that continues to be critical to the security of our country."[6] However, with the US now taking on the mantle of Empire in the post-Cold War period, plurilateral security arrangements, like NATO, are increasingly dominated by the hyper-power. This has caused Canada to seek out other plurilateral arrangements comprised of "lesser" states and that address security matters with a more normative, soft power approach. Canada uses the latter type of plurilateral arrangements not only to counter-balance US unilateralist tendencies and its use of hard power, but also to address "new" security issues.

Involvement in plurilateral arrangements for Canada is not limited to the security issue area. John Kirton ably demonstrates Canada's involvement in the Plurilateral forum of the G7. Kirton suggests, for example, that during the 1997–8 Asian-turned-global financial crisis, "Canada's behaviour was centered not on broad multilateralism, but on restricted membership plurilateralism, with an overwhelming emphasis on the concert that the G7 represented." He goes on to say that both universal multilateral and strictly regional solutions were insufficient to respond adequately to this crisis. This was so, particularly, because of the magnitude and nature of the financial crisis and its potential contagion, the paucity of IMF resources, the US failure to authorize its quota share increase, and the unwillingness of markets to trust the more universal intergovernmental multilateral institutions. The more universal multilateral body, the IMF, depended on the plurilateral body, the G7, for leadership in dealing with this particular crisis. Kirton comes to the conclusion that Canada's participation in plurilateral bodies like the G7 does not mean that the country is any less multilateral. In fact, he suggests that for Canada both multilateralism and plurilateralism are "mutually reinforcing parts of foreign policy." However, Kirton recommends that under those particular circumstances, "Canada's preferred forum should be the plurilateral G7, rather than the broadly multilateral IMF created at the core to cope with the global economy of 1945" (Kirton, 1999).

There is a sense that Canada, while continuing to be a major supporter of universal multilateralism, is drawn for pragmatic and practical reasons to "more selective plurilateral" clubs (Keating, 2001: 3). Apart from the G7/8, Canada is also part of the Group of Ten (G10) countries, which incidentally is made up of eleven industrial countries (Belgium, Canada, France, Germany, Italy, Japan, the Netherlands, Sweden, Switzerland, the United Kingdom, and the United States).[7] It is useful to recall the role that the G10 played during "the Nixon shock." When on 15 August 1971 US President Nixon announced domestic economic measures that were in clear violation of the multilateral Bretton Woods economic order, this was devastating to countries such as Canada that depended heavily on the US market. Canada tried, unsuccessfully, to utilize its bilateral channels to get the US to soften the blow of this new American economic policy on the Canadian economy, but the American secretary of the treasury resisted those appeals. So, as Tom Keating notes, Canada worked closely with the other members of the G10 "to minimize the damage" and "establish a sense of order and stability in the international monetary system" (ibid: 187). It must be borne in mind that collectively, the G10 members hold more than 53 percent of the votes in the IMF, "so they have more votes than all the other 172 members and have a collective veto on *all* decisions (Willetts, 2001). Therefore plurilateral groupings, like the G10, may be considered pragmatic arrangements for cobbling together solutions to certain global economic problems that may seem intractable to more universal multilateral bodies as well as to regional organizations.

Another example of a plurilateral arrangement is the Group of Twenty (G20) Finance Ministers Meeting. On 18 June 1999, at an World Economic Summit in Cologne that ushered in a global Financial Stability Forum (FSF) and the IMF's International Financial and Monetary Committee (IFMC), leaders of the G7 welcomed this move and declared a commitment to establish an informal mechanism "in the framework of the Bretton Woods institutional system, to broaden the dialogue on key economic and financial policy issues among systemically significant economies and to promote cooperation to achieve stable and sustainable world growth that benefits all" (G7, 1999). In fact, it should be noted that Canada proposed the establishment of the G20 body of Finance Ministers in the wake of the Mexican, Brazilian, and Asian financial crises, which has in a short time helped to modernize the structures of emerging economies (Canada, 2005b: 27).

The Canadian government, under Prime Minister Paul Martin, has championed this plurilateral body as an innovative attempt at "burden sharing, legitimacy and collective problem solving" (Canada, 2005b: 27) and at augmenting the existing global governance architecture. The most interesting feature of the G20 is its attempt at global representational democracy. This body is made up of members of the G7/8 plus Argentina, Brazil, China, India, Indonesia, Mexico, Saudi Arabia, South Africa, South Korea, Turkey, and the European Union (represented by the Council presidency and the President of the European Central Bank). The membership of the G20 is representative of "two-thirds of the world's population, and almost 60 percent of the world's poor" (Ibid.: 27). As Shepard Forman and Derk Segaar note, broadening the G7 to the G20 has "supplemented the damaged, technocratic, legitimacy of the existing regime for financial regulation with a degree of political legitimacy, based on its increased inclusiveness. As such the creation of the G20 represents the next stage in the evolution of informal consultation among industrialized countries and emerging markets (Forman and Segaar, 2006).

Prime Minister Martin wants to extend this experimentation with plurilateralism to bring together the leaders of a globally representative group of 20 countries (the L20) in order to tackle a wide array of problems that affect both the developed and the developing world (environment, education, public health, HIV/AIDS and other pandemics, etc.). The Canadian government sees this move as facilitating a new form of diplomacy and a new multilateralism that is both pragmatic and effective. Naturally, this kind of thinking reminds us of how antiquated the existing multilateral institutions and processes have become.

The need to get around old multilateral forms is something that the US has in common with Canada. Particularly since 1993, the US administration has demonstrated a dogged interest in plurilateralism as a way of getting things done, particularly when extant universal and regional multilateral institutions and processes seem unable to deliver. It is in this area of economic problem-solving that Canada and the US have tended to cooperate within pragmatic plurilateral structures.

During a speech at American University, President Clinton first indicated that the US administration would follow a pragmatic and flexible course in its international trade policy that combined multilateralism, regionalism and bilateralism. In effect, this was an indication of the president's desire to chart a middle course between free trade and managed trade. In order to secure support in Congress for the North American Free Trade Agreement (NAFTA), the US president had to find ways of appeasing individuals in domestic lobby groups (environmental, labour, and industry) who were concerned that free trade would hurt US industries, result in further environmental degradation, and eliminate certain American jobs. Clinton chose to institutionalize the ad hoc strategy of plurilateralism as a means of demonstrating his "middle of the road" approach.

This involved putting together coalitions of countries with which the US could conclude trade agreements, e.g. Canada and Mexico in NAFTA, the 34 Inter-American countries in the Free Trade Area of the Americas (FTAA), and the coalition between the US, Canada and countries in APEC. Satoshi Oyane (2001) writes that the 1995 Annual Report of the US Presidential Advisory Economic Committee explicitly dubbed this policy as plurilateralist. That Annual Report saw plurilateralism not as an alternative, but as a complement to multilateralism. It was seen then as an enabling process for carrying out negotiations between a small group of countries with similar interests, and then using the agreement reached on certain principles and norms to expand the circle and eventually gain broader agreement within more universal multilateral bodies like the WTO. It should be noted that Canada has been drawn into the vortex of the above mentioned arrangements, and is therefore a partner with the Americans in the development of this brand of multilateralism. However, in some cases, Canada has not always supported US attempts at plurilateralism. And, in other cases, the Canadian government has led the development of plurilateral processes which the US government has no intention of supporting. It would seem that Canada's pursuit of normatively-laden plurilateralism puts a great deal of tension in the Canada-US relationship. Certainly, Canada has a difficult time accepting plurilateral arrangements led by the US that are not compatible with universal multilateralism.

Some of the authors in this volume have suggested that the US-led global war on terrorism is something of which Canada ought to be a part. The impression given by these authors is that Canada is out of step with the US on this issue, as well as on other issues such as the ban on anti-personnel land mines and the establishment of the International Criminal Court (ICC). There is no doubt about the disconnect between Canadian and American positions on those issues. This final section of the chapter briefly analyses a plurilateral arrangement that clearly divides the two neighbours, i.e. the US-led coalition to fight a global war on terrorism.

9/11 AND THE US COUNTER-TERRORIST STRATEGY

When those fuel-laden aircraft crashed into the Pentagon and the World Trade Centre buildings on 11 September 2001, the US government naturally wanted to bring to account those responsible for planning and carrying out those terrorist attacks. These attacks had a profound impact not only on the American psyche but also on Canadians. Of the 3,000 people killed in that horrendous event, 25 were Canadians. Indeed, Canadians provided food and shelter to over 23,921 passengers and crew of 142 civilian aircraft that were diverted away from US territory immediately following the attacks.

Initially, the US pursued a multilateral approach to addressing this problem of global terrorism. It went to the UN where the Security Council passed Resolution 1368 condemning the 9/11 attacks, and reaffirmed Article 51 of the UN Charter which gives UN member governments the right to individual and collective self-defence. That Council resolution urged the international community to suppress terrorism and to hold accountable any individual or group who aided, abetted, supported or harboured the perpetrators, organizers and sponsors of terrorist acts. However, it soon became clear that the US would not depend on the UN to address this specific breach in its national security. Instead, the US looked to its allies in NATO to form a plurilateral coalition to wage a global war against the terrorists.

Canada was invited to be part of that coalition. It took measures to improve its domestic and border security. It signed and ratified 12 international conventions and protocols dealing with terrorism, and it joined the US in the attacks on al-Qaeda bases in Afghanistan. However, when the Bush administration began to pressure Canada to join the "coalition of the willing" in a military attack on Iraq, the Canadian government refused to be part of that plurilateral arrangement.

On this issue, the Canadian government showed a preference for acting within the universal multilateral framework. On 17 March 2003, Prime Minister Jean Chrétien speaking to the Canadian House of Commons said:

We believe that Iraq must fully abide by the resolutions of the United Nations Security Council. We have always made [it] clear that Canada would require the approval of the Security Council if we were to participate in a military campaign. Over the last few weeks the Security Council has been unable to agree on a new resolution authorizing military action. Canada worked very hard to find a compromise to bridge the gap in the Security Council. Unfortunately, we were not successful. If military action proceeds without a new resolution of the Security Council, Canada will not participate. (House of Commons, 2003)

Operating within the universal multilateral framework in this case allowed Canada to resist pressure from the world's hyper-power – a feat made more difficult because of Canada's proximity to the global hegemon.

Joseph Jockel and Joel Sokolsky claim in this volume that "there is no inconsistency between Canadian security and values, and the policies undertaken by the Bush administration" when it comes to the global war on terrorism, and that somehow Canada is more secure and stable as a result of the US policies in this area. Clearly, such a statement is highly contestable. For one thing, while Canada and the US share much in common with respect to security and values, there was a clear value difference between Canada's approach to addressing the problem of global terrorism and that of the Americans. That difference, as pointed out above in Chrétien's speech to the House of Commons, is directly linked to our government's position on universal multilateralism and the global rule of law. While Canada was highly supportive of the US war on terrorism, doubt was expressed within the Canadian government and among the Canadian people as to whether that "War on Terror" should extend to Iraq.

The Canadian government and a vast majority within the Canadian

population never bought the arguments put forth by the US administration that Iraq was a threat to the United States, or that Saddam
Hussein was somehow linked to the 9/11 terrorist attacks on American
soil. The secret Downing Street memo, written on 23 July 2002 and
released on 1 May 2005 in the British *Sunday Times*, demonstrates that
US policy (and Britain's) with respect to Iraq was deliberately linked to
the concocted idea that Iraq still possessed WMDs, that it was linked to
al-Qaeda, and that it was an imminent threat to the US. The following
excerpt from that memo is quite revealing:

The Foreign Secretary said he would discuss this with Colin Powell this week.
It seemed clear that Bush had made up his mind to take military action, even
if the timing was not yet decided. But the case was thin. Saddam was not
threatening his neighbours, and his WMD capability was less than that of Libya,
North Korea or Iran. We should work up a plan for an ultimatum to Saddam
to allow back in the UN weapons inspectors. This would also help with the
legal justification for the use of force. (Manning, 2005)

The memo points out that since regime change was not "a legal base
for military action" three other legal bases would have to be utilized:
"self-defence, humanitarian intervention, or UNSC authorisation." The
memo acknowledged that the first two could not be used as the basis
for military action in this case. But the British prime minister, Tony
Blair, felt that "it would make a big difference politically and legally if
Saddam refused to allow in the UN inspectors," noting as well, according to the memo, that "if the political context was right, people would
support regime change" (ibid).

In this case, Canada utilized its long-standing commitment to universal multilateral principles as a means of resisting US hegemonic
pressure to join the plurilateral coalition of the willing in bringing
about regime change in Iraq. It was not an easy decision, but it was one
based on the acknowledgment that plurilateralism ought to be compatible with universal multilateralism if such action is to be considered
legitimate. In this particular case, the invasion of Iraq was seen by the
Canadian government as an action outside the global rule of law and
one that undermined the multilateral institutions that both Canada and
the US helped to build at the end of World War II (Knight, 2005b). As
a result, the Canadian position on Iraq was much closer to that of most
European governments and certainly at odds with that of its hegemonic neighbour.

To stem any criticism from the US administration, the Canadian government has compensated for its refusal to join the US plurilateral
"coalition of the willing" in Iraq. Canada ranks among the largest

donors in the multilateral reconstruction effort in Iraq. To date Canada has committed $300 million to that effort, which includes providing emergency humanitarian assistance, the protection of civilians, the safety and security of aid workers, and the provision of food, water, shelter and health care. It had also earlier provided the UN with funds to assist with emergency preparedness and humanitarian relief in Iraq. Canada also pledged $100 million towards the International Reconstruction Fund Facility for Iraq – a fund co-managed by the UN and the World Bank. Finally, on 28 January 2005, the Canadian government contributed up to $7 million to support the multilateral International Mission for Iraqi Elections (IMIE) and has pledged to train Iraqi police, promote human rights and gender equality, contribute to the social and economic needs of Iraqis and assist the Iraqi people to usher in good governance.

CONCLUSION

If Canada has lost its place in the world, it may be because its leadership is having difficulties trying to find the most appropriate way to deal with a world order that is in flux. It is not the only country experiencing this moment of uncertainty and transition. The historical structures of world order are undergoing a reconfiguration that we haven't seen since 1648. It is important for Canadian policy makers to grapple with these changes – one of which is the emergence of rival multilateralisms.

I argue above that social network theory can help us understand the nature of the world order transformation and the complex web of overlapping governance networks within which the Canadian state manoeuvres. As demonstrated above, Canada's international policy is caught somewhere between universal multilateralist and plurilateralist tendencies. There are pragmatic reasons for wanting to be part of plurilateral processes. For example, such processes can help Canada address global economic problems that are not adequately dealt with by broader multilateral institutions. They can replace outmoded multilateral processes and institutions. They can act as a buffer between Canada's international policy and that of the US. They can augment and complement multilateral processes/institutions. They represent a new form of diplomacy and a new flexible and effective multilateralism.

It is about time that the Canadian government begins to reinvest in rebuilding its international role and reputation and in becoming the global citizen that it ought to be. This may require working across issue areas and across regions to establish new multilateral forums that address specific problems on a case by case basis. This may indeed require the furtherance of plurilateral multilateralism. However, the Canadian government must be careful as to which plurilateral process it becomes engaged in. While pragmatism, flexibility and effectiveness are important criteria for Canadian international policy, so too should representative democracy and global legitimacy. Thus, Canadian international policy should give preference to those plurilateral processes that strengthen and enhance universal multilateralism.

NOTES

1 Note that Canada has never lived up to the goal it set of earmarking 0.7 percent of its GNP to foreign aid. On 15 June 2005 the House Foreign Affairs Committee called on the government to make this commitment before the next Group of Eight leaders' meeting at Gleneagles, Scotland. This position has all-party support.
2 For instance, some of these outputs are contracted out to major international non-governmental organizations like Care Canada and the International Red Cross, and others are contracted out to individual academics or academic consortiums.
3 For a statement of Robert Cox's approach to world order, see Cox (1996: 85).
4 The list of 'like-minded' countries was drawn up by Steve Goose of Human Rights Watch.
5 The initial core group countries were Austria, Belgium, Canada, Germany, Ireland, Mexico, Norway, Philippines, South Africa, and Switzerland.
6 NATO has added 10 new members from eastern and central Europe since 1999. See also the "Defence" chapter of the *International Policy Statement* (Canada, 2005a: 25).
7 This Group consults and co-operates on economic, monetary and financial matters. Meetings are arranged at least one a year, in connection with the autumn meetings of the Interim Committee of the IMF, between the ministers of Finance and Central Bank governors of each member of the Group of Ten. The governors of the Group normally meet on a bimonthly basis at the Bank for International Settlements (BIS). The deputies of the Group meet about four times a year.

REFERENCES

Armstrong, David, Lorna Lloyd, and John Redmond. 2004. *International Organisation in World Politics*, 3rd ed. Houndmills: Palgrave Macmillan.

Burney, Derek. 2005. "Foreign Policy: More Coherence, Less Pretence." Simon Reisman Lecture in International Trade Policy, Centre for Trade Policy and Law, Carleton University, Ottawa, 14 March.

Canada. 2005a. "Defence" in *Canada's International Policy Statement: A Role of Pride and Influence in the World*. Ottawa: Department of National Defence (DND).

– 2005b. "Overview" in *Canada's International Policy Statement: A Role of Pride and Influence in the World*. Ottawa: Department of Foreign Affairs and International Trade (DFAIT).

Coate, Roger A., W. Andy Knight, and Andrei I. Maximenko. 2005. "Requirements of Multilateral Governance for Promoting Human Security in a Postmodern Era," in W. Andy Knight, ed, *Adapting the United Nations to a Postmodern Era: Lessons Learned*, 2nd edition. Houndmills: Palgrave Macmillan.

Cohen, Andrew. 2003. *While Canada Slept: How We Lost Our Place in the World*. Toronto: McClelland and Stewart.

Cox, Robert. 1996. *Approaches to World Order*. Cambridge: Cambridge University Press.

– and Michael Schechter. 2002. *The Political Economy of a Plural World: Critical Reflections on Power, Morals and Civilization*. London: Routledge.

Forman, Shepard and Derk Segaar. 2006. "New Coalitions for Global Governance: The Changing Dynamics of Multilateralism," *Global Governance* (forthcoming).

Friedrichs, Jorg. 2001. "The Meaning of New Medievalism," *European Journal of International Relations*, vol. 7, no. 4 (December): 475–501.

Group of 7 (G7). 1999. "Statement of G-7 Finance Ministers and Central Bank Governors," Washington, 25 September. Available at: <http://www.library.utoronto.ca/g7/finance/fm992509state.htm>.

Hampson, Fen Osler and Christopher Maule, eds. 1993. *Canada Among Nations 1992–93: A New World Order?* Don Mills: Oxford University Press.

Hartzog, Paul B. 2005. "Panarchy: Governance in the Network Age," *Panarchy.com*, 14. Available at: <http://www.panarchy.com>

Hettne, Björn. 2004. "Interregionalism and World Order," Paper presented at the 5th Pan European International Relations Conference, Netherlands Conference Centre, The Hague, 9–11 September.

House of Commons. 2003. *Debates*, 37th Parliament, 2nd Session, 17 March.

Ilgen, T.L. 2003. "Reconfigured Sovereignty in the Age of Globalization," in T.L. Ilgen, ed., *Reconfigured Sovereignty: Multi-Layered Governance in the Global Age*. Aldershot: Ashgate, 2003, p.6.

Keating, Tom. 2002. *Canada and World Order: The Multilateralist Tradition in Canadian Foreign Policy*, 2nd ed. Don Mills: Oxford University Press.

Keohane, Robert. 1990. "Multilateralism: An Agenda for Research." *International Journal*, vol.45, no.4 (Autumn).

Kirton, John. 1999. "Canada's Leadership Role in International Negotiations: The G7, IMF and the Global Financial Crisis of 1997–9," Paper prepared for an International Forum on *The Challenges of Globalization*, Bishop's University, 6–8 June. Available at: <http://www.g8.utoronto.ca/scholar/kirton 19990l/crisis6.htm>.

Knight, W. Andy. 1996. "Multilatéralisme ascendant et descendant: deux voies dans la quête d'une gouverne globale," in Michel Fortmann, S. Neil MacFarlane and Stéphane Roussel, eds. *Tous pour un ou chacun pour soi: promesses et limites de la coopération régionale en matière de sécurité.* Québec: Institut Québécois des Hautes Études Internationales, Université Laval.

– 2000. *A Changing United Nations: Multilateral Evolution and the Quest for Global Governance.* Houndmills: Palgrave Macmillan.

– 2005a. "Global Governance and Bottom-Up Multilateralism," in Claire Turenne Sjolander and Jean-François Thibault, eds, *On Global Governance,* Series on Governance. Ottawa: University of Ottawa Press (forthcoming).

– 2005b. "The US, the UN and the Global Rule of Law," *Review of Constitutional Studies,* vol. 10, nos. 1 & 2 (forthcoming).

Manning, David. 2005. "The secret Downing Street memo: Secret and strictly personal – UK eyes only," *Times On Line,* 1 May. Available at: <http://www.timesonline.co.uk/article/0,,2087-1593607_2,00.html#>.

Mathews, Jessica. 1997. "Power Shift," *Foreign Affairs,* vol. 76, no. 1 (January/February): 50–66.

Oudenaren, John Van. 2003. "What Is 'Multilateral'?" *Policy Review,* no. 117 (Feb/March).

Oyane, Satoshi. 2001. "'Plurilateralism' of the United States and its APEC policies." IDE APEC Study Centre, Working Paper Series 00/01 – No.5 (March). Chiba, Japan: Institute of Developing Economies (IDE). Available at: <http://www.ide.go.jp/Japanese/Publish/Apec/pdf/apec12_trade_0 5.pdf>.

Reid, Escott. 1977. *Time of Fear and Hope: The Making of the North Atlantic Treaty, 1947–1949.* Toronto: McClelland & Stewart.

Rosenau, James N. 1990. *Turbulence in World Politics: A Theory of Change and Continuity.* Princeton, NJ: Princeton University Press.

– 1992. "Governance, Order, and Change in World Politics," in James N. Rosenau, and Ernst-Otto Czempiel, eds. *Governance without Government: Order and Change in World Politics.* Cambridge: Cambridge University Press.

– 1997. *Along the Domestic-Foreign Frontier: Exploring Governance in a Turbulent World.* Cambridge: Cambridge University Press.

Ruggie, John Gerard. 1992. "Multilateralism: The Anatomy of an Institution," *International Organization,* vol. 46, no. 3 (Summer): 567.

Sakamoto, Yoshikazu. 1994. "A Perspective on the Changing World Order: A Conceptual Prelude," in Yoshikazu Sakamoto, ed, *Global Transformation: Challenges to the State System.* Tokyo: United Nations University Press.

Short, Nicola. 1999. "The Role of NGOs in the Ottawa Process to Ban Land-mines," *International Negotiation,* vol. 4, no. 3 (March): 481.

Vayrynen, Raimo. 2002. "Reforming the World Order: Multi- and Plurilateral Approaches," in Björn Hettne and Bertil Oden, eds., *Global Governance in the 21st Century: Alternative Perspectives on World Order.* Gothenburg: Almqvist and Wiksell International, 110–11.

Willetts, Peter. 2001. "The IMF as a Political Institution." Research Project on Civil Society Networks in Global Governance, London, City University of London.   Available   at: <http://www.staff.city.ac.uk/p.willetts/CS-NTWKS/PWUNESCO.HTM>.

Williams, Jody. 2002. "The Role of Civil Society in Disarmament Issues: Realism or Idealism?" Paper presented at Joint Conference, *A Disarmament Agenda for the 21st Century,* hosted by the United Nations Department for Disarmament Affairs and the People's Republic of China, 2–4 April. Available at: <http://www.icbl.org/campaign/ambassadors/jody_williams/realis m_vs_idealism?eZSESSIDicbl=09a79ad8322d093c58ba67d8e44b48ed>.

7 "Friends at a Distance": Reframing Canada's Strategic Priorities after the Bush Revolution in Foreign Policy

DANIEL DRACHE

The Bush revolution has dramatically changed the practice and principles of US foreign policy. Its commitment to regime change when needed, unilateralism when necessary and a disregard for international law when appropriate have opened a new page in global politics.[1] No country, no ally, no neighbour can be indifferent to the reframing of US priorities (Kagan, 2003).

In recent years, the US has consistently shown its support for international law to be conditional, preferring to keep its options open, picking and choosing between security and human rights at its own convenience. At the United Nations, a sea-change is under way after the UN refused to rubber stamp the US decision to rush to war. Condoleeza Rice, the US secretary of state, has called the new American approach to multilateralism "transformational diplomacy," by which it is meant that the United States must make the world conform to the needs and strategic interests of the new twin capstones of US foreign policy, the Homeland Security and Patriot Acts.[2] International agreements like the Landmines Treaty, the Kyoto Accord, and arms control agreements are further than ever down the US priority list. American priorities are being framed by the militarization of space and the reorganization of US Armed Forces, putting them on an attack and quick response footing, capable of going anywhere in the world in the shortest possible time.

Canada has been slow to react to the changed reality brought about by this American unilateralism. A complex, difficult, and demanding agenda is now facing Canadians, who at the level of raw sentiment, still want to cling to the much-tarnished ideal of Americans as our best friends and closest allies, words that Chrétien used after the 9/11 disaster to express Canadian solidarity.[3] But friendship, like any other strategic ideal, is subject to change and evolution. Canada's perennial question is what kind of friendship with the world's greatest power is possible and in our strategic interest. Canada's elite policy-makers have never fully addressed this basic question, and continue to respond to every new American president as though no change is needed, nor as if a real revolution in US foreign policy is likely (Martin, 1982). They are profoundly mistaken. And there is an answer.

Thoreau once wrote that "friends at a distance" make for the "longitudes" of life.[4] We ought to take his insight to heart. "Friends at a distance" is a good starting place from which to rethink the great border, security, and Canada-US relations. Disengagement, scepticism, prudential self-interest, building new strategic alliances, and support for international law and the UN offer a constructive alternative in uncertain times. In this light, this chapter will examine the growing divergence between Canada and the United States, as well as Ottawa's options in dealing with the Bush revolution, the myth of the border, the post-NAFTA reality, and the growing constituency of people who are opposed to the Bush doctrine. The conclusion will provide a practical examination of key elements of Canadian foreign policy which must be given equal weight.

WASHINGTON'S NEW CONSENSUS

The Bush revolution contains both style and content and Homeland Security has created a new frame for US governments to follow (Barber, 1996). It is the arms, legs, and nerve centre of Washington's national security doctrine, coordinating directing and overseeing US security needs. Homeland Security is now part of the fabric of American society and government and will outlast the Bush presidency. It is a permanent institutional change that Congress will not alter for a long time to come. The already large border effects on markets will soon become larger, and the impact on Canada will be even greater because so many agendas are in play.

Congress has used the Homeland Security Act to take control of its side of the fence (Drache, 2004). Many Canadians do not understand the extent to which US law and institutional arrangements have changed. Nor are Canadians particularly gifted readers of US presidential intent and the multi-centered diffuse nature of US politics. We are still operating in our old assumptions and belief in the power of good neighbourliness. Our business elites continue to believe in Bruce

Hutchinson's classic words that the border is "a perpetual diplomatic dialogue ... a fact of nature ... which no man thinks of changing" (NFB, 1976). However, Canadian folk singer Stan Rogers came much closer to the truth in his classic song "Northwest Passage." Canada has always been socially constructed, a fact that Rogers captures in his haunting lyric "tracing one warm line through a land so wild and savage ... I think upon Mackenzie, David Thompson and the rest who cracked the mountain ramparts and did show a path for me."[5] It is this social imagination which has to be imprinted on Canada's foreign policy.

On issues in which Canada has an interest as a NAFTA partner, like global free trade and WTO trade rules, conservative power in America is engaged in deep regime change at home while at the same time aggressively pursuing regime change wherever Washington deems its interests or security in danger.[6] It is absolutely bracing to read the Congressional Record and to see first-hand the policies, ideas, and beliefs of American legislators. However, Canadians don't read these reports, nor can CNN be relied on to provide fair and balanced coverage of American views.

For example, few Canadians have ever heard of Colorado Congressman Tom Tancredo (2001), who likened granting illegal Mexican migrants amnesty to "dismantle[ing] the border" and tantamount to a "death wish," and who also claimed that "the most significant threat we face to this country does not come from a home-grown terrorist; it comes from an immigrant, people who are here either legally or illegally, who are not US citizens, and are here to destroy this Nation." Nor have many heard of Texas Congressman Ron Paul, who has repeatedly sponsored bills to pull the US out of the UN altogether, due to UN "assaults on American sovereignty."[7] Even if these extreme views are in the minority, the record leaves little room to doubt just how aggressively the majority of Congress supports the Bush revolution as the strategic framework for home and abroad. The majority of Republicans want Bush to be even tougher on immigration policy, border issues, regime change and a host of other issues connected with global governance.

This dramatic shift in posture, values and goals has many implications for Canada. It means more trade disputes, beyond the dozens which have already been brought both to the WTO and to the NAFTA dispute-resolution tribunals, and it means more pressure on Canada to join the "coalition of the obedient" in defence and security matters (Canada, 2005b). It means Canadians have to address a status quo that is unravelling faster than anyone could have imagined when North America was first integrated as a market agreement under free trade rules.

Table 7.1 The Slippery Slope of Canadian Foreign Policy: Spin and Reality

Incident	Circumstances	Response	Outcome
Devil's Lake Diversion	In violation of Article IV of the Boundary Waters Treaty, North Dakota plans to divert waters from Devil's Lake into Manitoba.	The Bush administration refuses to overturn North Dakota's decision despite Canadian protestations that the diversion could jeopardize the health of Canada's ecosystem.	The US is unlikely to support the Canadian government's call for a joint investigation and hearing.
Softwood Lumber	The US has levied high tariffs on Canadian lumber exports due to what they say are artificially low stumpage fees.	Canada has taken the US to both the NAFTA and the WTO dispute resolution tribunals, and won.	Despite NAFTA and WTO decisions in Canada's favour, the US illegal tariffs are still in force.
Beef/Mad-Cow	The discovery in 2001 of an Alberta cow infected with Mad-Cow disease prompted a US ban on Canadian beef imports.	The US ban has cost Canadian producers an estimated $3 billion, leading to calls for greater government intervention.	The federal government has decided to provide one-time aid to Canada's producers, rather than invest in an inspection system that examines every cow that is slaughtered.
Cross-border pharmaceuticals	Canadian internet-based mail-order pharmacies have been illegally shipping Canadian drugs to the US.	Some US lawmakers want to legalize drugs imported over the internet from Canada.	Health Minister Ujjal Dosanjh is calling for a ban under the pretext that there will be a shortage in Canada, but in reality, the ban protects US drug company interests.

Table 7.1—*continued*

Incident	Circumstances	Response	Outcome
New security plan	The US has urged Canada to join it in forming a common North American security policy.	The Martin government has signalled a willingness to further integrate our security policies.	Canada will participate in the newly formed Security and Prosperity Partnership of North America.
Missile defence	The Bush administration wanted Canada to be an active participant in a joint missile defence system.	Canadian civil society strongly opposed participation in such a system.	Paul Martin surprised many by refusing to join the US plan, though Canada has provided the US with intelligence support.
End of the 'flash-and-dash commerce first' border	Under Homeland Security, visitors from Canada will be required to show a passport. It is a possibility that they will have to undergo a retina scan, and be fingerprinted.	The government misled Canadians by saying that Canada would get an exemption.	By 2008, Canadians will need full documentation to enter the US, or they will be turned back. The longest undefended border is now securitized and heavily policed.
Kyoto	The US is the only G8 country not to have ratified Kyoto.	Canada has signed onto Kyoto.	Canada is trying to use the G8 to convince the Bush administration to reduce emissions, but Bush is still saying 'No' to Kyoto.
Aid to Africa	Activists and civil society have been asking both Canada and the US to pledge 0.7% of their GNP in aid to Africa.	Both Canada and the US refuse to make such commitments, pledging instead to simply double their current aid.	Aid to Africa remains a low-priority for both countries.

As Table 7.1 shows, Canada is far from resolute in its dealings with Washington. If one were to construct a scale of compliance with Washington's definition of American strategic interests, it is revealing to discover that contrary to appearances, the Martin government has not been successful in defining a set of strategic interests for Canada. In the big picture, there are not only trade irritants, but also deeper issues that have not been forthrightly addressed, including human rights violations in Africa and the Middle East, environmental degradation in North America, and worldwide poverty eradication. Aside from the iconic decisions not to send Canadian forces to Iraq and to opt-out of North American missile defence for the time being, much of the Martin government's policy has been one of trying to massage the public's anxieties, rather than provide new leadership. It is well known that it was Pearson who provided the high benchmark of 0.7 percent of rich countries' GNP to be dedicated to foreign aid.[8] Forty years later, Canada still hasn't met the target despite having the strongest macro-economic numbers of the G7.

Washington has had a hard time accepting that Canada can say no to sending troops to Iraq and to North American missile defence, and yes to Kyoto and global arms treaties. It had been taking Canada's obedience for granted. But experience can be a great teacher. These signal events have not been isolated instances, but rather form the trend-line for a long-term policy shift which has yet to reach its conclusion. Still, Canada has yet to digest fully the American shift in mindset. For example, Allan Gotlieb (2004) and Derek Burney (2005), two of Canada's most respected and most senior diplomats have publicly rebuked Jennifer Welsh's purposeful idea that strategic foreign policy should be tied to human security and Canada's belief in multiculturalism. How could they come to this conclusion having read Romeo Dallaire's *Shake Hands with the Devil?* The more pertinent question is: Where does human security fit on their agenda for global governance? Is it simply placed after a comma in a very long realist sentence on state-to-state diplomacy?

Canada has to assess its own security needs in light of the Bush revolution in foreign affairs. Canadian policy-makers need to identify immediately both the core issues for cooperation and the benchmark areas where Canada will chart its own course of action. While hardline continentalists exhort Ottawa to "follow the leader" at all costs, they have failed to recognize that the world has changed. Putting faith in phrases like "a North American community of law" does not address the way the American Congress exercises its power and uses the rule of law only when it suits their interest (Gotlieb, 2005). Ottawa has come up empty-handed when it comes to protecting NAFTA's legal integrity. Gordon Ritchie is essentially correct when he argues that stripping NAFTA of its legal clout is very problematic. These kinds of tactics set precedents and can be "applied to everything from energy to agriculture" (Ritchie, 2005). NAFTA is poisoning the waters; making it very difficult for any Canadian government to reach agreement on terms acceptable to Canada and to Canadians on many other issues.

Anti-NAFTAists also run the risk of irrelevance. North American integration is a fact, and NAFTA is not going to be nixed; the strategic issue is to reduce its asymmetries and to look for partnerships elsewhere.[9] This takes a lot of hard thinking. Neither worn platitudes nor rigid template-thinking can define Canadian foreign policy in this complex global age.

MANAGING NORTH AMERICAN DIVERGENCE

The new policy challenge facing Ottawa is learning how to be a smart manager of the growing divergences in the North American security agenda. The long-run trend suggests that Canada-US relations are set to become more conflictual than conciliatory, and in the short-term, relations are going to be more acrimonious, as they have already begun to be. Initially, the Bush administration looked for external 'yes-elites' to support their homeland security agenda. Ottawa was the perfect candidate because rarely in four decades had Liberal diplomacy disagreed with Washington on any fundamental issue. The Canadian mindset was to take the edge off of Washington's tougher uncompromising stands, as it tried to do during the Cold War, Vietnam, or the countless behind-the-scenes diplomatic face-saving compromises (Heinbecker, 2004; Cooper, 1997).

As a middle power, Canada is instinctively drawn to the middle-ground. As a regional power, Canada is in a quandary because it is a regional player without a region. It has never made the hemisphere an integral part of its foreign policy. Brazil, Argentina, and Chile have never been priorities, where Canadian diplomats have invested in a long-term relationship that is basically narrowly commercial (Graham, 2004). At the same time, Canada faces the danger of declining global relevance as Europeans loosen their transatlantic ties, and Washington relies mainly on one or two key allies as its principal mainstays – Israel, the United Kingdom, and more recently, Australia. Without a basic reorientation, Canada will find itself marginalized and partner-less in a very tough and hardnosed age of power politics.

The Bush revolution has ended the functionality of the Pearson-Axworthy model as the policy frame for Canada to do business at the global level. This had been a powerful prism through which to balance realism and idealism. Now Canada needs to learn to navigate a much different world. The Rumsfeld-Bush game plan is to keep Canada and Mexico on a short leash. In a way that surprised experienced foreign-policy watchers, Ottawa ended up charting a moderately autonomous course from Washington on Iraq and Missile Defence. Historians will one day shed light on how Chrétien and Martin, neither of whom has an instinct for first principles, chose complimentary security policies for Canada, rather than common ones. More recently, in a minority government setting, this forward-momentum has not been difficult to maintain, since the government would face collapse if continentalists were the only force at the cabinet table. Still, the pressures for greater continental integration and less of a maple-leaf stance are never off the radar screen.

OPTION ONE:
ACCOMMODATING THE BUSH REVOLUTION

Canada can choose to support the Bush revolution in foreign policy in a variety of ways, such as incrementalism, ad hocery, stealth, default, or deliberate choice. The newest initiative, Independent Task Force on North America (2005), headed by John Manley and his Mexican and American counterparts, aims at deepened trilateral ties which would lock Canada even more closely into Bush's policy revolution. These trade proposals suggested by the Task Force have edged continentalism back towards the centre of the public policy agenda. Some of their ideas are vague, but Canadian policy-makers have targeted the conti-nentally-organized auto and steel industries upon which to build the new relationship (Chase and Keenan, 2005). However, with Chinese automakers in the next five years likely to take a healthy share of the North American auto market, and with one in three cars made in North America assembled in Ontario, the last thing that Ottawa should be negotiating is to move the industry's centre of gravity from Canada to the US. Clearly there is no strategic vision here, but just another ad hoc initiative taken by the Liberals, largely in secret without any public consultation.

The fear in business and elite circles is that Canada will miss the con-tinental trade boat by being too outspoken and by not being at the table on US terms. The new realities brought about by the Bush revo-lution haven't stopped Canada's business elites from acting as if nothing has changed (CCCE, 2004; Goldfarb and Tapp, 2005). Fortu-nately, public opinion is against any need for further integration. Cana-dians increasingly realize that Canada has all the access to the US market it will ever get, and even if Canada had 100 percent access, it doesn't have an industrial strategy to make significant headway in the American market in high-value high-tech industries. Compared to South Korea, Canada is a third-tier industrial power, without a full range of industries that are competitive outside of Canada's humongous auto sector. Stiglitz (2003), Sachs (2005), and Rodrik (1997) have all came to question the foundations of the Bush doctrine on free trade and economic integration. The best research underscores free trade's timing, sequencing, and how the opening of markets creates asymmetric payoffs in different countries and industries. This is particularly so in Canada, where a recent Statistics Canada study found that 65 percent of exports are now resource-based, confirming the Innisian model of staple-led growth.[10] Rocks, logs, and energy exports have created an international division of labour for Canada that is impossible to transcend with the existing policy mindset. With evidence like this, Canadian policy-makers will be tempted to take a serious look at our second option.

OPTION TWO:
BEING A NORTH AMERICAN SCEPTIC

This position is more consonant with the values and attitudes of modern Canada. Canadians support multilateralism, human rights, stronger international institutions of global governance, and the global redistribution of resources. Even on domestic North American issues, Canadians are more tolerant, more diverse, and more redistributive in their beliefs than Americans, as Michael Adams has shown in his studies of Canadian social values (Adams, 2003). Canadians have already begun a process of foreign policy reorientation, as evidenced by the Pew Global Attitudes Project, which found that 57 percent of Canadians favour a more independent Canadian approach from US policy, up from 43 percent just two years ago. At the same time, 75 percent of Canadians say Bush's re-election makes them less favourable towards the US (Pew, 2005). Canadians' attitudes and values have edged quite visibly towards those of social Europe. Ottawa needs to follow the Canadian public's lead.

Furthermore, the only way for any country to level the playing field is to use either the threat or the act of trade retaliation – a strategic weapon that Ottawa must explain to Canadians, but which may also result in US retaliation. At one time, the spectre of US retaliation was regarded as such a chilling prospect that no self-respecting trade expert would contemplate it. Yet this traditional viewpoint seems to have been challenged, as demonstrated in the case of Brazil's successful fight against US cotton subsidies, in which the US was forced to back down

(Chase and Keenan, 2005). Canadians must likewise look much closer at the benefits, as well as the costs, of using trade retaliation as a strategic instrument.

THE POLITICAL CULTURE OF THE BORDER

Some scholars think that NAFTA was supposed to create a system of North American governance, yet there are very few institutions that Canada and the United States commonly share. But there is indeed one very large and important institution: namely the border, which is created by geography, law and the state. The border predates NAFTA, has a long history, and is the primary mechanism for inter-governmental contact between Washington and Ottawa.

In our respective political cultures, the importance attached to the border could not be more striking. Canada and the US remain worlds apart in their views. For the US, the border is iconic. It is as significant to Americans as the flag, the constitution and the presidency. It is the embodiment of American sovereignty. It is the line in the sand for citizenship purposes, delineating between Americans and aliens. Each year, US border authorities aggressively remove over 200,000 migrants from the country; 71,000 for criminal offences and 120,000 for non-criminal reasons (Drache, 2004). Congress wants even tougher measures with which to remove any immigrant who breaches the tough, new and intrusive security regulations. By being steadfastly unwilling to grant undocumented Mexicans amnesty, Congress is signalling that it believes, today more than ever, that the security-first border is the frontline institution for citizenship and immigration matters.

For Canadians, the border has never acquired such magisterial importance. We think of the border as open, porous and undefended. Our idea of the border is largely a civic one. We value it because it protects Canada's programs, identity and cultural diversity. Our business elites, on the other hand, think of it as a necessary inconvenience which they would like to dismantle. No American corporation is as anti-border as the Canadian Council of Chief Executives.

Post-9/11, the fact is that the massive daily shipment of goods continues to move easily across the border for commercial purposes (98 percent of all truck traffic into the US is not inspected). Waiting times of 3 to 4 hours are considered reasonable, and these will be reduced further once new facilities are built to ease congestion at the Detroit-Windsor crossing. But for people, political refugees and immigrants, crossing the border remains a huge issue fraught with uncertainty. There are more stringent rules and many more tough custom's officials exercising their discretionary authority. This situation will not be easily regularized before it gets better.

THE POST-NAFTA BORDER
AND OPPOSITION TO THE BUSH DOCTRINE

The undefended, people-friendly, open border which Canada and the US once shared has disappeared forever. We haven't fully assimilated to the fact that the US assumes that in addition to being in charge of its side of the fence, it is by implication in charge of our side as well. Unlike the NAFTA negotiations, where compromises were made and a joint text emerged at the end of the lengthy process, US security changes are a unilateral work-in-progress. Fingerprinting, retina scanning, racial profiling, and security checks are now standard practice. The EU parliament is fighting the intrusive nature of these newly legalized practices as a violation of EU privacy rights. They may not win the day, but they will at least force the Americans into serious negotiations. Compromises may be possible. By opting to adapt rather than to innovate, Canada has chosen not to become part of a wider strategic alliance on this issue.

In this post-NAFTA age, the broadening and deepening of North American integration is largely a dead issue. There are some die hard supporters in the business community but there is no uptake by the public, the media, or by the NDP, the Bloc, or large parts of the Liberal Party. There is no new consensus here, nor is there likely to be one in Washington, where Congress looks not for genuine partnership but only to maximize its trade and security advantage. The benefits from the signing of NAFTA were frontloaded, and the macro effects on jobs and exports were much smaller than predicted. Originally, 450,000 new jobs were supposed to be created by NAFTA. In reality though, free trade may have cost Canada as many as 276,000 (Campbell, 2001). The productivity gap between Canada and the US has widened, not shrunk. Access to the American market was supposed to lead to bigger and more competitive Canadian firms capable of competing in the American market. Instead, a record number of our biggest firms have been taken over by US companies. With tariffs close to zero, access is no longer the issue. The new threat comes from China, India, and Vietnam. Mexico, Canada, and the US are losing jobs to the "Global South," and NAFTA is not the right strategy to address this wakeup call being sent to North American manufacturers to diversify, re-structure and re-invest in new labour-saving technologies.

One should not underestimate how opposed Canadians have been to the Bush revolution. In 2004, public opinion polling showed that over

60 percent of Canadians did not support the Bush agenda in Iraq, at the UN or on human rights (Sallot, 2003). There is now a large constituency which supports a fundamental reorientation in foreign policy; a constituency that did not exist when Trudeau toyed with the idea of a "third option" for Canada. Had it existed then, Trudeau may very well have engaged in a fundamental course correction. There is nothing romantic about re-thinking a country's strategic goals. Trudeau wanted to strike quite a different balance between pragmatic realism on the global stage and the constraints of Cold War politics. He wanted to push the boundaries of foreign policy to reflect more adequately Canadian society.

Canadians support complimentary policies towards the Bush revolution in foreign policy, not common ones. If there is one lesson that the last period has taught, it is that parallel policies, not compliant ones, offer Canada the best safeguard against a revitalized US imperial interest. Canadians see much merit in a made-in-Canada set of policies, and they do not want to be locked into the US chain of command in a trans-border institution that limits Canada's autonomy to act locally and globally in support of international law and the UN system of collective security. The majority of Canadians prefer human security to homeland security on the global stage.

The current fear is that governments have gone too far in fighting terrorism, and have ignored the rule of law and human rights. Such an approach fails to strike a balance between security and core Canadian values, and for that reason it is unlikely that Canadians will moderate their views or begin to support Bush's revolution in foreign policy in the foreseeable future.

NORTH AMERICAN SCEPTICISM: WHAT WOULD IT LOOK LIKE?

The United States will exercise disproportionate influence in establishing the rules of the international arena on security, global governance, North American integration, and over Canadian public opinion. As a result, Canada is going to have to make an extraordinary effort in these four strategic areas.

On Security

Canada has stepped up to the plate, spending over $10 billion as its contribution to improving North American security. But the reality is that there is no end in sight to US requests for Canada to do more. In fact, the 9/11 Commission found that many important security gaps and failures in the American system have been internal to the US, and that American authorities have not proceeded effectively to implement many practical, on the ground changes (see National Commission, 2004). In fact, American authorities are reluctant to have a 100 percent security-border, with the round-the-clock inspection of people and shipments which that entails, because this would undoubtedly paralyze the US economy as well as violate the privacy rights of its own citizens.

A recent study of high-level contact between Ottawa and Washington bureaucrats found that Canada has almost unlimited access to the US Office of Homeland Security at both policy and ministerial levels (Mouafo et al, 2004). Although Ottawa policy-makers have this high-level access, they should remain cautious of the fact that American priorities rank above Canadian concerns, and may ultimately restrain their options. Canada needs a strategy of continued, frank consultation with the Bush government, as well as reserving its right to follow an independent course of action whenever its strategic interests dictate. Paul Martin constantly asserts that Canada is an independent nation, but frequently is unable to add substance to its declarations.

Canada has not gone so far as the Homeland Security and Patriot Acts, which many US experts warn violate the first, fourth, fifth, and sixth amendments. US law authorities now have unprecedented sweeping powers to search, detain, and imprison without warrants. US police have used the new security legislation to hold individuals without counsel and without charges. At the border, Muslim Canadians and South Asian Canadians continue to be stopped, harassed, and questioned in contravention of their Charter rights.

Canada still does not have a sufficiently independent security policy from Washington. A security regime is not an exercise in supranationality; it must respect and enhance Canadian sovereignty. Canada has no interest in a common North American visa, identity card, political refugee policy or interdiction policy with the US. This mentality, which sees North American integration overshadowing every other major concern, is not viable or acceptable to the Canadian public.

So far there has been no Canadian public audit of the US Homeland Security Act and its impact both at the border, and behind it on refugees, immigrants, security and commerce. Ottawa needs a comprehensive and authoritative fine-grained audit, like the one Roy Romanow conducted for Canada's health care system. We also need a full-scale debate on the political, legal and strategic impacts of US Homeland Security. Ottawa needs to get its own house in order if it expects to be effective in making its voice heard.

On Global Governance and Human Rights

Canada used to be a leader in the area of global governance, but for too long has been relying on its past glories. Three decades ago, former Prime Minister Lester Pearson proposed that rich countries reserve 0.7 percent of their GNP to foreign aid. Despite its relatively strong economic indicators, Canada devotes a measly 0.26 percent of its GDP to aid, far below the 0.4 percent average for rich countries (Saunders and Clark, 2005). Canadian officials have set their expectations low, and have shied away from spending the political capital necessary to try and build a consensus around the 0.7 percent mark.

Despite what Paul Martin says, his government remains an out-rider in these areas. Ottawa continues to use a scatter-gun approach, emulating in many ways an American approach that has the resources but not the willpower to make a dent in global poverty, the single-most scourge of our time. But as a middle-power, finger-pointing at what the US or others don't do just makes Canada look hypocritical and smug.

What we can do is to set a high standard by engaging in new citizenship practices and acting on our international duty to protect those facing genocide and ethnic cleansing. Axworthy's contribution to human security and reform of the United Nations has been path-breaking and innovative. Leading up to the US war on Iraq, Canada collaborated closely with Mexico and other members of the UN Security Council, following a policy of caution and restraint in the hopes of building a compromise like Pearson had done in 1956 during the Suez Crisis. Once it became clear that no UN mandate for intervention would be forthcoming, Canadians mobilized in large numbers to oppose US actions. The moral and strategic imperative is not to divorce soft power, with its emphasis on diplomacy, persuasion and compromise, from the grubby hard power of market access, economic integration and collective security. Canada's capacity to act at the global level has to make soft power as important as hard power.

North American Integration

After a decade of North American integration, the macro-benefits of further integration are small, and whatever access has been achieved under NAFTA has already been realized. The most authoritative studies performed by Industry Canada argue that the low Canadian dollar, rather than free trade, has been responsible for Canada's export boom to the US (see Helliwell, 2000). Far more significant is that our access to US non-resource markets is not likely to grow until Canada has a clutch of home-grown multi-national corporations who can power themselves into the US market. But for a decade, Ottawa has been hostile to the practicality and effectiveness of having an industrial strategy, and have instead preferred to let NAFTA carry the burden. The major challenge that both pro- and anti-NAFTA sides agree on, is the need to shrink NAFTA's asymmetries (see Doran, 2000; and Drache, 2000).

Scepticism sends the message that we don't want to constitutionalize anything in any new NAFTA-plus deal that American business elites may try to sell to the Bush administration. Canada does poorly in trying to negotiate big deals, because there is no certainty that US trade politics will work to Canada's advantage. The North American sceptic view-point accepts that most of the present trade irritants will continue because the US Congress is not prepared to change its trade laws, which Destler described in his classic study of US trade politics as "arbitrary, ad hoc, and contingent" (1995). A sceptical policy process recognizes that divergences exist and instead of trying to minimize them or ignore them, tries instead to manage and exploit them in Canada's strategic interest.

Building Strategic Alliances

To be an effective middle-power requires Canada to build strategic alliances with the Global South and the European Union across a broad range of policy domains. When it comes to political refugees, the environment, and the provisioning of global public goods like clean water and affordable drugs, collaborating with other countries who share Canadian values and objectives is the only realistic way of advancing Canada's strategic interests.

Canada has over-invested in NAFTA, and as a result neglected its relations with the "Global South." It is not an unfair comment to say that Canada has failed to develop a strong relationship with Mexico, which could have been one of the primary benefits of NAFTA. After a decade of NAFTA, Canadian officialdom (as well as Mexican policy-makers) has very little idea of what relations between an emerging industrial nation and an established one looks like. Only 0.5 percent of Canada's exports are destined for Mexico. Civil society links are numerous and diverse, and there is much that needs to be done to make them more robust. Over 10,000 Mexican students now pursue higher education in Canada, but much more could be done. For example, immigration from Mexico to Canada is not that big, and could be encouraged. Canada could do much by the way of developmental and other types of exchanges with its southern-most NAFTA partner. Unless there is a large Mexican-Canadian resident community, it is unlikely that Mexican-

Canadian relations will broaden or deepen in the foreseeable future. Mexico is symbolic of the need for strategic alliances with countries from the "Global South." With 85 percent of our exports destined for the American market, and with the highest level of integration of any G7 member, Canada's relationship with Washington consumes all of the policy oxygen and energy of the Ottawa establishment (DFAIT, 2005a).

CONCLUSION

If Ottawa expects to be a more effective actor globally, it needs to connect with the Canadian public in ways that it has not chosen to do. Increasingly, foreign policy will have to reflect the social values of Canadian society, rather than, as in the past, the special interests of business elites. In a prescient article in *The Globe and Mail*, Gordon Pitts recently argued that the Canadian Council of Chief Executives has declined in influence in Ottawa partly because of its support for an outdated and economically deterministic set of policies (Pitts, 2005). At present, Ottawa is caught somewhere between denial and accepting responsibility, as it continues to do no more than react to policy changes coming out of Washington. Managing conflict will require increased focus and brains from Canada's policy elites. The Martin government must now accept that Canadian foreign policy has to constantly change, adapt, and innovate in this very charged global policy environment.

NOTES

Special thanks to Blake Evans for his meticulous assistance and many valuable suggestions in preparing this text.

1 For an acclaimed look at the Bush revolution in foreign policy, see Daalder and Lindsay (2003). For a less optimistic take, see Prestowitz (2003).
2 For a full-text version of the Homeland Security Act and the Patriot Act, respectively see <http://www.whitehouse.gov/deptofhomeland/bill/index.html> and <http://www.fincen.gov/hr3162.pdf>.
3 According to the Pew Global Attitudes Project (2004), 59 percent of Canadians still hold 'favorable opinions' of the US, a number significantly higher than any other G7 country, despite being lower than the 71 percent who held favorable opinions in 1999/2000.
4 "Nothing makes the earth seem so spacious as to have friends at a distance; they make the latitudes and longitudes." Thoreau wrote this in a letter to Lidian Emerson, 22 May 1843.

5 For Rogers' full lyrics, see <http://www.stanrogers.net>.
6 For comments on Mexican amnesty, see Huntington (2004) and Micklethwait (2004).
7 Paul made these suggestions to Congress, most recently in the proposed *American Sovereignty Restoration Act of 2005*, introduced on 8 March 2005. See H.R.1146, available at <http://thomas.loc.gov>.
8 When the Pearson Commission released its report in 1969, it based the 0.7 percent target on GNP. Today, development aid targets have been measured in terms of GDP, keeping the 0.7 percent target.
9 For a highly critical analysis of NAFTA, see Clarkson (2002).
10 See the 2002 Industry Canada report entitled, "Canada's Growing Relations: Relations with the United States."

REFERENCES

Adams, Michael. 2003. *Fire and Ice: The United States, Canada, and the Myth of Converging Values.* Toronto: Penguin Canada.
Barber, Benjamin. 1996. *Jihad vs McWorld.* New York: Ballantine.
Brock, Kathy and Kim Nossal. 2005. "Shattered dreams of tsunami aid," *Globe and Mail*, 5 July, A13.
Burney, Derek H. 2005. "Foreign Policy: More Coherence, Less Pretence." Simon Reisman Lecture in International Trade Policy, Centre for Trade Policy and Law, Carleton University, Ottawa, 14 March.
Campbell, Bruce. 2001. "False Promise: Canada in the Free Trade Era," in *NAFTA at Seven: Its Impact on Workers in All Three Nations.* Briefing Paper, Economics Policy Institute. Available at: <http://www.ratical.org/co-globalize/NAFTA@7/nafta-at-7.pdf>.
Canada. 2005a. *Canada's International Policy Statement: A Role of Pride and Influence in the World.* Ottawa: Department of Foreign Affairs and International Trade (DFAIT), 19 April.
– 2005b. "Dispute Settlement: Trade Negotiations and Agreements: Dispute Settlement." Ottawa: International Trade Canada (ITC), 29 March. Available at: <www.dfait-maeci.gc.ca/tna-nac/dispute-en.asp>.
Canadian Council of Chief Executives (CCCE). 2004. "New Frontiers: Building a 21st century Canada-United States Partnership in North America." Discussion Paper, CCCE, April. Available at: <http://www.ceocouncil.ca/en/view/?document_id=365&area_id=7>.
Chase, Steven and Greg Keenan. 2005. "New trade deal seeks close ties on auto and steel," *Globe and Mail*, 27 June, B1
Clarkson, Stephen. 2002. *Uncle Sam and Us: Globalization, neoconservatism, and the Canadian State.* Toronto: University of Toronto Press.

Cooper, Andrew F. 1997. *Canadian Foreign Policy: Old Habits and New Directions*. Scarborough: Prentice Hall.

Daalder, Ivo H. and James M. Lindsay. 2003. *America Unbound: The Bush Revolution in Foreign Policy*. Washington, DC: Brookings Institute Press.

Destler, I.M. 1995. *American Trade Politics: System under Stress*, 3rd ed. Washington: Institute for International Economics.

Doran, Charles F. 2000. "Convergence or divergence?" *Canada Watch*, vol. 8, nos. 4–5 (November-December): 61, 73–4. Available at: <http://www.yorku.ca/robarts/projects/canada-watch/pdf/cw_8_4–5.pdf>.

Drache, Daniel. 2000. "Integration without Convergence? The North American Model of Integration," *Canada Watch*, vol. 8, nos. 4–5 (November-December): 63–5. Available at: <http://www.yorku.ca/robarts/projects/canada-watch/pdf/cw_8_4–5.pdf>.

– 2004. *Borders Matter: Homeland Security and the Search for North America*. Halifax: Fernwood.

– 2006. *The Manufacturing of Dissent and Its Global Counterpublics*. London: Polity Press (forthcoming).

Goldfarb, Danielle and Stephen Tapp. 2005. "There are many ways to increase the effectiveness of the aid we give," *Toronto Star*, 6 July, A13

Gotlieb, Allan. 2004. "Romanticism and Realism in Canada's Foreign Policy," C.D. Howe Institute Benefactors Lecture, Toronto, 3 November.

– 2005. "A North American Community of Law." Address to the Borderlines Conference at the Woodrow Wilson International Center for Scholars, Washington, 27 February. Available at: <http://www.borderlines.ca/washington/speech_alangotlieb.phtml>.

Graham, John W. 2004. "Canada, Latin America and the Caribbean: What Sort of Amigo Are We?" Address to the Canadian Institute for International Affairs, Ottawa, 9 December. Available at: <http://www.focal.ca/pdf/speech CIIA_JWG.pdf>.

Harding, Katherine. 2005. "'Big development' over beef," *Globe and Mail*, 27 June, A4

Heinbecker, Paul. 2004. "Multilateral Cooperation and Peace and Security," *International Journal*, vol. 59, no. 4 (Autumn).

Helliwell, John. 2000. "Globalization: Myths, Facts and Consequences." C.D. Howe Institute Benefactors Lecture, Toronto, 23 October.

Huntington, Samuel. 2004. "The Hispanic Challenge," *Foreign Policy*, no. 141 (March/April): 30–45.

Independent Task Force on North America. 2005. "Building a North American Community." Report of the Independent Task Force on North America. New York: Council of Foreign Relations, May. Available at: <http://www.cfr.org/pdf/NorthAmerica_TF_final.pdf>.

Kagan, Robert. 2003. *Of Paradise and Power: America and Europe in the New World Order*. New York: Knopf.

Kissinger, Henry. 1973. *A World Restored*. Gloucester, Mass: P. Smith.

Martin, Lawrence. 1982. *The Presidents and the Prime Ministers: Washington and Ottawa Face to Face: The Myth of Bilateral Bliss, 1867–1982*. Toronto: Doubleday Canada.

Micklethwait, John. 2004. *The Right Nation: Conservative Power in America*. New York: Penguin Press.

Mouafo, Dieudonné, Nadio Ponce Morales, Jeff Heynen, eds. 2004. *Building Cross-Border Links: A Compendium of Canada-US Government Collaboration*. Action-Research Roundtable on Managing Canada-US Relations (Canada). Ottawa: Canadian School of Public Service.

NAFTA Secretariat. 2003. "Dispute Settlement: Decisions and Reports," 23 October. Available at: <http://www.nafta-sec-alena.org/DefaultSite/index_e.aspx?DetailID=76>.

National Commission on Terrorist Attacks. 2004. *The 9/11 Commission Report*. New York: W.W. Norton.

National Film Board (NFB). 1976. "Between Friends."

Pew Global Attitudes Project. 2005. *Views of a Changing World 2005*. Washington, DC: The Pew Research Center, 23 June. Available at: <http://pewglobal.org/reports/display.php?ReportID=247>.

Pitts, Gordon. 2005. "Tom's Club: Only chief executives need apply," *Globe and Mail*, 5 July, B10.

Prestowitz, Clyde. 2003. *Rogue Nation: American Unilateralism and the Failure of Good Intentions*. New York: Basic Books.

Ritchie, Gordon. 2005. "Who's afraid of NAFTA's bite? Not the US, whose dogged attacks on softwood lumber undermine trade agreements," *Globe and Mail*, 15 February, A21.

Rodrik, Dani. 1997. *Has Globalization Gone Too Far?* Washington: Institute for International Economics.

Sachs, Jeffrey D. 2005. "Investing in Development: A Practical Plan to Achieve the Millennium Development Goals," *United Nations Millennium Report 2005*. Available at: <http://www.unmillenniumproject.org/reports/fullreport.htm>.

Sallot, Jeff. 2003. "Canadians oppose US stand, poll says," *Globe and Mail*, 8 February.

Saunders, Doug and Campbell Clark. 2005. "G8 leaders back off 0.7% foreign-aid target," *Globe and Mail*, 5 July, A9.

Stiglitz, Joseph. 2003. *Globalization and Its Discontents*. New York: W.W. Norton.

Tancredo, Tom. 2001. Speech in the House of Representatives. Congressional Record, 6 November, H7841–H7846. Available at: <http://wais.access.gpo.gov>.

Welsh, Jennifer. 2004. *At Home in the World: Canada's Global Vision for the 21st Century*. Toronto: HarperCollins.

PART TWO

Giants Beyond the Continent

8 A BRICSAM Strategy for Canada?

JOHN WHALLEY and
AGATA ANTKIEWICZ

The term BRICSAM denotes a group comprising Brazil, Russia, India, China, South Africa, countries of the Association of Southeast Asian Nation (ASEAN), and Mexico. These countries have recently been the focus of major research projects, such as Goldman Sachs 2003 study, *Dreaming with BRICs: The Path to 2050*, and the Centre for International Governance Innovation's (CIGI) BRICSAM project. While membership in this group may appear somewhat arbitrary,[1] group members are essentially the set of more heavily populated, low and middle-income countries that are either rapidly growing or seem poised to achieve moderate to high rates of growth in the near future. The reason for focusing on these countries is that global economic power appears to be shifting towards them and away from the members of the Organisation for Economic Co-operation and Development (OECD)[2] or G7. The BRICSAM economies jointly account for over half of the world's population, and in the last four years have had average growth rates of around six percent.

The central feature of interest for Canada in this group is that current growth in the BRICSAM – if it were to continue on pace for a couple of more decades (and that may be a big 'if') – will likely yield export markets of increasing significance to Canada. Their emergence, therefore, provides an opportunity to diversify Canada's trade and industrial linkages away from the US. Thus, Canada may be poised to experience a progressive diminution in its relative integration with the US economy.

Canada's economy has become ever more engaged with the US since the end of the Second World War. Only 30 percent of Canadian wheat and resource-dominated exports went to the US in the later 1940s. After the Auto Pact in 1965, this share grew and was around 75 percent by the time of the 1987 Canada-US Free Trade Agreement. Following that agreement and the subsequent North American Free Trade Agreement (NAFTA), the share of Canada's exports going to the US grew even larger, and today it stands at around 85 percent. Investment flows are less dominated by the US, but are still large. Canada is now a net investor in the US, with the US receiving around 40 percent of Canadian investment outflows.

The prospect of a growing Canadian engagement with BRICSAM poses a number of challenges for Canada. BRICSAM trade growth, in contrast to that of the US, will likely be dominated by the exports of natural resources, despite the traditional Canadian aversion to becoming "hewers of wood and drawers of water." With resource export growth, the economic centre of gravity in the Canadian economy may well progressively tilt even more to the West and further away from Central Canada.

Canada will find itself ever more engaged with economies where both the social structure and modes of business are more traditional in orientation and less legalistic. Contacts and networking will become more central to market access, and the precise legal text of trade agreements will probably matter less. Trade arrangements and agreements will likely be sequentially negotiated, as much for the process of engagement they represent as for their specific content. Formal agreements may not ensure enhanced market access, but they may provide an entry; exploiting the consequent opportunities will then depend more on personal contacts and networks.

Thus, a pragmatic approach to securing access to markets in these economies suggests the need for a broader Canadian policy on trade and other related issues, rather than a focus on the World Trade Organization (WTO) and the negotiation of regional and bilateral agreements. For example, immigration policy may need to take into account the benefits of larger first-generation immigrant communities in Canada with direct network ties to BRICSAM countries. Similarly, proposed buy-outs of large Canadian resource companies by Chinese state-owned enterprises (SOE) may provide some benefits in the form of improved access to the superior distribution networks in China that are controlled by Chinese SOEs. Policy towards international agencies such as the WTO may also change as the BRICSAM countries either singly or jointly take a different approach to international economic issues. The recent proliferation of regional trade agreements outside of the WTO reflects, in part, overall frustration with WTO processes and the emergence of non-WTO fora for trade discussions.

If growth in the faster growing economies, such as China, continues at the current levels for several decades, there will be a historic transformation in the global economy with a major shift in global economic power, and a corresponding reorientation of global economic institutions. The adjustments implied for Canada could be among the most dramatic in the OECD given our current deep integration with the US. Developing a concerted strategy now for the changes that seem likely to occur makes sense. There is also some evidence that the BRICSAM are beginning to act jointly on certain fronts and a more active and pragmatic engagement of these countries, which reflects both humanitarian concerns (which remain central in the poorer BRICSAM countries such as India) and Canada's economic interests in gaining better market access, seems to be worth examination. The contention of this chapter is that it is in the Canadian interest to recognize these changes now and to modify policy accordingly in anticipation of the changes that may well come, and quite quickly.

THE BRICSAM

Some of the key features of the BRICSAM countries in terms of population, Gross Domestic Product (GDP), GDP growth rates, export growth rates, and savings-to-GDP ratios are set out in Table 1. Brazil, Mexico, South Africa, and Russia are considerably smaller in population than China, India, and ASEAN, but they all play the role of both large regional powers, and some are major players on the global political stage. Mexico has the highest per capita income of these countries and is differentiated by both being in the OECD and by its degree of integration within the framework of the OECD through NAFTA. In 2003, these countries accounted in total for 54 percent of the world's population and 12 percent of Global Domestic Product (GDP[W]).[3] Collectively they wield considerable economic power, as manifested in market size, anticipation of future growth in market size, capitalization of stock markets, combined reserves of central banks, ability to exercise power in international negotiation, and the emergence of nationally-based global corporations from these countries. The critical implication of the emergence of the BRICSAM countries is that economic power now seems to be tilting toward them and away from the OECD. The expectation is that with continued growth, this shift will become ever more pronounced, and after a couple of decades a historic transformation of the global economy will be well underway.

At the moment, GDP growth in the BRICSAM countries is uneven and high growth is more concentrated in the larger population BRICSAM countries of China, India, and ASEAN. Brazil, Mexico and South Africa

Table 8.1   A Summary of the BRICSAM Economies

	Population (million) 2003	GDP (USD billion) 2003	Domestic Savings/ GDP rate 2003	GDP (average annual growth)			Export of Goods and Services (average annual growth)		
				2002	2003	2004*	2002	2003	2004*
Brazil	176.6	492.3	23.8	1.9	-0.2	5.2	14.2	7.9	19.6
Russia	143.3	432.9	32.0	4.7	7.3	7.0	9.6	13.7	2.5
India	1064.4	600.6	28.1	4.1	8.6	6.9	21.2	7.0	13.1
China	1288.4	1412.3	47.0	8.3	9.3	9.5	29.4	26.8	27.0
South Africa	45.3	159.9	18.9	3.6	1.9	3.7	-1.4	-0.5	3.7
ASEAN	542.2	685.8	n.a.	4.3	5.0	6.3	n.a.	n.a.	n.a.
Mexico	102.3	626.1	18.2	0.7	1.3	4.4	1.5	1.1	3.7
Total BRICSAM	3362.5	4409.9							
OECD	914.6	28400.0	n.a.	1.6	2.1	3.4	1.8	2.5	8.0

*estimates

Sources: World Bank "World Development Indicators 2005", ASEAN Secretariat (www.aseansec.org), OECD (www.oecd.org).

are growing at a slower pace, but 2004 has seen elevation in their growth rates. There are also indications that this growth in the BRICSAM is accelerating and spreading. Chinese growth has been averaging perhaps 7–8 percent for some years now. After suffering a decline in per capita income of between 35 and 50 percent from 1991 until the Russian financial crisis in 1998, Russia's economic growth rate has since averaged around 6–7 percent annually, albeit with the assistance of high energy prices. Recent years have also seen a dramatic elevation in Indian growth and the estimates for 2004 are of 6.9 percent growth. Both Brazil and Mexico experienced higher growth in 2004 than in 2003, at 5.2 percent and 4.4 percent respectively. This pattern implies that the mean growth rate across the whole of the BRICSAM today, weighted by population, is in the 6–7 percent range.

Along with strong GDP growth, strong trade performance has also accompanied the emergence of most BRICSAM countries. Chinese trade growth has been especially strong and China is now the world's third largest trading country (behind the US and Germany). China's performance is consistent with the historical pattern, both at the level of individual economies and the global economy, of trade growing in a higher proportion than income or GDP. Thus the continued GDP growth in these economies raises the prospect of their rapidly taking a position of dominance in world trade. The absorptive capacity of the OECD for these exports may eventually provide a constraint to growth, though by that time intra-BRICSAM trade may take over as the engine of world trade. For now, BRICSAM trade is mainly with OECD countries; intra-BRICSAM trade is small, but is growing rapidly.

These economies also jointly account for over 50 percent of the world's population and on average have significantly higher population growth rates than the OECD. In 2003, population growth was 1.2 percent in Brazil, 1.5 percent in India, 0.7 percent in China, 1.5 percent in ASEAN, 1.4 percent in Mexico (only Russia and South Africa witnessed negative population growth in 2003: -0.4 and -0.1 percent respectively).[4] While these growth rates are sharply lower than those of two decades earlier, the prospect remains that on a population growth basis alone (before higher economic growth is considered), these economies will grow further in importance relative to the OECD in the next few decades. They exhibit higher savings to GDP ratios than is true of the OECD. Their foreign reserves are growing rapidly, with China alone having accumulated reserves of nearly US$610 billion by the end of 2004 (People's Bank of China, 2005).

These economies and societies, however, differ from those of the OECD. They have legal structures that, while clearly developing, are not as strong in terms of coverage and clarity of statute and enforcement as in the OECD. Their business and social structures rely more heavily on personal contacts, trust, and networks than in the case of most OECD countries. In addition, while state involvement in business is receding, government or communal enterprises are still a significant part of the industrial structure of BRICSAM. In China, for instance, the majority of the enterprise sector is in some way communally owned, often through complex and at times less-than-immediately transparent arrangements involving national, regional, and municipal governments, bodies such as research councils, and the military. For Canadians, doing business in these countries calls for a different approach than is used in other OECD markets; an approach that recognizes the distinctive features of the BRICSAM countries.

A central issue is whether these countries and their economies will slowly mature and develop in ways which move them closer to the OECD structure, effectively integrating into the OECD, or whether their distinctiveness will remain. In other words, can the OECD countries sit back in comfort knowing that the majority of the world's population will be joining them, or does the OECD have to think consciously, in a less inward-looking manner, about how the two groups will eventually be integrated?

Even though the BRICSAM countries share some of these broadly identified features, it is also important to emphasize their lack of commonality. The BRICSAM are far from being a singly entity with a well-defined common interest in all matters. China, for instance, is an exporter of manufactured goods while India's advantage seems to be in services; Russia is a large exporter of oil and gas to EU markets while Brazil (along with other non-BRICSAM countries in equatorial regions) is the custodian of significant environmental assets, and is now also primarily interested in market access for agricultural exports. Brazilian and Russian divergence in respect to their national interests in global environmental issues may have set them on somewhat of a collision course for the future.

Despite these differences, from Canada's perspective the common features of the BRICSAM countries are the important ones. Their size, strong growth, and reliance on an outward oriented growth strategy currently focused on access to OECD markets (primarily for manufactured goods) make them interesting as potential trading partners for countries such as Canada. In the past, Canadian policy towards these countries has largely been dominated by development, security, and governance concerns, interspersed with the protection of national group interests, as in the case of textile and apparel trade restrictions. But as BRICSAM countries grow, these traditional concerns will become increasingly subordinated to the need to secure access for trade and

Table 8.2   Canada's Trade with BRICSAM Countries (in US$ millions)

Country		2002	2003	2004
Canada	Total Exports	252,413.5	271,747.9	316,452.1
	Total Imports	222,147.2	239,709.2	272,955.2
	Trade Balance	30,266.3	32,038.6	43,496.9
Brazil	Total Exports	488.1	638.3	731.1
	Total Imports	1,213.1	1,421.8	1,798.6
	Trade Balance	-725.0	-783.4	-1,067.4
Russia	Total Exports	152.5	238.2	318.5
	Total Imports	242.1	576.0	1,063.4
	Trade Balance	-89.6	-337.8	-744.8
India	Total Exports	430.0	545.4	675.3
	Total Imports	844.7	1,015.5	1,211.1
	Trade Balance	-414.7	-470.1	-535.8
China	Total Exports	2,631.5	3,400.2	5,110.5
	Total Imports	10,190.9	13,250.9	18,510.9
	Trade Balance	-7,559.4	-9,850.7	-13,400.4
South Africa	Total Exports	161.9	226.2	279.8
	Total Imports	311.1	359.1	498.0
	Trade Balance	-149.2	-132.9	-218.2
ASEAN	Total Exports	1,576.2	1,645.5	2,135.2
	Total Imports	4,599.0	5,393.8	6,252.0
	Trade Balance	-3,022.7	-3,748.4	-4,116.7
Mexico	Total Exports	1,540.9	1,578.1	2,299.8
	Total Imports	8,114.9	8,695.0	10,300.8
	Trade Balance	-6,574.0	-7,117.0	-8,001.0
Total BRICSAM	Exports	6,981.1	8,271.9	11,550.3
	Imports	25,515.8	30,712.2	39,634.7
	Trade Balance	-18,534.7	-22,440.3	-28,084.4
BRICSAM Share	Total Exports	2.77%	3.04%	3.65%
	Total Imports	11.49%	12.81%	14.52%

Source: Statistics Canada and author's calculations

investment. In addition, and as economic power gravitates further to these economies, the key issue will become how to work jointly with them in pursuit of mutually advantageous global arrangements. How to pursue this interest and what it means for Canadian trade and other policies is at the heart of the discussion in this chapter.

Finally, it is worth noting that despite the growth in the BRICSAM, Canada's trade with these countries remains, in most cases, extremely small. Canada's trade flows with BRICSAM countries are shown in Table 8.2, which makes clear that these flows are dominated by China in terms of the level and rate of growth. Canada also runs trade deficits with all BRICSAM countries, some of which are equivalent to more than 60 percent of the total bilateral trade. If trade with the BRICSAM grows, Canada's exports to them will have to grow at a higher proportion than Canada's imports to avoid an unsustainable trade deficit. This situation is, for now, largely a reflection of the size of Canada's trade with the US, but it also re-emphasizes that the future adjustments necessitated by the emergence of BRICSAM countries may be considerably larger for Canada than for other OECD economies.

BRICSAM INTERESTS AND
THE EVOLUTION OF THE GLOBAL ECONOMY

It is essential to map out what the interests of the BRICSAM are in the global economic structure – to what extent a commonality of interest exists amongst these countries, to what degree do their interests diverge, and what do these interests suggest for the future of the global economy – in order to determine how Canada might position itself in response to these emerging powers.

We assume, for now, that the overriding and common interest in the BRICSAM currently lies in achieving high levels of sustained growth over long periods of time (the next 20–30 years) with a major focus on poverty alleviation within these countries (and especially in India). We will also assume, for the moment, that policy elites in these countries believe that to achieve this outcome strengthened engagement with the world economy is necessary, so as to generate high rates of outward oriented growth through trade and access to foreign markets, inward investment flows for infrastructure and human capital development, and the development of new export platforms.

Consequently, access to OECD markets is currently critical for the BRICSAM, with the future possibility of growing intra-BRICSAM trade possibly providing the key to further sustained growth. Intra-BRICSAM trade is small at the moment, and while this area will probably experience more rapid growth than their trade with the OECD, the OECD will remain their largest export markets for the next two decades. The size of their trade imbalances with the OECD (especially for China) poses major problems at the domestic level, and is the source of major pressure for export restraint.

As such, BRICSAM countries, unlike the EU and the US in the GATT in the 1960s-1980s, may be less concerned with achieving improved access to each others' markets via a reciprocal exchange of concessions than they might be in jointly achieving improved access to third country markets. And in these third country markets, they both are and will be competitors of each other. There is, for instance, considerable concern in countries such as Brazil and Mexico not only over growing Chinese penetration of their domestic markets (with resulting adjustment costs), but also over growing Chinese shares of US and EU markets at their expense. Non-India, non-China BRICSAM for now is permeated by a degree of fear of China.

As a result, while the BRICSAM may well seek to negotiate market access improvements on a multilateral basis, and remain committed to the WTO process, their competition with one another in OECD markets might make them especially attracted to bilateral – and hence exclusionary – trade arrangements. This impulse is already manifest in the wave of recent bilateral trade agreements that involve the BRICSAM. BRICSAM growth therefore, may well further elevate the importance of non-WTO regional agreements, and if anything, lower the profile of the WTO, much as we have seen in the last few years.

BRICSAM growth through trade also raises the key issue of whether the absorptive capacity of the OECD for their exports will become a constraint on their trade. China's exports, for instance, grew by 40 percent last year. Were they to continue growing at this rate for five more years, China's exports would likely exceed the current level of OECD imports. Clearly, something in this equation must change and the unanswered variable involves whether the currently small levels of intra-BRICSAM trade experience rapid growth.

BRICSAM countries also have an incentive in the area of international trade to negotiate jointly where possible. Their collective bargaining power will substantially exceed that of each individual BRICSAM country, and already Brazil, India, and South Africa are negotiating the creation of a trilateral commission to coordinate their trade policies.

In contrast to the OECD, inward investment flows are a more important policy consideration for the BRICSAM. They all have large pools of low-wage labour (effectively trapped in their own countries behind OECD immigration restrictions), which in combination with foreign capital and distribution systems would give them export platforms. This potential also gives them large leverage in attracting inward investments, to service both BRICSAM and OECD markets. A BRICSAM joint interest could therefore lie in the negotiation of co-operative arrangements to avoid competing amongst themselves for FDI.

BRICSAM countries will also increasingly have joint interests in the monetary sector, and especially to avoid providing fresh seigniorage benefits to the OECD by holding even more of the various OECD currencies, and US dollars in particular. China's reserves are now close to US$610 billion, and until recently much of this was held in US treasury bills, thereby granting the US large seigniorage benefits. This policy will likely change as holdings diversify into real assets and securities denominated in other currencies. The acquisition of OECD companies may also likely become part of BRICSAM activities, especially in the resource sector where such ties will help secure access to resource supplies and distribution systems in the OECD.

Of course, within this picture there will also be diversity of interest among the BRICSAM in respect to global arrangements. A Brazilian interest in forests is one, and Russian interests in oil and gas exports are another. A completely uniform BRICSAM strategy towards the management of the global economy will likely not emerge, but the impacts of outward oriented, large population, high growth economies with ever growing exports to the OECD will likely persist. Heightened interest in regional agreements, foreign investment, joint negotiation, and pragmatic approaches to international financial institutions may well define the emerging global policy environment.

The economic power which seems to be gravitating towards the BRICSAM countries has not been aggressively sought, nor has it been exercised in aggressive ways. The main concern of this group has been the achievement of high growth, and with it the poverty alleviation of, and improved welfare for its citizens. But the size of the BRICSAM is such that it is inevitable that power will accompany this growth and it will be exercised on the global stage. How the BRICSAM countries choose to exercise their power may well shape the global economy 20–30 years from now.

A BRICSAM STRATEGY FOR CANADA?

If the global economy is undergoing a large structural transformation, and if the pace of this change accelerates in the future, it makes sense for economies such as Canada's to anticipate the resulting shifts in power and to develop appropriate policy responses. This imperative is especially true for Canada given that our trade (and to a lesser extent investment flows) have been dominated by our bilateral relationship with the US. Some degree of regression in US interdependence and progressive elevation of BRICSAM engagement seems inevitable, and one of the essential first steps for a Canadian policy towards the BRICSAM is to recognize this shift. Canada also needs to recognize the present, sharply unbalanced nature of Canadian-BRICSAM trade and the large and growing trade deficits that Canada runs with the BRICSAM. If Canada-BRICSAM trade grows, Canada's exports to the BRICSAM will have to grow more rapidly than Canadian imports in order to be sustainable and beneficial for the Canadian economy.

What then are the key elements of a BRICSAM strategy for Canada? First, in terms of international economic architecture, we may need to accept a diminished role for both the WTO and the potential necessity of bilateral negotiation and networking with the more traditionally based and less legalistic BRICSAM countries. These countries are already active in bilateral negotiations, and the Canadian government should be prepared to engage with them in order to promote our interests in accessing their markets and their labour pools. This process will also require an identification and accommodation of BRICSAM interests. Given their size, bilateral negotiations with both India and China would seem to be a sensible way to proceed.

However, a BRICSAM strategy involves more elements than simply bilateral negotiation. One is a recognition that access to the markets of these economies relies as much on networks and personal contacts as it does on formal trade and other policy agreements. The formalities of trade agreements involving these countries may be better understood as forms of social processes, leading to the development of enhanced personal contacts. Therefore, it is necessary to recognize that these countries will remain less focused on legal structures and discourse and more on personalized traditional economies and societies than most of our OECD partners. Personal contact and networking will consequently be the key to trading success with the BRICSAM.

In addition, it may be important to recognize that pragmatism will be the hallmark of any successful BRICSAM strategy. Individual country differences within the BRICSAM need to be noted and kept in mind when planning Canada's strategic approaches to each. It is fundamental as well to consider how policy in non-trade areas will affect Canadian access to the BRICSAM. Canada might, for instance, approve Chinese SOE buyouts of Canadian resource companies on the grounds that the superior network of Chinese SOEs in China will improve Canadian export performance. Immigration policy in Canada might need to change to recognize the networking benefits to Canadian exporters of immigrant communities in Canada, a benefit which currently plays no formal role in the points system used to determine entry for new immigrants.

In the monetary sector, anticipating BRICSAM actions towards the global financial market will be important. If the world moves away from its heavy reliance on US dollars, Canada would be heavily affected due to our deep integration with the US.

The domestic adjustment implications of growth in the BRICSAM also need to be factored into any BRICSAM strategy. Canadian diversification in manufactured goods and growth in Central Canada since the 1990's has been based on, and fuelled by ever-deeper integration with the US, and especially within the automobile sector. While this integration will not end overnight, its relative importance may recede.

The precise elements of a BRICSAM strategy will clearly need careful consideration and articulation. Ultimately, Canadian policy needs to anticipate and reflect the profound changes that the world will face over the next few decades. As a trend that is already clearly identifiable, the emergence of BRICSAM is one central feature of the future global economy that Canadian policy makers can not, and must not ignore.

NOTES

This chapter draws on a presentation made and papers prepared for an initial project meeting on the BRICSAM countries (Brazil, Russia, India, China, South Africa, ASEAN, Mexico) hosted by CIGI, 27–28 May 2005.

1 Some have argued that Egypt or Nigeria could be included.
2 Some care has to be taken, as OECD membership has expanded and now includes Mexico. In the text we use the term OECD to refer to its traditional membership of wealthier, industrialized market economies.
3 The latter figure involves conversion at market exchange rates; at purchasing power parity rates the percentage is considerably higher.
4 For more detailed statistics, see World Bank, "Country Data Profiles Tables," available at: <http://www.worldbank.org/data/countrydata/countrydata.html>.

REFERENCES

Abreu, Marcelo de Paiva. 2005. "China's Emergence in the Global Economy and Brazil," *Integration and Trade Journal*, INTAL, Inter-American Development Bank (forthcoming).
Antkiewicz, Agata, and John Whalley. 2005. "BRICSAM and the Non WTO." CESifo Working Paper Series, *CESifo Group*, no. 1498.
– 2005. "China's New Regional Trade Agreements." Cambridge, MA: National Bureau of Economic Research, Working Paper No. 10992.
Cassim, Rashad, and Harry Zarenda. 2004. "South Africa's Trade Policy Paradigm – Evolution or Involution?" in E. Sidiropoulos, ed. *South Africa's Foreign Policy 1994–2004*. Johannesburg: South African Institute of International Affairs, University of Witswatersrand.
Dayaratna Banda, O.G., and John Whalley. 2005. "Beyond Goods and Services: Competition Policy, Investment, Mutual Recognition, Movement of Persons, and Broader Cooperation Provisions of Recent FTAS Involving ASEAN Countries." Cambridge, MA: National Bureau of Economic Research, Working Paper No. 11232.

Lloyd, Peter, and Penny Smith. 2004. *Global Economic Challenges to ASEAN Integration and Competitiveness: A Prospective Look*, REPSF Project 03/006a, Final Report, September.

People's Bank of China. 2005. "Executive Summary." *China Monetary Policy Report: Quarter Four–2004*. Available at: <http://www.pbc.gov.cn/english //detail.asp?col=6400&ID=509&keywor d=reserves>.

Rajan, Ramkishen S., and Rahul Sen. 2004. "The New Wave of FTAs in Asia: With Particular Reference to ASEAN, China and India," *Asian Economic Integration and Cooperation*. Manila: Asian Development Bank.

Shaw, Tim M. 2005. "Central African Perspectives on Globalization: Two Africas?" (forthcoming).

Shen, Danyang. 2005. "The Establishment of the Pan-Asian Economic Community: A Possible Mode for Economic Cooperation Among Russia, India, China, ASEAN and other Asian Countries," (forthcoming).

Virmani, Arvind. 2004. "Economic Performance, Power Potential and Global Governance: Towards a New International Order." New Delhi: Indian Council for Research on International Economic Relations, Working Paper no. 150.

– 2005. "A Tripolar Century: USA, China and India." New Delhi: Indian Council for Research on International Economic Relations, Working Paper no. 160.

9 Canada and Global China: Engagement Recalibrated

PAUL EVANS

The productive might of China's vast low-cost manufacturing machine, along with the swelling appetites of its billion-plus consumers, have turned China's people into what is arguably the greatest natural resource on the planet. How the Chinese and the rest of the world use that resource will shape our economy and every other economy in the world as powerfully as American industrialization and expansion have over the last hundred years (Fishman, 2005: 7).

China has mattered deeply to Canadians for 130 years despite vast asymmetries in power, influence, and size, and abiding differences in culture, values, political system, and level of development. Viewed over that broad sweep, relations have had three enduring pillars: human exchange dating back to the missionary period and the initial waves of immigration; commerce and the lure of the China market; and a strategic mission to assist China in entering the global community. This particular combination of human connections, commercial aspirations, and engagement ambitions has made the relationship distinctive, at least from the Canadian perspective. Compare what has been portrayed as a "special relationship" with China, for instance, to Canadian relations with India where the first component certainly has been present, the second intermittently, and the third not at all.

Positive relations with China for thirty-five years have paid dividends. Beginning with Pierre Trudeau, successive Canadian leaders have devoted careful attention to the management of bilateral relations with China — arguably more than to any country other than the United States. This exceptional commitment has produced a rich relationship in several areas and established a reservoir of friendship at high levels. The Team Canada missions beginning in 1994 and multiple visits by prime ministers and senior members of Cabinet have signalled Canada's recognition of China's importance – a gesture not lost on the Chinese leadership. Chinese leaders reciprocated with a string of high-level visits in the late 1990s, raising the overall level of bilateral diplomatic relations to what then President Jiang Zemin described during his 1997 visit as a "Trans-century Comprehensive Partnership," suggesting long-term positive relations, connections across a variety of sectors, and the absence of any strategic conflicts.

All three pillars of the China relationship need refurbishment in light of rising Chinese power and influence. Socially and culturally, the deepening web of human contacts is impressive but has not reached its potential. Economically, the Team Canada approach has run its course, two-way investment is of increasing importance, and the Canadian share of the China market is declining even as China has emerged as Canada's second largest trading partner in 2004, overtaking Japan.[1] Strategically, the historic mission of engaging China seems quaint or out-dated, not because strategies of isolation, containment and strategic competition are preferable, but because a Global China is no longer in need of engaging, at least not in the same way that it was in past.

The responses of the new Martin government, Canadian business elites, academics and the public involve the same ingredients of fascination and fear, admiration and cynicism, threat and opportunity that are evident in other nations in the Americas and Europe. The government's *International Policy Statement* (IPS) in April 2005 identifies the rising importance of China and other emerging markets. The prime minister visited China in January and Ottawa has launched several new initiatives focusing on the creation of Strategic Working Groups, energy cooperation, tourism, and air agreements.

Yet Canada, like the US, has not yet formulated a comprehensive policy response to the rise of China that recognizes its strategic significance in Asian, trans-Pacific and global contexts. This chapter will argue that the challenge posed by China is much deeper than short-term trade and investment matters. The emergence of an assertive China in a more closely integrated economy in East Asia is already altering the balance of power in Asia and shows signs of doing so on a global basis. Through a combination of its size and scale, production system, integration into regional and global supply chains, and increasing diplomatic self-confidence and weight, China is contributing to transformative processes that are beginning to reshape world affairs.

For reasons of asymmetries and differences, Canada and China cannot forge the kind of alliances and deep integration that Canada

enjoys with the United States and some of our Commonwealth partners including the UK and Australia. And for reasons of history and
values, there are limits on the depth and range of Sino-Canadian cooperation. This is made clear by simply invoking words like human
rights, Falun Gong, Tiananmen, Tibet or Taiwan.

Yet despite these differences, China's importance to Canada – in
bilateral terms and in respect to Canada's trans-Pacific, continental and
global objectives – is growing quickly and on a scale not imaginable
even a decade ago. A creative response depends upon stimulating a
deeper discussion at home, getting Beijing's attention, and balancing
competing priorities.

GLOBAL CHINA:
THE ECONOMIC AND HUMAN DIMENSION

Historians may well conclude that China's current rise in world affairs
is a re-ascendance to the position that it occupied for much of the past
two thousand years, a return to normalcy after a bad century or two.[2]
They have already noted that this is not the first Chinese rise after a
period of intense decline but the fourth (Wang, 2004). Yet a hundred
years ago China's chief global significance was as power vacuum, a
weak state, insignificant economy and a threat because of the prospects
of its fragmentation and collapse. Fifty years ago its significance was as
a revolutionary power intent on massive internal transformation and
supporting insurgency and change in its neighbours.

Twenty-five years after Deng Xiaoping's Open Door policies, China
is significant for a very different set of reasons. It is not just a burgeoning market economy, but now an economic force that is transforming the global economy. Consider the following:

- since 1978, the Chinese economy has grown at an average rate of
  about 9 percent per year, doubling more than three times over in that
  period, a surge that has no equal in modern history (Fishman, 2005:
  12).
- China now generates 13 percent of world economic output in purchasing parity terms, second only to the US. China is already the
  world's largest consumer of commodities including steel (it consumes
  more than twice as much as the United States), copper, coal and
  cement and is the second biggest consumer of oil after the US (*Economist*, 2004b: 12).
- China is now the world's third largest trader (after the US and
  Germany), with bilateral trade in 2004 of $1.1 trillion accounting for
  6 percent of the world's total. It is now Japan's largest trading

partner and Canada's second largest. China's *weekly* trade is now larger than its total annual trade in 1978. Its trade in 2004 was equal to about 70 percent of its GDP, Japan's to 24 percent (Overholt, 2005). Its trade with the United States increased 27.9 percent in 2004 to US$245.2 billion (USCBC, 2005). Bilateral trade with Canada increased 33.6 percent over the same period to C$30.1 billion (Asian Pacific Foundation, 2005).

- China received in excess of US$60 billion in FDI in 2004. The total accumulated FDI in the past 20 years is about US$555 billion (TDC, 2005). Out-bound FDI from China rose to about US$3.5 billion in 2004, while its accumulated outward FDI has increased from near zero in 1986 to over US$33 billion in 2003 (UNCTAD, 2005). There are estimates that outward-bound FDI in the energy sector alone in 2005 will exceed US$30 billion.
- China has about US$610 billion in foreign currency reserves. It now holds some US$224 billion of US Treasuries (USTD, 2005), sitting as the second largest creditor to the United States.
- China has more speakers of English as a second language than America has native English speakers. More people use the internet in China than in the United States.
- China has more than 300 biotech firms that operate unhindered by animal rights lobbies, religious groups, or ethical standards boards (Fishman, 2005). There are more than 750 foreign R&D centres operating in China (Zhang, 2005).

That China is now the world's dominant producer of manufactured goods including household electronics, toys, clothing and textiles is well understood. Less so is that it is also becoming a key producer of component parts and intermediate goods that are essential to increasingly refined supply chains in which research and development, software development, physical production and after-sales service are geographically dispersed but precisely integrated. And it is quickly moving into higher-end assembly and export including automobiles, trucks, aircraft, ships, telecommunication equipment, and machinery.

China has emerged as the shop floor of the world based on a distinctive production system. What might be called "post-Fordism with Chinese characteristics" involves a capacity to fuse high-end technology with low-wage, labour-intensive activity, cut-throat domestic competition, a reliable, docile, and capable industrial workforce, the availability of huge sums of foreign investment and technology, and the new appetites of a billion domestic consumers.

The fact that China is not just competing effectively in the global economy but changing it has two dimensions. First, relative prices are shifting as the price of manufactured goods and tradable services decrease and as the price for energy and non-renewable raw materials, including land, increase. This is strengthening the competitive forces that make manufactured imports less expensive, encouraging outsourcing of manufacturing and services, and increasing competition for investment and access to Chinese domestic markets. In this respect, the size and structure of its production system, argues Ted Fishman, "does not merely enable low-cost manufacturing; it *forces* it" (Fishman, 2004: 185).

Second, choices made by Chinese businesses, consumers and policy makers now have global impact. In no sector is this more visible than energy. China will soon be the second largest consumer of oil after the US and has been responsible for almost 40 percent of the increase in global consumption since 2000 (Downs, 2004: 23). When consumption of iron, steel, and minerals is taken into account, Chinese purchases are responsible for the majority of the 50 percent rise in the *Economist*'s commodity-price index over the past three years (*Economist*, 2004b: 1).

This global impact is amplified by the convergence and cumulative effect of development models in other developing countries, now likely to be referred to as "emerging markets," including India, Brazil and Vietnam. Though not identical in every respect, they do follow China's example by buying into globalization, welcoming FDI, maintaining a large governmental role in the economy, and keeping the capital account closed while systematically opening other parts of the economy. Competitive pressures generated by China on other low-wage countries forces them to lower labour rates and hence become even more attractive to foreign enterprises looking for low-cost locations. China is thus changing the future of work in both the developing and developed worlds. If Japan once played the role in Asia as the progenitor of a flying geese model of development, China is provoking a buffalo charge.

It is tempting but analytically misleading to treat China as another, albeit huge, emerging market. What separates China is partly a matter of scale and stage, but also includes political and diplomatic punch, the depth of the commitment to globalization and the breadth of market liberalization (Overholt, 2005: 6; Anderson, 2005: 25). Beijing is beginning to assert itself in multilateral economic fora such as the WTO and Doha Round, sometimes aligning in a supporting role behind Brazil and India on the Trade G20 issues, but more often opportunistically with both developing and developed countries.

These factors together do not guarantee that China's further rise is inevitable. Indeed, a host of commentators in the 1990s predicted the impending collapse of the Chinese economy and polity. China faces serious problems with its banking and legal systems, corruption, the rise of social unrest generated by growing inequities and human rights abuses, and severe environmental degradation. Decisions on governance and policy reforms in each of these areas will have a major impact on the ultimate trajectory of China's growth. And equally significantly, as one of the strongest supporters of globalization and liberalization in the developing world, it faces the prospect that its very success could trigger new protectionist forces in the developed world, limiting the access to American and European markets that remain the principal consumers of Chinese products.

But it would be unwise to underestimate China's transformative impact or to assume that China's rise has already run its course. The world is quickly adjusting to the fact that it is confronting a new breed of economic superpower with global reach and a peculiar set of domestic arrangements that mean China is becoming more powerful than many developed countries whose populations are much more affluent than the large majority of Chinese.

GLOBAL CHINA:
THE INSTITUTIONAL DIMENSION

Concomitant with its economic rise, China has become more self-confident, more sophisticated, more assertive and frequently more constructive in international institutions and processes dealing with a variety of issues ranging from economics and trade policy to non-proliferation, chemical and biological weapons, missile technology control, exports control and arms control and disarmament issues, pandemics, terrorism and trans-national crime. In a regional context, Beijing in the last decade has moved quickly through successive phases of defensive participation to active participation and leadership in groups including APEC, the ASEAN Regional Forum, the ASEAN + 3 process, and the Asia-Europe Meeting. It has played a key role in creating and hosting the Shanghai Cooperation Organization and the Six Party Talks focusing on the North Korean nuclear issue. In the United Nations, it has become a mature and responsible member of the Security Council and, while not always aligned with Canadian interest and perspectives, has demonstrated increasing commitment to the principles and activities of the organization.

China now works largely within the international system and has embraced most of the treaties, institutions, rules and norms that constitute that system. As claimed by two American authors, "not only does China now accept many prevailing international rules and institutions; it is also becoming a much more capable and adept player of the diplomatic game. When opportunities for cooperation exist, Beijing will bring much more to the table than in the past" (Medeiros and Fravel, 2003).

Multilateralism with Chinese characteristics tends to be state-centric, committed to conventional principles of sovereignty and non-interference, and dedicated to defending state interests against perceived challenges from non-state actors. On a variety of issues including climate change, Myanmar, Darfur, and aspects of the Doha round, Chinese and Canadian views do not coincide. But there is no question that China is a significant force in shaping outcomes and setting rules. One could say that most roads to international solutions now pass through Beijing.

A striking feature of China's rise is that it has been generally well received outside China. Despite concerns about the growth of Chinese military spending, its approach to Taiwan, and its policies in the South China Sea, policy makers in Asia have praised China's "soft power" and efforts to reassure neighbours. David Shambaugh correctly observes that most observers in Asia now see China "as a good neighbour, a constructive partner, a careful listener, and a non-threatening regional power" (Shambaugh, 2005: 64). Public opinion polls tend to be favourable. A 22–country BBC poll conducted in December found that China is viewed as playing a significantly more positive role in the world than either the US or Russia and more on par with the UK. Though most are negative about rising Chinese military power, most are positive about its rising economic power (PIPA, 2005).[3]

IMPLICATIONS FOR CANADA

For most Canadians, China is no longer an exotic place on the far side of the world but a part of daily life. Immigration and tourism have changed the demographic composition of our major cities. A trip to Wal-mart, a stop at the gas pump, or the negotiation of a mortgage rate all connect with China-generated forces that simply didn't exist a decade ago.[4]

As in every other G7 country, Canadians are confronting a range of policy choices necessitated by the rapid rise of the Chinese economy and the production system of which it is a part. Many of these changes are a product of the broader forces of globalization, but the China dimension adds an extra edge and urgency.

Regarding domestic competitiveness and corporate deregulation, the "China price" puts enormous pressure on producers in virtually every manufacturing sector. In the competition for foreign investment, low-cost wages and tax breaks are losing their allure. Those investing in developed countries are looking for pools of skilled labour they cannot find in countries like China along with logistical and communications support necessary for coordinating globally partitioned labour forces (Keidel, 2005: 3). Foreign firms need to compete with Chinese partners at the same time that they cooperate with them in benefiting from supply chain innovation.

The consequence for trade policy is that this outsourcing and new division of labour means that countries in Europe and North America need to brace for substantial trade imbalances and job losses, not just because of the appetite for low-priced goods manufactured in China but also because of their necessary and often profitable investments in Asian-centred supply chains. In the US in particular the need to maintain strong domestic demand comes at the cost of long-term trade deficits with the rest of the world. Trade disputes based on domestic concerns about job loss, despite China's remarkable level of liberalization after its WTO entry, are bound to increase.

Regarding labour force restructuring, almost every low-end manufacturing and service job is vulnerable, thus magnifying the need for more flexible and better educated work forces. If there are no low-tech industries remaining, only low-tech firms, the pressures for skills upgrading are formidable. Social inequalities and differences in income distribution are increasingly difficult to control, as they are in China itself.

The implications specific to Canada include the following.

- Increasing prices for commodities, natural resources and energy based in large part on growing Chinese demand.
- Increasing trade and investment volumes with China accompanied by a growing trade and, at least in the short term, investment deficit. In addition to formulating rules to protect Canadian investment in China, a major new development is the prospect of increasing substantially larger Chinese investments and acquisitions in Canada. The increased volume of trade poses major issues for air and port infrastructure and has the potential to affect the course of deeper North American integration.
- Increased pressure for Chinese professionals and business people to emigrate to Canada and to press for more flexible visa, taxation and citizenship rules.
- Increased opportunities in areas of non-tradable services including education, health care and tourism. The level of human interactions is destined to grow, perhaps dramatically, with significant implications for new opportunities in connecting immigration, education and tourism. There will be new pressures for alterations in visa, citizenship and taxation rules.

- Increased opportunity, and need, for working with Chinese officials on virtually the full spectrum of Canadian diplomatic and developmental priorities.

The Martin government has responded to these challenges in several ways. The *International Policy Statement* notes that China is "poised to become the most important national economy in the 21st century" (Canada, 2005b: 17) and is at the heart of regional and global supply chains that are vital to the Canadian and world economy. It also notes that China's rise will put new pressures on Canadian manufacturers, reduce the price of consumer goods and increase the price of commodities including oil. The most surprising element of the analysis of China is that it is not placed in a special category of its own but in the category of emerging markets and "new powers in the developing world" (Canada, 2005a: 22) along with India and Brazil. It's interesting that Mexico receives more coverage in the IPS than China. There is a commitment to doubling the volume of bilateral economic interaction by 2010 and a recognition that successful relations with Asia are key to other policy objectives, including the Responsibilities Agenda, forging a new multilateralism, tapping into East Asian value chains bilaterally and as part of North American supply chains.

The government's policy agenda has continued the tradition of high-level contacts including the prime minister's own visit to China in January 2005 which created bilateral Strategic Working Groups to facilitate regulatory policy dialogue, promoted cooperation in science and technology, energy and multilateralism, and safeguards for foreign investment; and resuscitating inter-departmental consultations on China as part of a "whole of government" approach. Though China is not one of the Canadian International Development Agency's (CIDA) 25 "development partners," it seems certain to receive continuing bilateral support based on the criteria of strategic importance and diasporic connections to Canada. The two governments have negotiated a major expansion in bilateral air services and an agreement in principle for Approved Destination Status from Beijing, facilitating a much larger inflow of Chinese tourists into Canada.[5] And the federal government has strongly supported the BC government's Asia Pacific Gateway Strategy designed to augment port, air, and rail links connecting Canada to Asia.

ENGAGEMENT'S OBJECTIVES AND INSTRUMENTS

Equally important to the commercial and human connections to global China are the implications for Canada's diplomatic objectives abroad, the most fundamental of which remains the creation of a rules-based multilateral system. No one denies that in the last decade Beijing has become a more active and engaged participant in a full range of multi-lateral institutions, no longer interested simply in matters of recognition and status but grappling with a set of domestic, international and global policy challenges that will determine whether it can achieve the developmental objectives at home and the regional and global role abroad that its leaders espouse. It is a near certainty that China will be a powerful actor in most, if not all, of the global policy areas that affect Canada in the decade to come, ranging from the Doha Round to UN reform and L20 aspirations.

The disagreement amongst observers begins with the nature and depth of Chinese commitments. Where some see China as an increasingly responsible multilateral player, others argue that "China has little problem setting the rules of the game and no problem breaking them" (Fishman, 2005: 294). The fact that China is increasingly embedded in international institutions and is beginning to play a leadership role in them does not mean that our interests, values or views will automatically converge.

Beneath the debate about current Chinese behaviour is a deeper one about longer-term Chinese perspectives on world order. Is the purpose of being a strong and powerful nation to join the system or change it? Does China want to adjust to current international rules or create new ones? If so, what new rules? Is China wed to a nineteenth century conception of hard shell sovereignty or is it adjusting to twenty-first century realities?

The last frontier of engagement may be the compelling but complex challenge of understanding, and more ambitiously, shaping Chinese attitudes about world order and its role in it. Foreigners can no longer decide China's destiny or dictate its policy preferences. What unfolds in China will reflect calculation, the reaction of other major states, and in broader terms, the great forces of nationalism, consumerism and cosmopolitanism that are reshaping Chinese society and its own sense of identity.

If any country can work with China on how it understands and approaches multilateral institutions, it might be Canada. This is not to suggest that Canadians should overestimate our influence or the difficulties of getting Chinese attention. Nor can they be smug about having the monopoly on righteous international behaviour, have unrealistic assumptions about shaping any great power's outlook, or underestimate the time and resources that it will take to have even a serious multi-level dialogue on these matters. Whether Canadians can influence the development of Chinese positions in these policy areas is an open question, but Canada can benefit from the exchange and potentially play a catalytic role in restructuring the framework of global institutions to provide more benefits to the global south.

This ambitious objective will depend on governmental support at high levels from both sides. The bilateral Strategic Working Groups that were initiated in 2004 include a focus on multilateralism and energy cooperation. And through existing CIDA-sponsored programs there are good working channels for dialogues on human rights, legislative reform, and environment issues.

Canada also may need new mechanisms operating outside government and government control to reach its destination. Marcel Masse's idea in 1981 that Canada's aim in China should be "the multiplication of contacts at the thinking level" remains relevant. The task now is to get beyond broad-based contacts and dig more deeply in several policy areas, multilateralism among them, where partnerships of mutual interest are needed and feasible. It will be necessary to augment and leverage the already extensive set of private contacts between Canada and China – especially those involving Canadians of Chinese descent – for business development and the projection of Canadian diplomacy more generally.

This might be the time to create an instrument, separate from our bilateral aid program, to maximize the impact, visibility, and effectiveness of policy research and dialogues. This could take the form of a new Centre for Canada-China Partnerships, similar in design to the National Committee on US-China relations in the US, and possibly connected to the revitalized Asia Pacific Foundation of Canada (APFC). To maximize flexibility and creativity, it would be independent of government but closely informed about governmental priorities on both sides. Its task would not be simply to review and restate existing policies but to look for areas of cohesion and opportunity, especially on issues that are just over the horizon and will be important in a two to three year time period.

THE STRATEGIC CONTEXT

Users of Single Lens Reflex cameras are familiar with a focusing device that contains a small circle separated by a median bar. The object to be photographed is in focus when the images on both sides of the bar are clear. Getting both sides of the bar clear is particularly complex in Canada-China relations, especially when the American factor and competing regionalisms are the object of interest.

The first and most important of these is China's relations with the United States. Canadian policy is not made in Washington but the course of US-China relations has major consequences for the context in which Canadian policy makers must act. In some respects, US-China relations have never been better. Politically, both governments have found common ground on several issues including fighting terrorism and constraining North Korea's nuclear program.[6]

Economically, two contradictory trends are operating simultaneously. The level of economic interaction has never been higher, measured in the number of US firms doing business and investing in China, the volume of two-way trade, and the purchase of US Treasury Bonds. China is thus financing US deficits, lowering inflation and interest rates and sustaining the economic boom. At the same time, there are increasing trade frictions that are stimulating protectionist responses inside the US and pressures for reevaluing the Chinese Yuan, both aimed at limiting the impact of the Chinese production system which is perceived by some commentators as a major factor in US job losses.

The deeper strategic issue in US-China relations is how Washington views the significance and implication of China's rise. For some, China is not just a strategic competitor but a potential peer competitor. The idea of a looming and inevitable clash influences large segments of thinking in Washington, framed by Robert Kagan (2005: 1), who treats it as axiomatic that "rarely have rising powers risen without sparking a major war that reshaped the international system to reflect new realities of power."

These concerns have a material foundation reflecting an unmistakable shift in the diplomatic and economic balance of forces in Asia. The United States, India, Japan and China all play leadership roles in a much more complex regional system that combines alliances, new regional institutions, a much more dynamic and integrated regional economy, and a rising sense of Asian interdependence. There is mixed evidence on whether China is now attempting to use regional processes and its new Asian influence to counter-balance or undermine American presence in the region (Evans, 2005: 211–15). There is little disagreement that China will be far more likely to do so in the future as its material capacities strengthen, raising a very new kind of challenge for China's neighbours. Robert Sutter correctly observes that "few Asian leaders adhere to a Chinese-led order in Asia" (Sutter, 2005: 5), and few Asian leaders want to choose between the US and China.

There are signs of a growing coalition inside the United State determined to alter US-China relations. It includes human rights and democracy activists appalled by political conditions within China, politicians concerned about job losses and trade deficits, industries and unions hurt by the Chinese production system, and security analysts frightened by China's growing military and political capacity. These may well produce new tariffs and protectionist measures designed to stem job loss and put additional pressure on Beijing to revalue the Yuan. They are almost certain to violate the WTO and existing trade regulations, summoning up the perennial Canadian fear of American unilateralism and exceptionalism.

The implications of these trends are immediately relevant to the future prospects of Taiwan. While Chinese thinking may be showing new flexibility on issues of sovereignty and non-interference on a global basis, none of this is evident in its approach to Taiwan. Beijing's growing economic power and diplomatic influence are gradually reducing Taiwan's sphere of diplomatic influence, and the steady modernization of the Chinese military is slowly but inexorably shifting the regional military balance. The room for manoeuvre by other countries in playing a constructive role in the cross-Straits relationship is shrinking. In Canada, the Conservative proponents of Bill C-357, the recently-proposed "Taiwan Affairs Act," are calling for the equivalent of the confirmation of Taiwan's statehood; permitting in effect private visits by senior Taiwanese officials, the use of the name "Taiwan" in its representative office in Ottawa (it is currently The Taipei Economic and Cultural Office), and supporting Taiwan's entry into multilateral institutions. While passage of the bill seems unlikely, if enacted it would have devastating consequences for all three pillars of the Sino-Canadian relationship.

Though some may wish it, there are no realistic prospects for Canada being a mediator in resolving or mitigating these deep strategic tensions between the two most important countries in the world or across the Straits of Taiwan. What Canada can continue to do is avoid supporting any kind of alliance system that would be targeted at containing China and instead encourage both Washington and Beijing to look for moderation and mutual accommodation. Few Canadian policy makers feel that a clash is either desirable or inevitable. And fewer and fewer Canadians hold to the notion that Canada can use trade or aid conditionality as a way of influencing Beijing on matters like human rights.

The second split image to be brought into focus is the future course of emerging regionalisms in North America, East Asia and across the Pacific. In addition to maintaining and enhancing economic and security linkages to the US, Canada's intermittent commitment to forging deeper trilateral relations within North America will not be easily squared with deeper connections to China and a burgeoning East Asia. For the moment Canadian thinking about connecting across the Pacific and connecting within the North American continent are only loosely linked and are in some ways contradictory.

China is now playing a central role in the intensifying economic transactions within East Asia and in the efforts to build intra-Asian institutions including the ASEAN+3 process. The emerging regionalism in East Asia is not being constructed independent of the US – indeed, America and Europe remain major markets for a considerable percentage of the finished goods produced in East Asia – but it is occurring without American (and Canadian) participation.

There are tensions between Canadian commitments to trans-Pacific and continental futures. One domain in which this is already emerging is natural resources (including nickel and uranium) and energy. As the Chinese demand for oil continues to soar, Chinese firms are looking for investments and long-term supply agreements in at least 18 oil-producing countries around the world including Australia, Iran, Sudan, Libya, and Indonesia. In mid-2004, Minmetals explored the possibility of acquiring Noranda, though the deal did not materialize. Several dozen Chinese oil delegations visited Canada soon after Paul Martin's trip to China in January 2005. For a period it looked as if there would be "more thunder than rain" (Jiang, 2005: 7). The rain began as drizzle in spring 2005 when the China National Offshore Oil Corporation purchased for $150 million a 17 percent common-share stake in MEG Energy Corporation, a minor player in the Alberta oil sands. It turned to a light shower in June 2005 when Sinopec announced the purchase of a 40 percent stake in Syneco Energy's bitumen mining operation for $105 million, with a commitment to a larger outlay of $2 billion when construction begins for a larger oil sand project that includes an option to transport its share of the crude produced for export across the Pacific. These purchases are linked to the possibility of new pipelines being built to bring Alberta oil to the West Coast for shipment to Asia (Brethour, 2005; McKenna, 2005).

Though these do not yet compare to the scale of acquisitions and long-term supply agreements that China is striking with Australia, Venezuela or Iran, they reflect Chinese interest in energy diversification and may be the portent of more to follow in outward-investment. This prospect raises difficult policy and regulatory issues for Ottawa. Some of these centre on rules for foreign investment in a situation where the investor is state-owned Chinese firms, the target is what some feel is a strategic resource, and there are commercial and political concerns in the US about the sales. While some in the Alberta oil patch feel there are enough future reserves to satisfy North American and Asian demand and that there are advantages to Canada in diversification of markets, American analysts have already voiced concerns about Chinese penetration into energy markets in several countries in the Americas including Venezuela, Brazil, Peru, Mexico and Canada. The specific concerns focus on security of North American supply, unfamiliar competition for Canadian crude and the possibility of China gaining strategic advantage in America's backyard and fuelling anti-Americanism. These concerns will likely deepen if the level of Chinese investment increases significantly and if plans for new pipelines to ports on the West Coast are realized.

The tension between greater opening to China and Asia, meeting the needs of closer connections to the US and fulfilling North American aspirations is surfacing in other issues as well, including visas, refugee and immigration policies, border management and port security. At the level of trade policy, proposed FTAA's with Asian countries can raise new complications for NAFTA. Canada's decision to enter into free trade negotiations with South Korea is largely motivated by dreams of penetrating the Korean market and intentions to use Korea as an entry point into the East Asian production networks in which China is a central node. Problems of rules of origin, particularly in the auto sector, are going to make the negotiations especially difficult.

At the level of trade policy, Canada's best option is to continue to promote trans-Pacific processes including APEC and the ASEAN Regional Forum that connect North America to Asia rather than choosing one or the other. And from a commercial perspective, there are clear advantages in pursuing both a gateway Pacific strategy at the same time that Ottawa deepens contacts and access within North America. But in making choices about Canada's relationship with the United States and accommodating a rising China in the context of a more integrated East Asia, Ottawa is struggling with how to create an integrated strategy that puts both North America and Asia into focus simultaneously. There has been to date very little systematic thinking about how to do this.[7]

CONCLUSION

North America can be conceived in one of two ways when China is read into the equation. The first is as a protective wall against an East Asian region and a Chinese production system that will generate a new global economy and enormous adjustments in North America and Europe, as well as Asia. The second is as a means for increasing competitiveness that will allow Canada to prosper from deeper integration into the supply chains and export markets of Asia.

Decisions about dealing with China thus represent fundamental choices about dealing with a form of globalism which China has embraced with astonishing competitive success. Reactions to a global China thus may mark either the beginning of a deeper and more complex era of globalization or a decisive chapter in its demise. And the stakes are significantly higher as China's rise presents a plausible challenge to a unipolar world order.

NOTES

The author thanks Julie MacArthur for research assistance. This essay draws on Paul Evans and Yuen Pau Woo, "Canada and a Global China: From Special Relationship to Policy Partnership," a paper commissioned by the Department of Foreign Affairs in Ottawa in April 2004. The paper was later posted on <http://www.dfait-maeci.gc.ca/cip-pic/library/china-en.asp>.

1 China's outward FDI has increased from near zero in 1986 to over US$33 billion in 2003 (UNCTAD, 2005). Canada's share was just 1.05 percent of that total, at US$339 million, down from 1.5 percent in 1997 (Asia Pacific Foundation, 2005).
2 China has been the world's largest economy for much of recorded history. It had the highest per capita income until the fifteenth century and was by far the biggest economy into the early nineteenth century at which point it still represented 30 percent of world GDP. By 1950, using PPP calculations, it had fallen to less than 5 percent (*Economist*, 2004a).
3 An Ipsos-Reid poll of Canadians and Americans conducted in April 2005 and released two months later indicates that about 60 percent of Canadians do not see China's emergence as a threat to world peace and about 40 percent believe China "will soon dominate the world." By comparison, 54 percent of Americans indicated they see China as a threat to world peace and 54 percent are concerned about the level of Chinese investment in the US. 45 percent of Canadians indicated they were concerned about the level of Chinese investment in Canada, 51 percent that China is a serious threat to jobs in Canada, yet 61 percent see China's economic development as an opportunity and 68 percent that expanding trade relations with China is a good idea because it helps reduce trade dependence on the US (Ipsos-Reid 2005). And a Pew Poll puts this in comparative perspective by indicating that 58 percent of Canadians hold a favourable view of China, almost equal to the 59 percent who hold a favourable of the US but below the 78 percent who hold a positive view of France (Pew, 2005: 11).
4 The Wal-Mart-China connection is extraordinary. In 2003, Wal-Mart purchased US$15 billion worth of goods from Chinese suppliers. Somewhere between 10 and 13 percent of Chinese exports to the US are to Wal-Mart. If Wal-Mart were a nation, it would be China's fifth-largest export market ahead of Germany and Great Britain. Wal-Mart's trade

with, and in China accounts for 1.5 percent of China's GDP (Fishman, 2004: 153–4). It is a factor in our mortgage and lending rates (one estimate has it that a Chinese decision to stop buying US Treasury bonds would raise Canadian interest rates by up to 3 percent). It affects every trip to the gas station because of the fact that a full 25 percent of increased oil consumption is based on Chinese demand.

5 This could be significant as estimates including those by the Economist Intelligence Unit foresee the number of Chinese travelers increasing from about 16 million in 2001 to 49 million in 2008 to 100 million by 2015 (cited in Larenaudie, 2005).

6 David Shambaugh analyzed 35 regional security issues in Asia and concludes that there is a convergence between US and Chinese views on 16 of them, divergence on 8, and uncertainty on 11 (Shambaugh, 2005: 92).

7 As seen in two recent reports on Canada-US and Canada-US-Mexico futures, little effort has been focused on integrating trans-Pacific and continental priorities. See "Building a North American Community" (CFR, 2005) and "Renewing the US-Canada Relationship" (American Assembly, 2005).

REFERENCES

The 105th American Assembly. 2005. "Renewing the U.S-Canada Relationship," Report on the Meeting at Arden House, New York, 3–6 February. Available at: <http://wwics.si.edu/topics/pubs/US-Canada.pdf>.

Anderson, Jonathon. 2005. "The End of the China Love Affair," *Far Eastern Economic Review*, vol. 168, no. 5 (May): 20–6.

Asia Pacific Foundation of Canada. 2005. "Inward Foreign Direct Investment from Asia." Available at: <http://www.asiapacific.ca/data/trade/general_dataset6_fromasia.c fm>.

– 2005. "Canada's Bilateral Trade with Asia." Available at: <http://www.asia-pacific.ca/data/trade/t2_withasia.cfm>.

Brethour, Patrick. 2005. "Canadian oil could be headed to China under latest deal," *Globe and Mail – Report on Business,* 1 June.

Canada. 2005a. "Diplomacy," in *Canada's International Policy Statement: A Role of Pride and Influence in the World.* Ottawa: Department of Foreign Affairs and International Trade (DFAIT), 19 April. Available at: <http://www.dfait-maeci.gc.ca/cip-pic/ips/ips-en.asp>.

– 2005b. "Overview," *Canada's International Policy Statement: A Role of Pride and Influence in the World.* Ottawa: Department of Foreign Affairs and International Trade (DFAIT), 19 April. Available at: <http://www.dfait-maeci.gc.ca/cip-pic/ips/ips-en.asp>.

Council on Foreign Relations (CFR). 2005. *Building a North American Com-*

munity. Report of the Independent Task Force on the Future of North America. New York: CFR. Available at: <http://www.cfr.org>.

Downs, Erica S. 2004. "The Chinese Energy Security Debate," *The China Quarterly*, vol. 177 (March).

Economist. 2004a. "The real Great Leap forward," 2 October, Special Section: 6–9.

– 2004b. "A hungry dragon," 2 October, Special Section: 12–13.

Evans, Paul. 2005. "Between Regionalism and Regionalization: Policy Networks and the Nascent East Asian Regional Identity," in T.J. Pempel, *Remapping East Asia: The Construction of a Region*. Ithaca: Cornell University Press, 195–215.

Fishman, Ted. 2005. *China Inc.: How the Rise of the Next Superpower Challenges America and the World*. New York: Scribner Publishers.

Freeze, Colin. 2005. "Canadians see silver lining in China's cloud, poll says," *Globe and Mail*, 10 June.

Hong Kong Trade Development Council (TDC). 2005. "Market Profile of Chinese Mainland," 8 June. Available at: <http://www.tdctrade.com/main/china.htm>.

Ipsos-Reid. 2005. *A Public Opinion Survey of Canadians and Americans about China*. Report prepared for the Canada Institute of the Woodrow Wilson International Center for Scholars and the Canada Institute on North American Issues, June. Available at: <http://www.wilsoncenter.org/events/docs/Ipsos-Reid%20Survey%20on%20Can-US%20Attitudes%20toward%20China%20%5BJune%202005%5D.pdf>.

Jiang Wenran. 2005. "Fuelling the Dragon: China's Quest for Energy Security and Canada's Opportunities," *Canada in Asia Series*. Vancouver: Asia Pacific Foundation of Canada. Available at: <htpp://www.asiapacific.ca/analysis/pubs/pdfs/can_in_asia/cia_fue ling_dragon.pdf>.

Keidel, Albert. 2005. "China's G8 Impact." Paper presented at the *How Is China Shaping Globalization?* conference, Shanghai, 18 March. Available at: <http://www.carnegieendowment.org/publications/index.cfm?fa=print&id=16728>.

Larenaudie, Sarah Raper. 2005. "Luxury for the people!" *Time Magazine*, Special Edition (Spring). Available at: www.time.com/time/2005/style/030105/luxury_for_the_people__24_pri nt.html>.

McKenna, Barrie. 2005. "China advances into South America have US on edge," *Globe and Mail*, 24 May.

Medeiros, Evan S., and M. Taylor Fravel. 2003. "China's New Diplomacy," *Foreign Affairs*, vol. 82, no. 6 (November/December).

Overholt, William. 2005. "China and Globalization," Testimony to the US-China Economic and Security Reviews Commission, Washington, 19 May. Available at: <http://www.uscc.gov/hearings/2005hearings/written_testimonies/05 _05_19_20wrts/overholt_william_wrts.pdf>.

Pew Global Attitudes Project 2005. "American Character Gets Mixed Reviews," 23 June 2005. Available at: http://www.pewglobal.org.

Program on International Policy Attitudes (PIPA). 2005. "'China in the World' 22 Nation Poll." Available at: <http://www.pipa.org/OnlineReports/BBC-worldpoll/030505/html/bbcpo ll3.html>.

Shambaugh, David. 2005. "China Engages Asia: Reshaping Regional Order," International Security, vol. 29, no. 3 (Winter): 64–99.

Sutter, Robert. 2005. "China's Rise in Asia – Promises, Prospects and Implications for the United States." Occasional Paper Series, Asia-Pacific Center for Security Studies (February): 1–11.

United Nations Conference on Trade and Development (UNCTAD). 2005. "Firms in Developing Countries Rapidly Expanding Foreign Investment, Transnational Activities," Press Release 2005/018, 30 May.

United States Embassy in China. 2005. "Investment Climate Statement – China," Economic Section Report. Available at: <http://www.usembassy-china.org.cn/econ/021705inv.html>.

United States Treasury Department (USTD). 2005. "Foreign Holdings of US Treasuries". Available at: <http://www.treas.gov/tic/mfh.txt>.

US-China Business Council (USCBC). 2005. "US-China Trade Statistics and China's World Trade Statistics." Available at: <http://www.uschina.org/statistics/tradetable.html>.

Wang, Gungwu. 2004. "The Fourth Rise of China: Cultural Implications," China: An International Journal, vol. 2, no. 2 (September): 311–22.

Zhang, Yongjin. 2005. "China Goes Global." London: Foreign Policy Centre. Available at <http://fpc.org.uk/fsblob/449.pdf>.

10 Re-engaging India: Upgrading the Canada-India Bazaar Relationship

RAMESH C. KUMAR and
NIGMENDRA NARAIN

The new realities of the twenty-first century present significant challenges as well as opportunities for Canada. Geography, history, national security and economic imperatives will continue to keep Canada largely focused on managing its relationship with the US. However, just as the US responds to the shifts in global power balances brought about by the recent economic achievements of a number of large, fast-growing, developing countries, Canada too will have to take a fresh look at its relations with a number of them and redefine its policies and priorities in accord with the emerging opportunities (see Whalley, this volume). If Canada does take the initiative, invests the necessary resources and is innovative in its approach, the BRICSAM group presents enormous economic opportunities for Canadian goods, services and investment. Moreover, increased economic engagement might open political channels that could be quite helpful for achieving Canada's larger global interests in the area of human security, development aid, disaster relief, refugee resettlement as well as disarmament and non-proliferation of weapons of mass destruction (WMDs).

This chapter examines Canada-India relations and argues that the new realities present an excellent opportunity to re-engage India. Canada has recently taken some steps in this direction by making a number of, mostly economic, overtures towards India. However, Canada's India policy, ranging in the past from indifference to neglect, presents an image that is best described as a "bazaar relationship": shopping around for one-off trading opportunities but lacking a sustained and diversified relationship.

What is needed instead is a coherent, comprehensive approach, backed with real initiative and resources, that will not only enable Canada to deepen and broaden its relationship with India to further its national and global interests, but will also recognize India's status as an emerging economic power. The chapter first details some reasons why it is in Canada's interest to re-engage India. It then summarizes the current state of affairs in preparation for an analysis of how Canada could pursue such a policy of re-engagement in terms of economic interaction, civil society relations, and cooperation in multilateral areas such as nuclear non-proliferation, international security, developmental assistance, and peace keeping. The chapter concludes with some general remarks on the challenges that lie ahead.

WHY INDIA?

India is a very large nation, accounting for nearly one sixth of the world's population. Although it is defined as a low income country on the basis of income per capita, it is the fourth largest economy in the world in purchasing power parity terms. India's arrival on the world economic scene has been impressive despite being overshadowed by China's rise, which began almost a decade earlier. For the past decade and a half, India has been experiencing the second highest average rate of economic growth. At 6.5 percent, it is second only to that of China and according to some observers the long-run prospects may even be better than those of China (Purushotaman, 2004; Huang and Khanna, 2003; Singh, 2002). With an estimated middle-class of 200–300 million capable of Western consumption levels, India presents a very promising market for expanding Canadian trade and investment. Moreover, India is producing a surplus of highly educated professionals, in information technology (IT), health services, as well as business and finance, who are being courted worldwide. In this new era of more liberal trade and investment regimes, Canada cannot afford to ignore these opportunities if it wants to retain its status as a major trading nation.

India, relative to most other developing countries, also possesses greater political, economic and social similarities to Canada. Like Canada, India is a stable federal parliamentary democracy, with an independent common law judicial system and a large, well-trained bureaucracy. It is multi-lingual, multi-religious, multi-cultural and multi-ethnic, and nearly 300 million Indians can speak, read and write English. Moreover, its economic and financial institutions are better developed than any other developing country. Re-engagement with

India, therefore, should be relatively much easier compared to most other large BRICSAM countries.

There are also foreign policy issues that favour re-engagement. India and Canada share some common values and foreign policy goals. India, like Canada, has been long interested in peacekeeping and peace-making activities, and was a major source for peacekeeping troops and other personnel to Africa in the early sixties and to Sri Lanka in the 1990s. India is also a significant refugee receiving country. In the seventies, India hosted millions of refugees fleeing from East Pakistan (Bangladesh), and absorbed many of the refugees from Uganda and the rest of East Africa. The same was also true in the early years of the on-going conflict in Sri Lanka. Even today, large numbers of refugees regularly cross into India from Bangladesh, Nepal and Myanmar. Finally, India has also started to share in the responsibilities of international disaster-relief. Following the recent Indian Ocean Tsunami disaster that had devastated the Indian territory of Andaman and Nicobar Islands as well as parts of the southern state of Tamil Nadu, India only accepted multilateral agency aid for long-term reconstruction, while its naval ships and military personnel were the first to arrive in Sri Lanka and Indonesia with medical and other relief supplies. These are but some of the areas where Canada and India share similar goals and could assist each other.

A re-engaged India could also be an important ally in advancing the cause of multilateralism in global governance, an objective marked for renewed initiative by the current government in its recent statement of foreign policy (Canada, 2005b). As India gains in stature, it is bound to play a more significant role in the running of some of the global institutions. As an active participant in the Uruguay Round of trade negotiations, it was an important member of the coalition that was successful in interlinking the success of the TRIPS agreement with concessions on the MFA. More recently, it has been instrumental, in cooperation with the EU, the US, Australia and Brazil, in putting the Doha round trade negotiations back on track by bringing about the July 2004 accord, following the failure of the ministerial conference in Cancún in the preceding year. At the time of this writing, the same group was also huddling on the sidelines of the OECD meetings in Paris to try and help the free trade negotiations to meet the deadline for the signing of a draft deal in Hong Kong in December. India is currently a member of the G20 Finance Ministers Meeting, the group largely responsible for global financial management, and would be a significant player in the L20 group, proposed and supported by Canada. Engaging India in a significant manner could thus be a source of generating positive externalities in the cause of multilateralism.

CURRENT STATE OF THE RELATIONSHIP

From 1947 to 1974, Canada-India relations were mostly cordial and co-operative, though largely uneventful. Escott Reid, a one-time Canadian high commissioner to India, has characterized this period as one of "special relationship" but the reality, according to others, was quite different: the relationship might have been a pleasant one, but it was never very deep.

Following India's successful testing of a nuclear device in 1974, there emerged a real hiatus in the bilateral relations that has yet to be fully bridged. While, over the years, there were sporadic acts of cooperation such as the sanctioning of South Africa, Canada-India relations have been marred by sharp disagreements over a number of issues, including Canada's handling of the activities of certain Canadian individuals and groups in support of the Sikh separatists in the Punjab, the Air India disaster in 1985 and related matters, as well as India's second series of nuclear tests in 1998. In fact, Canada's reaction to the second set of nuclear tests was even more dramatic than in 1974, with the quick imposition of trade sanctions and a generally tougher stance against India. For example, Foreign Minister Lloyd Axworthy expressed in late May 1998 Canada's commitment to "voicing vigorous public opposition to any move to legitimize any new nuclear-weapon state," arguing specifically that "India, 'has forfeited any claim to a permanent seat on a body created specifically to preserve peace and security as well as enhance the international order'" (Ditchburn, 1998; *Edmonton Journal*, 1998). In its newly found economic and military self-assuredness, the Indian government reacted equally sternly by immediately cutting funding to the Shastri Indo-Canada Foundation, curtailing other cultural linkages, and generally remaining indifferent to economic relations. Overall, both sides had once again reacted too strongly. For Canada, according to Rubinoff, its human-security and non-proliferation multilateral agenda had again trumped its "bilateral interest with India ... [with] adverse consequences for political, economic, and cultural linkages" (Rubinoff, 2002: 838).

Fortunately, the acrimony this time did not last long. Following US President Bill Clinton's visit to India in March 2000 and that of the Russian President Vladimir Putin in October 2000 – signalling perhaps a growing shift in global opinion in favour of India – Canada began taking steps towards rebuilding the relationship. In March 2001, Foreign Affairs Minister John Manley announced Canada's new plan for "re-engagement with India," including the lifting of many of the trade sanctions in April 2001 (Canada, 2001). As the US moved and continues to move closer to India in the wake of 9/11, the Canadian government also signalled its intention to give Canada-India relations greater importance. This shift in policy was indicated by a flurry of high-level visits to India and numerous trade missions at all levels of government over the next four years, but especially those of Prime Ministers Chrétien and Martin in 2003 and 2005, respectively. The Indian government reciprocated, most significantly in September 2002 when the Indian Minister of External Affairs Yashwant Sinha met in Ottawa with his Canadian counterpart, Bill Graham. The meeting led to an understanding that disagreements would not prevent Canada-India engagement in other common interest areas. Clearly, given the dearth of activity prior to 9/11, Canada has recently been working to re-gain lost ground in its relationship with India, and is finding needed reciprocation.

While the recent initiatives have generated some political good will, they mostly focus on strengthening economic relations with India. This focus, according to some observers, may once again be to the detriment of efforts "at coming to terms with India's regional political and strategic role" (Wiebe, 2003: 1). Nonetheless, given the divergent positions on various issues and given the current state of economic engagement between the two countries, it may not be too bad an idea to *start* the process of re-engagement by cultivating the trade area (Delvoie, 1998).

THE ECONOMICS OF RE-ENGAGEMENT

The economic interaction between the two countries, one developed and one developing, is best revealed through describing trade, aid and investment and technology transfers. Canada has always been a major trading nation, with over 40 percent of its national income generated through international trade. For reasons of geography and history, however, Canada's trade relations barely extend beyond the US, which takes in 80–85 percent of Canadian exports and supplies over two thirds of Canadian imports. Canada's total bilateral trade in 2003 was valued at US$611 billion ($272 billion of exports plus $239 billion of imports). India accounted for a miniscule 0.2 percent share of exports and 0.4 percent share of imports.[1]

The picture is similar for foreign investment. Over the years Canada has become a net creditor nation, and by 2002 Canadians owned $432 billion of foreign assets compared with $349 billion of domestic assets being owned by non-Canadians. Of the $432 billion, $202 billion was invested in the US, while another $106 billion was situated in Western

European countries. Canada's total direct investment in India was merely $144 million in 2002 and $184 million in 2003. Moreover, these meagre amounts are very thinly distributed over a number of different sectors, including banking, insurance and finance, telecommunications, mining and energy and the environment. Similarly, in 2002, Indian investors owned only $29 million of Canadian assets, though in recent years Indian direct investment in Canada increased by nearly 250 percent, from $18 million in 1999 to $62 million in 2003, mostly in the IT sector.[2]

Recent ministerial missions to India have repeatedly emphasized the goal of doubling trade flows by the year 2003. This objective was first stipulated by the Department of Foreign Affairs and International Trade (DFAIT) in its 1998 India Trade Action Plan, and was subsequently rolled into the South Asia Trade Action Plan. While Canadian exports in 2003 did register an increase of 26 percent over the previous year, the calculations done on behalf of the Asia Pacific Foundation of Canada (APFC) suggest an average rate of growth of slightly over 6 percent over the fifteen-year period from 1985 to 2003. If this growth rate is projected to the future, there is little likelihood that Canada will be able to achieve this objective for at least another decade (Assanie et. al., 2003). Setting unrealistic targets does not re-engagement make! Canada would be much better served if it were to invest some effort to obtain, on the one hand, a better understanding of the rapidly changing economic environment in India, and, on the other, a more realistic appreciation of its competitive advantage. In this regard the APFC study makes some important observations.

First, Canada's exports to India are still dominated by commodities, with raw materials comprising nearly one-third of the total. Manufactured goods and transport equipment make up 20 percent and 13 percent of the total, respectively. The rate of growth of Canadian exports to India has lagged behind our exports to other emerging economies. Over the 1985–2000 period, Canadian exports to India grew at the average annual rate of 6.2 percent, placing India in the 19th position, just ahead of Russia, on a list of 20 emerging economies, and this growth was concentrated in the category of food and live animals. Finally, Canadian exports to India have tended to be highly volatile. To improve on this spotty record of trade engagement, Canadian policy makers and businesses will need to be more cognizant of their own current and future strengths and advantages, more coherent in linking these to the priority sectors in the government's South Asia Trade Action Plan, and more aware of the India's rapidly changing economy and economic policy.

On the basis of a detailed analysis of 182 industries at the 3–digit

SITC level, the APFC study identifies 32 different industries in which Canada may possess export advantages relative to other OECD countries. Some of these, such as mining and minerals, are priority sectors in DFAIT's action plan. Other areas of advantage are mostly in crude materials or low value added manufactured goods. Other Action Plan priority sectors, such as electricity generation, transmission and distribution, emerge as possible candidates for expansion on the basis of Canada's comparative advantage relative to all producers, not just OECD ones.

Comparative advantage, however, changes over time. Changing Indian demand and future competition from India's other suppliers will be the principal determinants of the extent and nature of these shifts. Canadian exporters and policymakers will have to be continuously alert to the changes taking place in the Indian economy to maintain their advantage.

In view of the limited success Canada has had so far in significantly increasing its trade with India, it is not surprising that in the recent foreign policy review statement, the Martin government seems to be advancing enhancement of Canadian investment as the better option for greater involvement in the Indian economy. Given the relatively small FDI flows into India (US$2–3 billion per annum) and even smaller levels of Canadian direct investment stocks in India, it may not be a bad strategic choice as the prospects cannot but be for future growth.

Although India's economic success to date has been achieved without a reliance on foreign capital, more recent Indian governments have come to appreciate more its role in further accelerating India's rate of growth. Consequently, they have undertaken a series of policy reforms to enhance India's attractiveness to foreign investors (Singh, 2002; Nayar, 2000). A number of sectors from finance to insurance to telecommunications, previously closed to foreign investment, have been made open, even allowing in some cases majority participation by foreign investors.

Canadian investment in India has generally targeted telecommunications, environment, energy and mining, and there have been some notable successes. But clearly there are other areas of mutual interest such as the development and construction of highways and transportation systems, generic pharmaceuticals as well as software development that remain largely unexplored.[3] India and Canada could also collaborate in third country projects by combining Canadian technology and expertise with well–trained and technologically skilled Indian labour. In this regard, undertaking joint ventures in civil construction, infrastructure development, machine tools, power generation and transmission equipment, telecommunication, engineering designs and computer software in Africa, the Middle East and Southeast Asia would appear to be the most promising.

Of course, success in the various options outlined above depends once again upon how Canada responds to these opportunities. For its part, India has been laying the necessary groundwork to welcome Canadian involvement. It has already signed a comprehensive treaty to avoid double taxation and prevent tax evasion. A bilateral investment promotion and protection agreement is currently under negotiation between the two countries (*Economic Times*, 2005).

Despite some recent successes in oil and natural gas exploration (Saran, 2005: 24), however, Canada has generally been too cautious in responding to the opportunities offered by the Indian economy, mostly operating, according to the *Times of India*, "under the radar" (Rajghatta, 2004). Canada has not only been late in arriving in India, it has also done little to create a favourable image of Canadian exporters and entrepreneurs. In a recent survey, the APFC has found that Canadian business personnel in India are less well known than their Australian and Japanese counterparts, rank behind those from Singapore in providing a favourable business climate, and are definitely not seen as entrepreneurial. Canada is also not associated with high quality products, or seen as a leader in science and technology.

Yet another contributing factor has been the inability of Canadian businesses to build on success. For example, in the 1990s, Canadian firms were actively engaged in building roads and highways in India, but these have now been displaced by Italian competitors. Similarly, the recently completed elevated rail system for the city of Delhi, a major urban transportation project, was financed by the Japanese and built by the Koreans, even though Canada has considerable expertise in both sectors. Similar examples in other sectors are easily found (Rajghatta, 2004). Unless Canada adopts a more pro-active stance in dealing with these issues, it is likely to lose even more ground to its competitors.

CIVIL SOCIETY PATHS
FOR RE-ENGAGEMENT

Civil society relations between Canada and India have a long history. Indian migrants have been coming to Canada for over a hundred years, and other linkages through cultural, scientific and academic exchanges, and through development assistance, have existed ever since India's independence. Can these traditional linkages facilitate the process of re-engagement?

Foreign aid and development assistance have slowly gone out of fashion. Despite recent pledges to increase development assistance budgets beyond the 0.23 percent of Gross National Income (GNI) level provided in 2003, Canada's relative rank in the donor tables has been roughly maintained largely as a consequence of other countries being even more miserly. India's share of Canada's meagre foreign aid flows ($2.8 billion in 2003) has been a paltry $31 million, less than both Bangladesh and China and less than 33 cents for every Indian citizen. In the light of the paltry sums involved, the Indian government announced in June 2003 that it would no longer be "accepting government-to-government bilateral assistance directed to Central and State government entities from a number of donors, including Canada" (Canada, 2003a). After current programs end in 2007 (India, 2005a), CIDA will "continue its development work in India through programming with Canadian partner organizations and through multilateral institutions which comprise the majority of Canada's assistance to India" (Canada, 2003a). In addition, the Canada Fund for Local Initiatives operated by the Canadian High Commission in Delhi, currently worth $800,000, will continue, at least for now, to be available to "[support] small projects which provide technical, economic, educational, cultural or social development assistance to local populations in India" (Canada, 2005a). While policies could change, it appears, however, that development assistance will provide only negligible opportunities for re-engagement.

While ODA has declined as an avenue for interaction, Canadian businesses have slowly become more engaged in India. Two of the key organizations facilitating this process are the Indo-Canada Chamber of Commerce (ICCC), which brings together over 200 Indo-Canadian business leaders and local organizations in order to provide technical support, discussion forums, and networking opportunities, and the Canada-India Business Council (C-IBC), which tries to assist businesses that are attempting to enter the Indian market (Montgomery, 1991). The two organizations regularly host events in both Canada and India that bring together high-ranking officials and government leaders from both countries. They also organize trade missions with government officials, and generally facilitate business relations between the two countries (India, 1988). The APFC does similar work in building linkages between Canada and India, working with both the private and public sectors in the areas of trade, development, and exchanges.

A more visible government role, however, remains essential. Canadian businesses need knowledge about India and Indian business practices, and about possible commercial opportunities that await them. Moreover, as the Indian government devolves economic development and planning matters to lower levels of government, the information needs of Canadian business will increase and become more complex. Evidence of these needs were apparent at the March 2003 roundtable on Clean Development Mechanisms, during which it was noted "that companies require facilitation support, including assistance with ... obtaining financing" (Canadian High Commission, 2003). Indeed, at least since the 1980s, organizations such as the C-IBC, ICCC and the Conference Board of Canada have been urging the Canadian government to engage India in a more concerted manner in order to facilitate Canadian business entry into the Indian market. What is required in essence is substantive investment, in funds as well as personnel, to develop adequate in-house information and expertise to help Canadian businesses navigate the semi-dismantled Indian License Raj, especially at the state-level. DFAIT can carry out the task all on its own, or, to somewhat lessen its burden, may enrol the Indo-Canadian community for assistance.

After China, India is the second largest source of immigrants to Canada. Since 2000, well over 20 thousand Indians have immigrated to Canada each year, constituting over 10 percent of Canada's total annual in-take (Canada, 2003b). As Haroon Siddiqui points out, roughly 600,000 members of the 25 million strong Indian diaspora live in Canada (Siddiqui, 2005). These 600,000 Indo-Canadians are engaged in a variety of social, economic, and political activities. The strength of their socio-economic presence is starkly seen in the nearly $250 million earned by the Toronto-area wedding-related retailers from the Indo-Canadian wedding market alone (Siddiqui, 2005). As regards to their political involvement, Indo-Canadians are active across the entire political spectrum in the federal parliament, provincial legislatures, and municipally. It is only sensible for Canada to harness the talent and resources of the Indo-Canadian community to help in the process of re-engaging India.

SECURITY RE-ENGAGEMENT

Compared to the opportunities for re-engagement through economic and civil society relations, security issues present a much narrower band of possibilities. The most promising area of cooperation is in counter-terrorism. India is eager to cooperate on the basis of domestic considerations alone, quite aside from the broader threats associated with 9/11. Foreign policy changes under Canadian Foreign Ministers Graham and Manley have de-linked Canada's security disagreements with India from its desire to enhance economic relations, facilitating progress on security cooperation. The most visible dimensions of this progress are the 2003 Chrétien-Vajpayee and the 2005 Martin-Singh joint statements (Canada, 2003c; India, 2005b). The India-Canada Joint Working Group on Counter-terrorism (ICJWGCT) was established in 1997 to formalize cooperation in the investigation of the 1985 terrorist bombing of the Air India flight. This was "the first such working group established by India" (Canada, 2003c), with senior officials from the political, counter-terrorist, and law enforcement backgrounds and agencies meeting to discuss substantive terrorist-related security issues including narco-trafficking, terrorist financing, cyber-terrorism, intelligence-sharing, aviation and maritime security, and multilateral action (India, 2005c). What is most notable is that even after 1998, when bilateral relations had hit an all-time low, the Group continued to meet. Besides this bilateral mechanism, India is also a potential supporter of Canada's multilateral initiatives to deal with terrorism, as illustrated by its support of Canada's G20 Finance Ministers initiative to impede the financial operations of terrorist groups. Indeed, as India seeks greater global cooperation to deal with terrorism, all Canadian initiatives on the issue are likely to find ample support in New Delhi.

The other security goals of Canada that will likely secure India's support are best pursued through multilateral mechanisms, such as the UN. For instance, Canada is identified globally with peacekeeping. As India now consistently ranks in the top five suppliers of peacekeepers, there are opportunities for cooperation through joint exercises and information sharing. There may also be a convergence of interests in reforming peacekeeping, such as Canada's support for a UN Rapid Reaction Force. Canada's desire for a greater role in disaster relief management, especially in Asia, could also be pursued. India demonstrated its own disaster relief capabilities after the 2004 Tsunami, particularly in its rapid assistance for Sri Lanka. Canada could enhance the effectiveness of its Disaster Assistance Response Team (DART), while India would be able to leverage its own limited resources, by coordinating their relief efforts during future crises.

Canada's objectives in reforming global governance are also likely to find some resonance in New Delhi. Canada has been a leader in the G20–finance and L20 initiatives. India supported these initiatives despite some misgivings (shared by others) that they may deflect attention from more pressing governance issues, such as the structural reform of the UN in general, and the reform and possible expansion of the Security Council in particular.

Despite these areas of common security interest, a broader engagement with India on security issues is likely to suffer from at least two

significant limitations. First, Canadian goals in hard security areas –
weapons of mass destruction (WMD) and nuclear non-proliferation –
will not receive India's support. Canada wants India to sign onto the
Non-Proliferation Treaty as well as the Comprehensive Test Ban
Treaty. In contrast, India's voluntary adherence to non-proliferation
reflects its view of these treaties as discriminatory, and it argues instead
for eradicating all nuclear weapons.[4] Similarly, Canada's push for the
International Convention to Ban Landmines (ICBL/Ottawa Protocol)
and the establishment of the International Criminal Court (ICC/Rome
Treaty) was opposed by the Indian government, which saw them as
inimical to India's national interests, limiting in particular its options
in Kashmir. In hard security matters, India's policies are premised on
its regional hegemony and status as a nuclear power. Unless Canada
develops a better understanding of India's interests in these regards, the
room for mutual support and cooperation on traditional security
matters will be very limited.

Second, since 9/11, the shifts in Canada's security relations with the
US are also an obstacle to closer ties with India. As Kapur (1988),
Rubinoff (2002), and others have consistently argued, the Canada-US-
India triangle has been the key context for Canada-India relations.
During the Cold War, Canada was seen as a channel between the US
and India, though one that was frequently skewed in favour of the US.
In contrast, Canada's influence in Washington is diminishing (see
Burney, this volume) while, since 9/11 at least, India's direct access has
increased. India's warming relations with the US is visible in the direct
American engagement of India on security issues through joint military
exercises, counter-terrorism discussions and cooperation, and the
resumption of supplies of military goods, including F-16 fighter jets
(*Times of India*, 2005). In the past, Canada, along with India and other
middle-powers, used multilateralism to limit American power. Now, as
a regional and nuclear power itself, India is much more ambivalent
about the necessity of multilateral restraints. In these matters, and even
in the area of counterterrorism, Canada may find that in the triangu-
lar relationship, it will be the one that is increasingly out of step with
its partners.

Neither of these two limitations, however, should dissuade Canada
from the modest engagements suggested above. Upgrading the current
relationship will not quickly remove the political consternation on the
security side, but a total lack of interaction on the security front will
cripple the efforts to build a deeper and broader relationship over the
long haul. The current on-off policies limit Canada's foreign policy
goals in global security management. In contrast, a sustained security
re-engagement with India will allow both countries to enhance coop-

eration in areas of mutual interest, and manage their differences more constructively when interests diverge.

CONCLUDING REMARKS

The picture of Canada-India relations outlined above is one of missed opportunities, interspersed with sporadic successes that were never fully capitalized on by either side. Uninspired relations between the two countries must now confront the changed reality of the twenty-first century. Canada's recent initiatives to re-engage India, with a focus on upgrading economic linkages first, hold out significant promise for a more sustained relationship. While one should not over-estimate the future possibilities of the relationship, it is hard to imagine that a deeper economic engagement will be in the way of a deeper political engagement. To ensure greater success this time around, however, Canada will have to invest additional resources to improve its in-house information and expertise on the Indian economy. Given the enormous economic opportunities India currently presents, and the future possibilities for political cooperation in several areas of national and global interest to Canada, the investment will eventually pay for itself several times over.

Nonetheless, Canada-India relations face many challenges. First and foremost, as discussed by Rubinoff (2002), Tremblay (2003) and most directly stated by Wiebe (2003: 2), of the APFC, "Ottawa must accept the reality that India is a nuclear power and work with it as an equal, just as we do with other nuclear-armed democracies." India's status as a nuclear power leaves it indifferent to multilateral mechanisms and impervious to external pressure when it comes to settling contentious regional issues such as Kashmir, refugee flows, and the sharing of water. More helpful is the flipside of India's regional and nuclear power, which is its desire to be a key player in global initiatives, ranging from counter-terrorism to the L20, and from disaster relief to peacekeeping. Consequently there are many opportunities for Canada to work with India in the pursuit of objectives such as disarmament and non-proliferation, while simultaneously re-engaging with it on non-security issues.

In summary, as Canada now confronts split images in terms of its foreign policy, it also faces split images in its relationship with India. While recognizing these differences, it is still possible to envision a more sustained and coherent relationship that skilfully blends the existing political, economic and social linkages into a better-focused, less bazaar-like, and more cohesive foreign policy towards India.

NOTES

The authors would like to thank Jackie Bonisteel, Gwen Cottle and
Rocio Ilera for their research assistance.

1   The data are taken from the statistics database of the WTO, complied
    under 'Trade Profiles' and 'International Trade Statistics, 2004,' both of
    which can be accessed on the web.
2   The FDI statistics are taken from the UNCTAD document "FDI Profile:
    Canada," available from its web-site and promotional information com-
    plied by the High Commission of India, Ottawa and available upon request.
3   Nearly 80 percent the relevant land mass of India remains unexplored for
    oil and natural gas exploration. India also lags significantly behind China
    in road construction and highway development. The last two areas also
    represent major opportunities for outsourcing, although Canada is at
    times a competitor in IT.
4   According to the Department of National Defence (DND), India may be
    preparing to conduct more tests because the 1998 tests may have "fallen
    short of [their] planned potential" (Canada, 2002).

REFERENCES

Assanie, Nizar, et al. 2003. "Canada-India Trade: Retrospect and Prospects,"
    Canada in Asia: Foreign Policy Dialogue Series, vol. 2003, no. 2 (Septem-
    ber). New Delhi: Asia Pacific Foundation of Canada and National Council
    of Applied Economic Research.
Canada. 2001. "Statement by the Minister of Foreign Affairs on Re-engage-
    ment with India." Ottawa: Department of Foreign Affairs and International
    Trade (DFAIT), 21 March.
– 2002. "India and Pakistan." Ottawa: Department of National Defence
    (DND), Policy Group. Available at: <http://www.forces.gc.ca/admpol/eng/
    doc/strat_2000/s000_07_e.htm> .
– 2003a. "Canada establishes new partnership with India," Press Release.
    Ottawa: Canadian International Development Agency (CIDA), 10 October.
    Available at: <http://w3.acdi-cida.gc.ca/cida_ind.nsf/o/740994dafod48ebb
    85256dbb0067ea19?OpenDo cument>.
– 2003b. "Facts and Figures 2003 Immigration Overview: Permanent Resi-
    dents." Ottawa: Citizenship and Immigration Canada (CIC). Available at:
    <http://www.cic.gc.ca/english/pub/facts2003/permanent/14.html>.
– 2003c. "Partners for the 21st century joint statement by India and Canada."
    Ottawa: Department of Foreign Affairs and International Trade (DFAIT), 24
    October.

– 2005a. "Canada announces comprehensive tsunami disaster relief, rehabilitation and reconstruction assistance." Press Release. Ottawa: Office of the Prime Minister (DMO), 10 January. Available at: <http://pm.gc.ca/eng/news. asp?id=381>.

– 2005b. "Overview," in *Canada's International Policy Statement: A Role of Pride and Influence in the World*. Ottawa: Department of Foreign Affairs and International Trade (DFAIT), 19 April. Available at: <http://www.dfait-maeci.gc.ca/cip-pic/ips/overview-en.asp>.

Canadian High Commission to India. 2003. "RFI-CII Roundtable on the Clean Development Mechanism in India," Summary Report on Bilateral Roundtable on Clean Development, New Delhi, 4–5 March. Available at: <http://www.dfait-maeci.gc.ca/cdm-ji/round_table-en.asp>.

Delvoie, Louis. 1998. "Canada and New India: A New Beginning?" *The Round Table*, vol. 345 (January): 51–64.

Ditchburn, Jennifer. 1998. "Use Canada as example: Axworthy," *Kingston Whig–Standard*, 27 May, 13.

Economic Times. 2005. "WTO talks may miss July deadline," 2 May.

Edmonton Journal. 1998. "India defiant in face of economic sanctions; Stock exchange rises, Clinton burned in effigy; Nuclear Test Fallout," 15 May.

Huang, Yasheng and Tarun Khanna. 2003. "Can India Overtake China?" *Foreign Policy*, no. 137 (July/August): 70–81.

India. 1988. "Canada and India." New Delhi: Department of External Affairs (DEA).

– 2005a. "Canadian Bilateral Economic Assistance to India." New Delhi: Ministry of Finance, Administration and Bilateral Cooperation Division. Available at: <http://finmin.ninc.in/the_ministry/dept_eco_affairs/admin_divisi on/na_canadian_assistance.htm>.

– 2005b. "India-Canada Joint Statement." New Delhi: Ministry of External Affairs (MEA), 18 January.

– 2005c. "Joint Statement, India-Canada Joint Working Group on Counterterrorism." New Delhi: Ministry of External Affairs (MEA), 12 April.

Kapur, Ashok. 1988. "South Asia: The Diplomatic and Strategic Setting", Arthur G. Rubinoff, ed., *Canada and South Asia: Issues and Opportunities*. Toronto: University of Toronto Press.

Montgomery, Melinda. 1991. "The Indo-Canadian Connection," *CA Magazine* (English ed.), vol. 124, no. 1 (January): 8–9.

Nayar, Baldev Raj. 2000. "The Limits of Economic Nationalism in India: Economic Reforms under the BJP-Led Government, 1998–1999," *Asian Survey*, vol. 40, no. 5 (September): 792–815.

Purushothaman, Roopa. 2004. "India: Realizing BRICS Potential," Global Economics Paper No. 109, *Goldman Sachs*, 14 April.

Rajghatta, Chidanand. 2004. "Moaner's decline, neighbour's pride," *Times News Network*.

Rubinoff, Arthur. 2002. "Canada's Re-engagement with India," *Asian Survey*, vol. 42, no. 6 (November): 838–55.

Saran, Rohit. 2005. "Mani for Oil," *India Today,* 28 February, 24–5.

Siddiqui, Haroon. 2005. "Diasporas have much to contribute," *Toronto Star*, 23 January, A17.

Singh, Nirvilar. 2002. "Miracles and Reforms in India-Policy Reflections," *Asian Survey*, vol. 42, no. 5 (September): 708–22.

Times of India. 2005. "India, US hit snags over Iran, F-16s to Pak," 16 March.

Tremblay, Reeta Chowdhari. 2003. "Canada and India: Broadening and Deepening Relationship," *Canada in Asia: Foreign Policy Dialogue Series, 2003–2004.* Vancouver: Asia Pacific Foundation. Available at: <http://www.asiapacific.ca/analysis/pubs/pdfs/canadaindia4_14octo 3.pdf>.

Wiebe, John. 2003. "A Call for reality in Canada-India relations," Editorial. *Asia-Pacific Foundation of Canada,* September. Available at: <http://www.asiapacific.ca/analysis/pubs/pdfs/india_summito3_oped .pdf>.

11 Canada-Russia Relations: A Strategic Partnership?

BOGDAN BURUDU and
DRAGOŞ POPA

Canada's recently released *International Policy Statement* (IPS) (Canada, 2005) includes among its new foreign policy priorities the need to realign bilateral relationships and develop novel networks outside North America. Russia, alongside China, India, and Brazil is generally considered one of the emerging global actors to be targeted, and as a result, warrants special attention in the light of growing linkages and mutual interests.

A country of 17 million sq km and 145 million people, holding claims to 20 percent of the world's fresh water resources and to 40 percent of the circumpolar Arctic territory, Russia is a full G8 member and holds a permanent seat on the United Nations (UN) Security Council. It remains a global power, a status that Canada-Russia relations strive to reflect. Rapidly moving away from the state of affairs characterizing the Cold War period, these relations witnessed a continuous development throughout the 1990s and focus currently on security, development, and environmental issues.

Especially in the post-9/11 international security environment, the Canadian and Russian leaders have pledged repeatedly to cooperate in the fight against global terrorism and in preventing the spread of nuclear weapons. Canadian Prime Minister Paul Martin has also reiterated his strong backing for Russia's accession to the World Trade Organization (WTO), which will likely happen by the end of 2005. While not neglecting the benefits of increased bilateral trade under the auspices of the WTO, Canada sees the primary benefit of accession to be the strengthening of the rule of law in Russia that will hopefully follow from the exposure to binding (i.e. strictly enforced by interested parties) trade rules.

Augmenting the capacity of the Russian state is essential in order to continue successfully the transformation of the Russian polity and economy. However, the apparent disconnect between the people and the state, a sign of a weak democracy, impedes Russia's ability to clearly identify the public interest – crippling the chances of successful policy-making. As a result, Russia needs to create a functioning democracy within a strong and effective state. Encouraging this effort has been a key area of interest for Canada, although Western efforts in facilitating the transformation of Russia's domestic political and economic life have consistently received a lukewarm response from Moscow, when they have not been rejected altogether.

Canada's new IPS steers away from this mentoring approach, which characterized Canadian positions vis-à-vis Russia during the 1990s, and instead identifies further opportunities to advance a mutually agreed upon agenda in the international realm. It promotes not only "a new multilateralism that emphasizes global responsibilities and a reformed multilateral system that tackles major global issues," but also the idea of "building new networks (beyond North America), key to both our interests and values" (Canada, 2005: 2). While this new emphasis has the potential to strengthen relations significantly, Canada may find its interest in Russia diminishing if the latter does not maintain the status of a major player. Russia's position in the world could be overshadowed by the rise of new international giants such as India and China, whose emergence could accordingly shape its relations with Canada.

This chapter will offer an overview of Russia's status almost a decade and a half since the collapse of the Soviet Union and will investigate key topics of interest to Canada-Russia relations. It will explore not only areas of relatively successful collaboration, but also areas of contention, involving Russia, Canada, and the larger Western community. The chapter will argue that Russia is still seen by Canada as a major international player and that important issues bind the two countries together, but that the potential for a strategic partnership has not yet been reached, and may not be reached at all in the foreseeable future if Russia's standing in the international arena does not improve rapidly.

RUSSIA PROFILE

Russia lives in historic times, with great events unfolding and eventual outcomes uncertain. History has seen Russia go through the painful building of the Communist system at the beginning of the twentieth century and now, following the demise of the Soviet Union, the country has to endure the tumult of reversing that transformation. Unfortunately, neither journey can be described as pleasant: dismantling an elaborate and highly structured economy and society – painfully built over almost eight decades – is bound to be incredibly difficult. Fourteen years into the process, Russia still grapples with the difficult transition from dictatorship to democracy, and from a centrally planned economy to a market economy.[1]

Experts studying this complex transition process loathe the comparison between the current efforts to reform the Russian polity, economy, and society and the vast Soviet experiment undertaken by Communists during the last century. After all, Russia is now moving in the "right" direction. The fact remains that the whole endeavour is overwhelming and requires profound changes that took centuries to unfold in the West under the pressures of the Industrial Revolution, and more recently, globalization. It is very much a transformation by design, but unlike the Communist social experiment, it faces expectations (and possibly a political imperative) of immediate positive results. Reality has moderated the initial hopes and at the present time it is hard to enlist constant support for reforms from the same people that were asked, over several decades, to build the Communist society that now needs to be dismantled.

In the economic realm, the transformational recession in Russia and the rest of the Soviet bloc countries was expected. However, its extent was a surprise. Indeed, such a significant drop of output during peacetime was unprecedented in world economic history. The decline in production is comparable to the losses caused by the Great Depression. The drop in real incomes and the growing income inequality put tremendous strain on the Russian society. The increased insecurity, and not only of the economic sort, did not generate constructive political efforts to respond to these challenges. The accompanying significant decreases in average life expectancy and increases in crime rates have not led to a strong societal reaction, but rather to complacency and lost hopes. This outcome is not unique to Russia; indeed, it characterizes all the laggards among Central and Eastern European (CEE) transition countries.

Wiping the slate clean is not a recipe for success unless there are effective institutions that will replace the discarded ones in a timely manner. Russia somehow lacked the ability to put those new institutions in place, both in the economic and political spheres. The result was a "failing state," without the capability to prevent breakdown in the health care system, further degradation of the environment, rise in levels of crime, and endemic corruption. Even more importantly, the lawlessness of the business climate that ensued led to levels of foreign investment well below what authorities hoped for, and was certainly much less than what the smaller economies of Central and Eastern Europe were able to absorb. This outcome, in turn, had far deeper consequences. Not only did the economy not rebound as expected, capital stocks actually deteriorated. More importantly, Russia lost a key ingredient to successful transformation: the pressure foreign capital provides in terms of introducing new technologies, breeding competition, injecting institutional and organizational expertise, and instilling inherent support for the rule of law.

Not all has been wasted in the years following the 1991 collapse of the Soviet Union. The hyperinflation of the early 1990s and the currency crisis of 1998 are past, though the consumer-price inflation rate is likely to remain in double digits for 2005, despite the government's target of 8–9 percent. 2004 was a bumper year for foreign direct investment, though inflows were partially offset by US$8 billion in capital flight, marking the acceleration of a problem endemic during the 1990s. Most likely, this capital exodus represents the reaction to the Yukos affair, revealing the extent of the damage it has done to the business environment in the eyes of domestic investors.[2]

Russia's economic reforms have advanced considerably since Vladimir Putin became president in 2000. The early reform period (2000–02), focused on deregulation and tax reform. Subsequent progress in sensitive areas such as utilities restructuring and housing reform has been slower, partly because of the large, unwieldy and corrupt bureaucracy. But the economy grew at the healthy rate of 7.1 percent in 2004. Sky-high international oil prices helped balloon Russia's exports to more than US$180 billion per year, leading to a current-account surplus of US$60 billion in 2003 (*Economist*, 2005). Unfortunately for Russia, most experts expect a decline in world oil prices in 2006. This may slow down the GDP growth and decrease the fiscal and current-account surpluses.

Due to the follies of central planning and the presence of abundant natural resources, heavy industries including fuel, energy and metallurgy are dominant in Russia's industrial sector. Large enterprises still dominate Russia's economy, while the small and medium enterprises that provide the bulk of economic growth in developed and some developing economies are scarce due to high taxes and excessive regulation. The large, incumbent enterprises are more likely to use ties with the bureaucratic apparatus forged during Communist times to get the upper hand in fighting any emerging competitors. This process slows down reforms in both the industrial sector and the bureaucracy.

Political challenges remain as well, especially the strengthening of democracy in Russia. Some observers argue that by drawing former Soviet bloc countries, such as Georgia and Ukraine, into the democratic fold, the West encourages Russia to become more democratic and embrace core Western values itself. Clearly, this does not seem to be the way Russia sees things. Russia resents the eastern expansion of the North Atlantic Treaty Organization (NATO) and the European Union (EU), as well as aggressive Western support for democratic movements in the "near abroad countries." It is debatable whether palpable successes on the economic and political fronts in these countries would provide enough incentives for Russia to follow suit.

In addition to US President George W. Bush's repeated criticism of Russia's stance on democracy, the co-chairmen of the Russia Democracy Caucus in the US Congress, Rep. Chris Cox (R-Calif.) and Rep. Tom Lantos (D-Calif.), have recently introduced a bill that urges the US President to suspend Russia's membership in the G8, given its lack of progress toward becoming a free and democratic society. "Russia has failed to complete a successful transition from Communism to free enterprise, and from a Soviet police state to a stable, securely democratic society. Vladimir Putin needs to show that his nation belongs in the same league with the other G-7 members," they argue in a joint statement (Thomas, 2005). From a similar position, Hugues Mingarelli, Director for Eastern Europe, Southern Caucasus and Central Asian Republics in the European Commission's Directorate General for External Relations, pointed out that "EU decision-makers had grave doubts about Russia's readiness to uphold the EU's values," especially in the areas of domestic political life and interventions in former Soviet space (cited in Chapman, 2004: 22).

No Canadian foreign policy is complete – or ought not to be – without tackling the issues that Canada's American and European counterparts have raised in relation to Russia. Canada is hurting its own interests, and those of its closest friends and allies, if it continues to be one of the least vocal critics of Moscow. By putting pressure on Russian decision-makers to abandon the newly found Russian version of a third way – that is, a compromise between Communism and Western democracy and a market economy, (which in its current form only benefit the country's elites) – Canada can advance both Russia's long-term interests and those of the West.

Recent experience with European enlargement shows that reform laggards accelerate their efforts only after the accession talks are well under way. Russia might not feel compelled to advance on the road of democratic reforms before gaining enhanced access to Europe's elite clubs is more than a distant prospect. Until then, Russian President Vladimir Putin or his successors can continue to simply sell oil to the West and supply promises to act responsibly when it comes to, for example, supplying nuclear enrichment know-how, hardware components and fuel to countries such as Iran. As long as Russians in general, and Mr Putin in particular, crave a seat at the world's top tables, the West (including Canada) can find ways to quell the uncertainty of democracy in Russia and further the mutual interests of prosperity and security.

Russia has the potential to regain its status as a major global player and of remaining a key partner to the USA, the EU, and China, if it can manage to overcome significant constraints. There is a serious demographic crisis on the horizon as a consequence of low birth rates and inadequate health care, coupled with a potentially severe HIV/AIDS problem. The US Census Bureau predicts that Russia will have a lower life expectancy in 2010 than it did in 1991. Adopting effective HIV/AIDS prevention measures is going to be a key factor to reverse this trend. Reforming its economy, by diversifying it away from an excessive reliance on the energy sector and improving governance at all levels, are imperatives for Russia at this point in time. Dealing with the localized tensions and conflicts within Russia and along its southern border is also a priority. Tackling these challenges in a timely fashion may keep Russia on track to become one of the up-and-coming economic powers (National Intelligence Council, 2004).

However, most recent analyses on Russia's position in the world emphasise its sharp loss of influence in the international arena after the end of the Cold War. This is a phenomenon most clearly seen in Russia's "near abroad." It is also apparent in other parts of the world, such as the Middle East, where its predecessor, the Soviet Union, had been perceived as a major international player. From one of the world's two superpowers, Russia's international status has been reduced in the past decade to, at best, that of a tolerated member of influential clubs such as the G8. With "an overall life expectancy below Cuba's and even Iraq's" and a domestic "income gap approaching Latin American levels" (Levitov, 2005), a questionable record of political freedoms and systemic economic problems, Russia is struggling to define its place in an increasingly competitive world, while finding itself in a clearly unenviable position.

DIMENSIONS OF
CANADA-RUSSIA RELATIONS

A number of areas of cooperation illustrate the convergence of Canadian and Russian views on many topics of key interest to the two countries and the international community. The growing level of official and private linkages between Canadian and Russian partners indicates the desire of both Ottawa and Moscow to strengthen bilateral relations. Rather than focussing on improving domestic developments in Russia, recent Canadian efforts have concentrated on promoting bilateral approaches to international political issues: programs against proliferation of weapons of mass destruction (WMD), the fight against international terrorism, challenges and opportunities in the Arctic region and joint collaboration within the framework of multilateral organizations.

Given Canadian concerns about Russian domestic developments such as widespread corruption, inefficient bureaucracy, ineffective government, rampant organized crime, an ever-changing legal system, and an unreliable judicial system, the level of economic cooperation between the two countries remains low. The technical assistance provided by Canada to tackle these issues and other social problems is received at top political levels with reservation; seen as potentially useful, yet condescending. Ottawa's involvement with countries in Russia's near abroad further complicates its relations with Moscow and even the areas of stronger bilateral cooperation are marred by issues that are of significant concern to Canada.

One area of Russian-Canadian cooperation of key importance to both countries is the Global Partnership Program. Initiated at the G8 Kananaskis Summit in June 2002, its main goal is to provide financial and technical assistance to Russia for the destruction of chemical weapons, the dismantling of nuclear submarines, the employment of former weapons scientists, and the disposal of fissile materials. The G8 leaders agreed to raise up to US\$20 billion over ten years for this program, with Canada covering up to C\$1 billion over ten years. The Canadian contribution is concentrated on the dismantling of Russia's decommissioned nuclear submarines and the destruction of its stockpile of chemical weapons. The program is beneficial to all parties, since it provides Russia with much-needed resources to eliminate dated weaponry and meet international obligations, while reducing the risk of international terrorists and rogue states acquiring weapons of mass destruction. In the new, post-9/11 global security context, both countries, along with the other G8 members, can emphasize their commitment to non-proliferation principles through participation in this program. Unfortunately Canadian involvement has been slowed down recently by allegations that Russia has misused program funds. Western and Russian defence critics have warned repeatedly that money could be diverted by the Russian government or agencies of the Russian armed forces toward Moscow's weapons-making programs. They have also argued that more transparency is needed in Russia to assure Western donors that the allocation of funds reflects their intended purposes.

Closely related to the goals of the Global Partnership Program are the efforts to eliminate the threat of international terrorism. Canadian and Russian officials meet regularly, both on a bilateral basis and in the framework of various international organizations, to discuss the two countries' response to this growing threat. In late 2004 in Ottawa, Canada hosted bilateral multi-disciplinary consultations on the Campaign against Terrorism, Organized Crime, Illegal Migration and Drug Trafficking. The NATO-Russia Council, established in May 2002, is one of the key multilateral venues for Canadian-Russian consultations on counter-terrorist strategies and non-proliferation of weapons of mass destruction.

Despite significant progress in advancing this common agenda, Canadian officials, including Prime Minister Paul Martin, have expressed their uneasiness about the use of counter-terrorist tactics by Russian troops in Chechnya[3] and the alleged human rights abuses in this separatist region. While Canada and Russia share the same goal of preventing terrorists from striking the two countries and threatening the international community, they sometimes disagree over the best course of action. Cooperation in the war against terrorism seems to be reasonably fruitful, although much of it happens in the realm of intelligence sharing, which prevents the broader public from assessing it.

Canada and Russia have largely transcended the state of suspicion that characterized their Cold War relations, and cooperation on specific security issues is sincere. Occasionally, however, information on Russian intelligence efforts to penetrate Canadian military targets (O'Flynn, 2004), attempts by Moscow to regulate the way Canadian media cover stories on Russia and terrorism (Oziewicz, 2004), or accusations that Canadians have joined insurgents fighting against Russia (Freeze, 2004), provide a reality-check on bilateral cooperation in this area. For example, in 2002 two Russian diplomats were expelled from Canada for activities "inconsistent with diplomatic status" (Aubry and Bronskill, 2002). Two Canadians were expelled from Russia in a tit-for-tat response. Amy Knight, a specialist in Russian security affairs asks, "Why would the Russians still be spying on the West if they need its cooperation in fighting terrorism, joining the North Atlantic Treaty Organization and encouraging economic investment in their country?" (Knight, 2002). One possible answer is that the overall relationship between Russia and the West (including Canada) is not necessarily more than the sum of their specific projects of cooperation. More succinctly, Russia is the West's new best friend as long as the situation suits Moscow.

Despite such hurdles, the Canadian and Russian governments have continued attempts to strengthen security-related linkages. Many of the two countries' common interests are advanced through multilateral frameworks, especially at the United Nations, an organization that both Canada and Russia actively support. For example, prior to the onset of the Iraq War in early 2003, both countries expressed their support for multilateral diplomacy and the use of the United Nations in solving the USA-Iraq standoff. Both countries seem to regard collective peacekeeping operations and the involvement of international organizations in providing solutions to transnational problems as serving not only the interests of the global community, but also their own strategic interests in a unipolar international order. Canada and Russia's similar stance on subjects such as the Iraq War, the Kyoto Protocol, the resolution to Middle East conflicts, the fight against global terrorism and other topical areas of action offers a solid basis to improve bilateral relations. Dealing with climate change, for instance, requires, by its nature, solutions devised and implemented in a multilateral setting.[4] There is considerable scope for cooperation between Canada and Russia in this area. While it may very well be that the two countries promote multilateralism for different reasons, the fact remains that Canada and Russia find common cause in articulating support for it, and in using it as a framework for cooperation.

Nevertheless, disagreements on specific issues between Canada and Russia on various international issues do emerge, and are most evident in the operations of the Organization for Security and Cooperation in Europe (OSCE)(especially in Chechnya) and in relations with countries on Russia's borders. Recent attempts by Russia to consolidate its position in its near abroad, even to create a new political and economic space as a counterbalance to the European Union and other such blocs, have been disturbed. Several former Soviet states have discovered new interests in cooperation with, or integration into the West. The withdrawal of the GUAM group, consisting of Georgia, Ukraine, Azerbaijan and Moldova,[5] could even threaten the de facto existence of the Moscow-led Commonwealth of Independent States

(CIS). According to James Sherr of the Conflict Studies Research Centre, Mr. Putin has repeatedly presented the CIS as a new "economic and strategic space" with aspirations to "mirror EU integration," within which a "single economic area," created around a core consisting of Russia, Belarus, Ukraine, and Kazakstan would be established (cited in Chapman, 2004: 34). Western support for GUAM activity could inadvertently, or purposefully, undermine CIS integration efforts.

Canada is actively encouraging the process by which former Soviet countries are integrated into the West, and is widely seen as one of Ukraine's strongest supporters on this path. Not only was Canada the first Western country to recognize Ukraine's independence in 1991, "Canada has consistently stressed Ukraine's importance to its allies in a variety of multilateral settings and has played a truly notable role in facilitating Ukraine's return to the European and world community" (Dalkie and Dutkiewicz, 1997: 271). Canada has significant economic links with another GUAM member state, Azerbaijan, with the two countries cooperating in the petroleum and energy transmission sectors.

Canada has also been one of the strongest supporters of all Central and Eastern European countries' integration into Western structures such as NATO and the European Union. Since most of these countries were "assigned" to the Soviet area of influence after the end of the Second World War, Russia expressed its desire to maintain the same geopolitical arrangement following the demise of its Communist empire. European and North American efforts toward CEE integration into the West are in conflict with Russia's regional interests and this has complicated Canada's relations with Russia. For example, Canada was the first country to voice its concerns with respect to Russia's involvement in the 2004 presidential elections in Ukraine.

An area of active cooperation concerns the Northern dimension of the two countries' relations. Canada and Russia are neighbours across the Arctic Ocean. They share, as Arctic countries, common challenges and they benefit from their rich Northern cultures and natural resources. The two countries' cooperation on pan-Arctic issues is already decades-long and they are actively engaged in an effort to reinvigorate it, especially after Canadian Governor General Adrienne Clarkson's visit to Russia in late 2003, which gave a significant boost to the Northern dimension of Canada-Russia relations.

Canadian-Russian cooperation in the Arctic has intensified and continuously diversified since it was promoted in a 1987 speech by then-Soviet President Mikhail Gorbachev. Two years later, then-

Canadian Prime Minister Brian Mulroney was instrumental in bringing Canadian constituencies to the table, by actively involving them in the setting up of an Arctic Council (Stoett, 2000: 93–4). Created in 1996, it consists not only of eight Arctic states – Canada, Denmark (Greenland), Finland, Iceland, Norway, Russia, Sweden, and the USA – but also of permanent representatives of Aboriginal peoples. Yet, in spite of concrete activities within this promising framework, experts on the Arctic region point out that Canada's "ever-growing preponderance of trade and commerce flowing south seems to run counter to the often-voiced but rarely acted on visions of opening up the North" (Koring, 1998: 51).

Moreover, as Canada intensifies its efforts to reinforce claims over its Northern territories, a potentially growing problem is the alleged violation of Canadian sovereignty by Russia, and others. Many Russian and Western nuclear submarines are said to enter Canada's Arctic waters regularly, and many defence and economic analysts argue that the problem will only worsen if global warming were to open up commercial shipping routes between Europe and Asia through the Northwestern Passage.

Nonetheless, the current Russian Ambassador to Canada, Georgiy Mamedov, believes that the prospects of this new maritime route are more than encouraging. Dubbed the "Arctic Bridge," this navigational path would link Churchill, Manitoba, with Russia's northwestern port of Murmansk. This waterway would be one of the quickest routes to transport oil and liquefied natural gas into central Canada and the United States. Once the route is in place, Canada would make money on transit fees, and it could also significantly increase the merchandise trade between the two countries. However, there are several hurdles that need to be overcome: the costly infrastructure needed for such a venture at both ends; the risks attached to possible damage to the environment; and the costly security measures to reinforce Canadian claims to the Arctic waters (which are contested by the US). While this project has a lot of potential for improving economic linkages in the future, many challenges will need to be overcome.

Similarly, there are challenges to current economic relations. To insulate itself from the risks of excessive reliance on its energy resources, Russia needs to diversify its economy. This process requires strengthening the rule of law and undertaking the necessary structural reforms to unleash market forces. There are several benefits to this strategy. First, a diversified economy will lead to the creation of a middle class, the ticket to building a viable democracy in Russia. Second, a budding economy will stop the capital flight and attract foreign direct investment, creating longer term benefits. Last but not least, diversification can also reduce income inequality and other social problems.

The Russian Ministry of Industry and Energy announced earlier this year a series of mineral resource tenders that will take place in 2005, some of them considered of strategic importance. In a separate statement, the government made clear that foreign owned or controlled companies would face restrictions in participating in such tenders. This apparent economic nationalism does not bode well for the Canadian companies operating in the Russian energy sector, or for the economic environment in general.

According to Statistics Canada, the turnover of trade between Russia and Canada reached c$1.4 billion in 2004. Canadian imports from Russia amounted to c$1.08 billion dollars, representing 0.4 percent of Canada's imports and 0.14 percent of Russia's exports. Oil, steel, metals and fish made up the bulk of Canadian imports from Russia. Canadian exports to Russia added up to c$317 million in 2004, representing some 0.1 percent of Canada's exports. Canada sent to Russia mainly oil and gas equipment, building product, tobacco and pork products. Comparatively, Canada's volume of trade with South Korea or Australia is four times larger. While there is a lot of potential here, and while 2004 witnessed a big spike, bilateral trade with Russia has yet to take off.

Canadian foreign direct investment (FDI) in Russia reached c$221 million in 2003, down from a peak of c$627 million in 1996. For comparison, Canadian FDI in Malaysia was four times larger in 2004, while reaching eight times as much in Spain. The total Canadian accumulated investment in Russia amounts to c$1.2 billion. More than half of all Canadian investment takes place in the mining industry, with significant amounts in food processing and construction industries. Barrick Gold Corp. invested c$200 million dollars in Russia in 2003–04. Other notable investors include Nortel Networks, Bombardier, SNC-Lavalin, and McCain Foods. Russian FDI in Canada in 2003 amounted to c$50 million.

Why is the level of bilateral trade and investment cooperation so far below its potential? The precarious state of the rule of law in Russia, insecure property rights, an unreformed judicial system prone to corruption, frustrating red tape, and a policy regime marred by uncertainty are several factors that come to mind. The Team Canada trade mission to Russia yielded considerably less than advertised, and countless reports in the media document the predicaments of Canadian companies such as Norex, Kinross Gold, and Pan American Silver at the hands of their Russian partners (Trickey, 2002). The scenario is common: after Canadian firms spend millions to set up a joint venture, their local partners use legal technicalities in order to break contracts and take control of the firm (see Webster 2002, and Saunders, 2002). Despite recent signs of improvement – Petro-Canada is spending lavishly on a natural gas project – serious problems remain. In the words of former Canadian Prime Minister Jean Chrétien, "the negative experience of some Canadian investors has tarnished the Russian market in the eyes of many" (Cattaneo, 2004: A1).

For the 2004–05 fiscal year, CIDA has a budget of C$17.8 million, funding about thirty active programs in Russia, which are largely in the area of governance.[6] Anecdotal evidence shows that the Russian partners at the grassroots level highly value Canadian cooperation. Among the most far reaching programs are those helping to increase the efficiency and effectiveness of courts and the judicial system in general, those helping the nascent Russian civil society get off the ground, and those providing expertise and policy guidance to the Russian Government at all levels in matters of fiscal federalism, regional economic development, and problems of the Russian North. There are signs that the majority of these programs will wind down by the end of 2007. The knowledge of Russia's government, economy and society that has been acquired through these CIDA projects could be of value in guiding Canada's future policies towards Russia, including in trade issues related to WTO accession.

Russia started the negotiating process to join the World Trade Organization some ten years ago and Canada has been one of the strongest supporters of Russia's bid to enter the WTO. Russia's bilateral negotiations with the USA and Japan have reportedly been successful, and while talks continue with 15 more countries, it seems likely that Russia will be in a position to join the WTO by the end of 2005. Together with improved access to important markets, WTO membership would also help improve Russia's status and economy, though some important sectors such as agriculture could be hit hard by the removal of subsidies.

The Canadian and Russian space programs constitute another important sector to advance the two countries' common interests. The Canadian Space Agency (CSA) has strengthened relations with its Russian counterpart, especially since the disaster involving the US space shuttle Columbia in early 2003. The temporary grounding of all NASA shuttle flights that followed emphasized the high level of Canada's dependency on the United States space program. Although not without its problems (e.g., lack of sufficient funding), experts point out that Russia's space program is still matched only by NASA (Foglesong and Hahn, 2002: 138).[7] Nonetheless, the return to flight of the US space shuttle, in which Canada is expected to play a significant role, would reinvigorate the traditional collaboration between the CSA and its US counterpart. Canada-Russia cooperation in the areas of sports and the arts has its role as well in maintaining and advancing bilateral relations, but cannot be regarded as linkages of strategic importance.

ASSESSMENT

Canada is deeply interested in having Russia improve the functioning of its democracy and economic system – even more so now that Russia struggles to overcome the Soviet legacy and rethink its place in the world. Integrating Russia deeper into the Euro-Atlantic and global order is a prerequisite to its accelerated transition towards Western norms and principles. Chastising or trying to isolate it on the world scene is counterproductive as it plays right into the hands of authoritarian tendencies. How can Canada best facilitate the democratization process in Russia?

Inventing a new Russian polity is certainly possible but it will take time. After all, the relatively successful liberal democracies and market economies in the West took several centuries to develop themselves. In addition, they did not have to shed the heavy baggage inherited from a Communist dictatorship stretched over three quarters of a century, including a distorted economy, ingrained corruption, a bloated and incompetent bureaucracy, and widespread nationalistic prejudice. While fully recognizing how both pride and capacity will limit Russia's openness to foreign ideas, Canada should continue to offer Russia support in redesigning its institutions.

Most Canadians would probably find repugnant a heavy handed, top-down, authoritarian process of implementing political and economic reforms. However, Russian traditions favour the existence of a powerful, charismatic leader (be that a tsar, a party secretary or a strong president) who would show the way and channel society's efforts into an important national project. Grassroots movements are less likely to dominate the Russian political process. Therefore, care should be taken in striking the right balance between the two approaches. What some people decry as the authoritarian excesses of President Putin may be necessary steps in mending an exceedingly weak state. On the other hand, unchecked power, due to a feeble parliamentary system and an emasculated media, breeds systemic failure and endemic corruption, as several decades of Communist rule has forcefully illustrated.

Currently, the West seems to favour another method of putting pressure on Russia to democratize: the encouragement of the "orange wave," a somewhat collective push toward political reform by Ukraine, Moldova, and some states in the Caucasus. It simply seems easier to reform smaller states than larger ones, though it is also true that propitious domestic conditions were ripe for such movements. The hope was that these movements could have a positive spill-over into the Russian political and economic environment, by leading to the creation of a broader geographical area of democracy, economic development and stability. The knee-jerk reaction by Russia, however, was to try to oppose those changes because they are seen as a blatant diminution of its influence in the region. After all, the Kremlin considers this region as its own backyard and the increased closeness of these countries to the West, in spirit if not in geography, is deemed as an affront and a direct challenge to Russia's economic and security interests.

The changes in Russia's international status have led other countries to revise their foreign policies vis-à-vis this former superpower. Canada is no exception and what seems to be Ottawa's wait-and-see strategy is by no means unique among Western countries. Although it is in Canada's best interest to anchor Russia in the West and to ensure that its reform efforts contribute to a politically democratic and economically viable environment in the larger Eurasian area, the efforts of Western countries to promote this goal are often contentious. While cooperation in areas such as energy resources, in which Russia is still a leader, seems to benefit everyone (except for a handful of other energy suppliers), Canada and other Western countries' active efforts toward democratization in the former Soviet space seem to run counter to Russia's interests in maintaining its influence in the area.

In the end, one of Canada's great difficulties in its relations with Russia is how to reconcile its democratic values with Russia's questionable democratic credentials and its neo-imperialist tendencies in the near abroad. The West generally feels a certain uneasiness in dealing with a country that seems to support only half-heartedly the human rights and economic freedoms of its own citizens and those of its neighbours. The Russian Government's intervention in Chechnya has raised particular concern among Western states.

Canada is not in a position to steer Russia in the right direction, but it still has an obligation to itself and to the international community to support Russia's efforts toward democratization and economic liberalization and stabilization. A broader question is whether, in a unipolar world, Canada can achieve more in terms of its relations with Russia on its own, or with the US as a partner. Most likely, Canada will pursue its commercial interests primarily in a bilateral framework, while continuing to pursue security concerns in a multi-lateral setting.

Russia will certainly face some competition from rising powers such as Brazil, India, and China, and the interplay of these actors will define the emerging geopolitical landscape. If it fails to reposition itself among the club of respected international powers, Russia runs the risk of plunging into authoritarianism and squandering the reform dividends accumulated so far. Furthermore, Canada and its Western partners would lose interest in their relations with Moscow. Should Russia's political and economic situations not substantially improve in the short and medium run, it is likely that the BRICSAM group (see Whalley and Antkiewicz, this volume) could become known as the BICSAM.

NOTES

1 The joke goes like this: it is relatively easy to make fish stew out of an aquarium, but it is impossible to make an aquarium out of fish stew.

2 In 2003, the Russian Government froze 44 percent of the shares in Yukos, one of the world's largest private oil companies, and in 2004 it charged Yukos with tax evasion, after arresting its Chairman and Chief Executive Officer Mikhail Khodorkovsky. Critics accused the Russian Government of attempting to put the company into bankruptcy because of the political activity of Mr. Khodorkovsky and other individuals linked to Yukos.

3 A recent ruling by the European Court of Human Rights (February 2005) accused Russia of "serious violations" in Chechnya, "including torture and extra-judicial killing."

4 On the plus side, only a few countries or political entities (the US, the EU, Russia, China, Japan, and India) are responsible for two thirds of all carbon emissions and this fact could make an agreement more likely. Unfortunately, there are significant hurdles to overcome. At the country level, government regulation will prove itself very costly and the complying costs for firms will be large. At the multilateral level, some countries will balk at the constraints brought about by the concerted action (see the US position on Kyoto) while other will see their main export revenues threatened (OPEC, Russia).

5 As a recent development, Uzbekistan announced its decision to pull out of this organization; it effectively distanced itself from GUAM activities several years ago, while joining the organization in 1999, two years later than the four founding member states (the name of the organization was GUUAM during Uzbekistan's membership).

6 Further information on CIDA's activities in Russia can be found on their website. Available at: <http://www.acdi-cida.gc.ca/CIDAWEB/webcountry.nsf/VLUDocEn/Russia-Overview>.

7 Canadian astronauts have seen the Russian program and especially the idea of flying the much less technologically developed Soyuz spacecraft as a less desirable option.

REFERENCES

Aubry, Jack and Jim Bronskill. 2002. "Expelled Russians were military attachés," *Ottawa Citizen*, 10 December.

Canada. 2005. "Diplomacy," in *Canada's International Policy Statement: A Role of Pride and Influence in the World*. Ottawa: Department of Foreign Affairs and International Trade (DFAIT), 19 April. Available at: <http://www.dfait-maeci.gc.ca/cip-pic/IPS/IPS-Diplomacy4–en.asp>.

Cattaneo, Claudia. 2004. "PetroCan makes bold Russian bet," *National Post*, 24 September, A1.

Chapman, John. 2004. "Russia and Europe: European Policy Summit," Report on *Russia and Europe* conference. Brussels: Friends of Europe, May.

Dalkie, Karen, and Piotr Dutkiewicz. 1997. "Canada and Ukraine: Cooperation in the International Arena," in Tetiana Stepankova, Piotr Dutkiewicz and Maridula Ghosh, eds, *Ukraine in Transition: Politics, Economy, Culture*. Kiev: Akademia Press.

The Economist. 2005. "Country Briefings – Russia," 13 July. Available at: <http://www.economist.com/countries/Russia/index.cfm>.

Foglesong, David, and Gordon M. Hahn. 2002. "Ten Myths about Russia: Understanding and Dealing with Russia's Complexity and Ambiguity," *Problems of Post-Communism*, vol. 49, no. 6 (November/December): 3–15.

Freeze, Colin 2004. "Possible ties with Chechen insurgents probed," *Globe and Mail*, 16 October.

Knight, Amy. 2002. "Spy another day: They're back," *Globe and Mail*, 13 December, A15.

Koring, Paul. 1998. "Foreign Policy and the Circumpolar Dimension," *Canadian Foreign Policy*, vol. 6, no. 1 (Fall): 51.

Levitov, Maria. 2005. "Russia Seeking Its Place between Rich and Poor," *Moscow Times*, 15 February, 5.

National Intelligence Council. 2004. "Mapping the global future: Report of the National Intelligence Council's 2020 Project." Washington, November. Available at: <http://www.foia.cia.gov/2020/2020.pdf>.

O'Flynn, Kevin. 2004. "Sex, spies and mini-mikes bug Canadian military," *Moscow Times*, 1 June, 4.

Oziewicz, Estanislao. 2004. "Globe reporter criticized by Kremlin," *Globe and Mail*, 5 November.

Pankratyeva, Yelena. 2002. "Russian, Canadian officials discuss strategic stability, arms," *ITAR-TASS*, 10 December.

Saunders, John. 2002. "Norex woes continue in Russia," *Globe and Mail*, 10 June.

Stoett, Peter. 2000. "Mission Diplomacy or Arctic Haze? Canada and Circumpolar Cooperation," in Andrew F. Cooper and Geoffrey Hayes, eds, *Worthwhile Initiatives? Canadian Mission-Oriented Diplomacy*. Toronto: Irwin Publishing.

Thomas, Cal. 2005. "US needs to voice displeasure with Russia," *Myrtle Beach Sun News*, 6 May, A5.

Trickey, Mike. 2002. "Team Canada fails to score in Russia," *Ottawa Citizen*, 16 February.

Webster, Paul. 2002. "Ripped off in Russia," *Maclean's*, 20 May, 64–5.

12 Canada and Brazil: Confrontation or Cooperation?

ANNETTE HESTER

By any measure Brazil is a country of considerable, and rising, importance. In terms of area it is the largest country in South America, and third largest in the hemisphere, after Canada and the US. With 176 million people, it is the most populous country in South America, and second only in the region to the US. Its GDP is US$492 billion (World Bank, 2004), the largest in South America and fourth largest in the hemisphere. Although it also has the most unequal income distribution in the hemisphere, increasing stability and growth have brought masses of new consumers: individuals who are opening their first bank accounts, buying cellular phones, fridges, stoves, and other consumer products. Unlike other large emerging markets such as India and China, Brazilians have very similar tastes to North American consumers, making them a ready market for Canadian exports; in terms of trade, the Brazilian market is the potential jewel of the hemisphere (see Whalley and Antkiewicz, this volume).

But these factors alone do not convey the importance of Brazil. The country has been working diligently at creating a key role for itself among Latin American countries. It has made leadership of the region a cornerstone of its foreign affairs strategy – often provoking resentment among some neighbours, especially Argentina – by successfully acting as a moderating voice. Globally, Brazil has advanced the role of developing countries in the WTO and it is pushing for a much bigger role in the UN. What promise does an ascending Brazil hold for Canada?

The year 2005 started on a positive note for relations between Canada and Brazil, but the relationship is lately once again showing signs of strain. Buoyed by an unexpectedly positive visit by Prime Minister Paul Martin and International Trade Minister Jim Peterson to Brazil in November 2004, negotiations for a limited-scope trade agreement between Canada and four-nation Mercosur[1] trade alliance got off to a quick start.[2] As well, Canada identified Brazil – along with India and China – in its *International Policy Statement* (IPS) of April 2004 as one of the "emerging giants." All these gave reason for cautious optimism.

The two governments appeared to be looking for ways out of the predicament that has plagued the bilateral relationship for 15 years: a string of unrelated events, such as the Lamont/Spencer case, in which two Canadians were convicted in the kidnapping of a Brazilian industrialist, and the Bombardier and Embraer aircraft subsidy dispute.

Their optimism was based on several factors: the two countries are avowed multilateralists that want to see the World Trade Organization's Doha Ministerial Conference succeed, are co-operating in bringing a new peacekeeping model to Haiti, have similar security issues relating to vast unprotected territories – the Amazon and the Arctic, and Brazil is supportive of Paul Martin's L20 initiative, which would expand the G8 into a gathering of 20 world leaders. On the bilateral file, trade volumes have not increased substantially in the last decade, possibly as a consequence of trade tensions, but the two countries are starting to talk about a trade agreement (in the context of Mercosur). On the investment front, figures tell a surprising story – the stock of Brazilian investment in Canada now surpasses the stock of Canadian investment in Brazil. Clearly, this is no longer a relationship between unequal players, one developed and one developing.

This evolving relationship reflects the realities of the newly globalized world where the power relationships break the mould. Unfortunately, tensions are likely to flare again. This time, the point of contention is the Canadian federal and provincial governments' likely support for the development of Bombardier's C-series regional aircraft,[3] while Brazil's Embraer developed its new series without government handouts. An equally significant sore point is the Martin government's lack of support for Brazilian aspirations for a permanent seat at the United Nations Security Council.

And, as a further damper, the one positive file – the current market-access negotiations between Canada and Mercosur – is under threat of unravelling because the Martin government is unwilling to give Canadian negotiators a realistic mandate. The problem is that the joint declaration, issued by Martin and Brazil President Luiz Inacio Lula da

Silva in November 2004, sets the negotiations within the framework of
the Free Trade Agreement of the Americas (FTAA).[4] The current FTAA,
agreed to by all 34 member countries in Miami in November 2003,
requires that consensus be achieved on a common set of rights and
obligations before further bilateral or multilateral market access deals
are made. And yet, negotiations to that end have stalled. In an attempt
to conclude a trade agreement with a developed nation,[5] Brazilians and
the Mercosur are busily preparing demands and offers for market
access to specific products, services and investments.[6] Canadians,
however, feel bound to the offers they presented in the last round of
FTAA negotiations before November 2003. Canada, then, runs the risk
of upsetting Brazil by courting a negotiation it is unable to participate
in, and it runs the risk of losing a unique opportunity to gain a "first-
movers" advantage in one of the most promising emerging markets in
the hemisphere.

Good intentions on the part of both governments can only go so far.
To improve on the bilateral relationship and break the pattern established in the last two decades, goodwill needs to be accompanied by
clarity of vision and a consistent and coherent plan of action. Moreover, this relationship must be understood in the context of its interaction, influence, and impact on Canada's dealings with the US, the
hemisphere, and evolving global geopolitics. It is important past
lessons are learned and mistakes are not repeated. Towards these ends
this chapter will draw insights from five specific events/files: the
Lamont/Spencer affair, the Rio Eco 92, the Bombardier–Embraer
dispute, the Canadian ban on Brazilian beef and beef by-products, and
the FTAA negotiations. The conclusion will consider the implications of
future Canadian and Brazilian relations for our position vis-à-vis the
US, Americas, and the world and discuss how these lessons can be
applied to future dealings with Brazil.

FROM THE BEGINNING TO NOW

Historically, Canada's relationship with Brazil has been primarily positive. Canadian presence in that country dates back to just before the
turn of the twentieth Century, when the Brazilian Traction, Light and
Power company – which in the 1970s became Brascan Corporation –
laid down the tram tracks in São Paulo and later provided electricity
for both São Paulo and Rio de Janeiro (McDowall, 1988). Light, as
the company was known in Brazil, was a household name and an
important player in the country's political landscape. Alcan was
another significant Canadian investor in Brazil. It discovered the
bauxite mines – in which it still has an interest – in the north of the

country, and for more than 50 years was a leader in the country's aluminum market.

As positive as the relationship was, it was equally narrow and shallow, particularly after power and investment giant Brascan sold its utilities assets to the Brazilian government in 1979. Brazil went from accounting for more than 10 percent of total Canadian investment stock abroad to a paltry two percent (Daudelin, 2002: 264).

In the 1980s, Canadian investment in Brazil reflected that country's economic stagnation, which resulted from the oil crisis of 1979 and the debt crisis of the 1980s. Between 1981 and 1992, the GDP increased at an average annual rate of only 1.4 percent and per-capita income declined six percent. Gross investment, as a proportion of GDP, fell from 21 percent to 16 percent.[7]

But while the 1980s was a lost decade economically, there was a monumental political shift – from military dictatorship to democracy. In 1984, millions of Brazilians took to the streets demanding the right to vote in presidential elections.[8] After months of negotiation and political compromise, in January 1985, José Sarney Costa became the first civilian president in 20 years. Not surprisingly, Canada found itself much more at ease dealing with a democratic Brazil. Signs of improved economic and political engagement between the two countries emerged over the next two decades.

In economic relations, Canada emerged as a strong player in the Brazilian aerospace-satellite sector, starting with Canada's Spar Aerospace's winning bid to build Brazil's first communication satellites (Data Communications, 1984: 58). Subsequently, Pratt & Whitney landed the contract to provide engines for Embraer's regional turboprop Brasilia, and much later, Canadian Aviation Electronics opened its first flight simulator training centre outside Canada in São Paulo. In other sectors, a syndicate of 14 Canadian banks negotiated a debt restructuring agreement with the Brazilian government in the 1980s, Nortel arrived in 1992, and Nexen Chemicals entered Brazil with the purchase of Aracruz (Lake, 1989: 42).

Improved economic linkages went hand in hand with cooperation on other fronts, including co-operation in international trade negotiations in the 17–nation Cairns Group pushing for agricultural reforms. Other signs included cooperation over the Rio Eco 92 environmental conference, the chemistry between former Prime Minister Jean Chrétien and former President Fernando Henrique Cardoso, the creation of the Canadian Chair in Brazilian Studies[9] and, recently, the close relationships between union activists in Québec and President Lula and some trusted advisors.

These improvements, however, only translated into modest trade and investment growth. Brazilian exports to Canada only rose from $880 million (expressed in 2003 US dollars) in 1990 to $1.42 billion in 2003, while Canadian exports to Brazil barely moved at all: $542 million (expressed in 2003 US dollars) in 1990 to $597 million in 2003. Canadian investment in Brazil fared better – from $862 million (expressed in 2002 US dollars) to $2.74 billion in the period from 1990 to 2002. And Brazilian investments in Canada have surged from $166 million (expressed in 2002 US dollars) to $834 million in the same period.[10] Moreover, when the US$5.6 billion purchase of Canada's Labatt beer maker by the Brazilian beverage producer AmBev enters the 2004 statistics,[11] Brazilian investment in Canada will leap far ahead of Canadian investment in Brazil.

Several events seemed to overwhelm the otherwise improved conditions for better economic and political relations. While the reasons for Canada's lacklustre performance extend beyond the sour intergovernmental relations, one should not discount their impact. And it all started with the most unlikely events.

THE LAMONT/SPENCER STORY

On 17 December 1989, as millions of Brazilians went to the polls to vote in the first direct presidential elections in almost three decades,[12] a high-tension drama was taking place in a residential neighbourhood in São Paulo. The televised negotiations for the release of kidnap victim Abílio dos Santos Diniz, a local supermarket magnate, ended with Diniz being freed and the kidnappers filing out of the house into a police bus. Two of those kidnappers were Canadians: Christine Lamont and David Spencer (Vincent, 1995: 3). Christine's devoted mother spent the next 10 years in relentless pursuit of their freedom. (They were finally transferred to a Canadian prison on 20 November 1998.)

Her media crusade, which involved Canadian and Brazilian politicians, church officials and community activists, was premised on the couple's innocence, the "Midnight Express" conditions of their imprisonment; and the unjust and "third world" legal system in Brazil. It all left a bitter aftertaste, cost the pair an extra four years in jail, and led to years of fence-mending by Canadian officials in Brazil.

While space does not permit a full discussion of the details of this fascinating case, it is clear there was an enormous gulf in the Canadian and Brazilian perceptions of these young idealists' motivations and actions. For a typical Canadian, who for years had heard about the plight of left wing movements in Central America – particularly in Nicaragua and El Salvador – it was hard to imagine these two fresh-faced, middle-class Canadians were anything but well-intentioned young activists. It wasn't until an explosion in a bunker in Managua, Nicaragua, in 1993, which revealed a cache of documents linking the pair to terrorist organizations, that Canadians could see what Brazilians felt all along – these two individuals were criminals on a misguided liberation campaign.

Brazilians had just achieved success after a decade-long campaign for democracy. By the time Lamont and Spencer joined the cause, Brazil was well on its way to free and fair elections. And by then, it was preposterous to think that foreigners would be using criminal activity in Brazil – the ransom demanded was US$30 million – to finance liberation of the oppressed. Having secured a peaceful transition from dictatorship to democracy and, more importantly, without help from Canada, Brazilians were angry with their portrayal in the Canadian media as citizens of a third-world backwater. The final straw was the Brazilian congress's apparent capitulation to Canadian diplomatic pressure.

An interview by Canadian journalist Isabel Vincent in late 1993 with Brazilian journalist Boris Casoy captured Brazilians' outrage: "I was ashamed to be Brazilian," Casoy is quoted as saying. "It was a matter of principle. The Brazilian congress [which ratified the prisoners' extradition treaty] was kneeling before Canada, one of the world's seven richest countries. I just couldn't stand by and watch our country be pushed around so badly by an arrogant First World nation" (ibid: 166). The treaty did not receive final presidential approval, allowing the Canadians to be sent home, until 1998, when then-Prime Minister Jean Chrétien engaged in some quiet diplomacy with Brazil's President Fernando Henrique Cardoso. The bitterness of this case was such that it overshadowed one of the biggest events of the decade – Rio Eco 92.

RIO ECO 92

The Earth Summit, or Rio Eco 92, chaired by Canadian Maurice Strong, was attended by 105 heads of state, at least 1,400 participants and 8,000 journalists. More than 15,000 people participated in NGO activities related to the event. Although 153 governments signed each of the climate change and biodiversity conventions, the consensus was that the "Rio Declaration" was a disappointment. From that day on, however, the environment became a major political issue (Runnals, 1993: 141). For Canada and Brazil relations, the Rio Eco summit was an unusual confluence of individuals, interests and circumstances, and this time, at least, in a good sense.

While John Bell was Canadian ambassador to Brazil, from 1987 to 1990, one of the most discussed issues was the plight of the indigenous people of the Amazon. International media and a host of high profile Canadian environmentalists were reporting on the struggles of Chico Mendes – the Amazon rubber tapper and union organizer – his call for action to protect this pristine environment, and his subsequent murder in 1988, two months before the first Meeting of Indigenous Peoples of the Xingu convened to bring international attention to plans to build a hydroelectric dam on the River Xingu.

Canada's involvement in environmental discussions stretches back to 1972, when it assigned Strong to the 1972 United Nations conference on Human Environment – the Stockholm conference. Although Brazil's involvement was much more recent, both countries were competing to host the next UN environmental conference. Then, Bell, Canada's ambassador, and Brazilian Ambassador Flecha Lima made a deal: Canada would support Brazil's bid to host the conference if Brazil would support a Canadian as secretary general of the event (Bell, 2005). That is how the Earth Summit ended up happening in Rio with Strong as secretary general.

There were a series of firsts during this conference: the first time NGOs participated in the preparations for official positions; the first time a Canadian minister for the Environment – Jean Charest – held daily briefings with NGOs and civil society; and the first time the Brazilian government interacted with government officials and NGOs on an equal basis. But the event also represented a lost opportunity. In the academic articles, reports, and writings that followed the conference, including two chapters in the 1993 edition of *Canada Among Nations*, there is no evidence this event brought Brazil and Canada together (see Cooper, 2004). In that respect at least, nothing was gained in the bilateral relationship.

Given the conflicts Brazil and Canada were about to encounter in the lucrative and leading-technology market of regional aircraft, capitalizing on good partnerships would have gone a long way.

THE BOMBARDIER AND EMBRAER DISPUTE

Much has been written about the bitter dispute between Canada and Brazil on the export subsidies for the regional jets built by Bombardier and Embraer. There has been some excellent political and economic analysis of the subject, starting with Jean Daudelin's fluid piece in the

2002 edition of *Canada Among Nations*. Daudelin describes the scenario and explains why governments could not afford to cut subsidies to such politically sensitive companies, concluding that "The two governments and their bilateral relationship have been taken hostage by the companies they have sponsored, and they will likely remain so until some outside intervention frees them" (Daudelin, 2002: 274).

Andrea Goldstein and Steven McGuire's authoritative 1994 paper explores why the two countries would choose to wage a trade war that would benefit just one firm, to the detriment of consumers and other domestic producers. Their conclusion? "Both Canada and Brazil have made aerospace a cornerstone of their technology policies and neither can afford to abandon the field to the other side" (Goldstein and McGuire, 2004: 564). Finally, Peter Hadekel's superb book provides a detailed history of Bombardier and explores the ins and outs of rival Embraer (Hadekel, 2004).

Since the late 1980s and early 1990s, Embraer and Bombardier have seen each other as direct competitors for the regional jet market. The leader, Bombardier, apparently thought its rival would falter. But, by 1996, it realized Embraer was a serious competitor that wasn't going to play by the established rules of the game (ibid: 191).

The battle for the success of Embraer's ERJ regional jet was a battle for the survival of the company itself. It had spent years developing the plane, securing deals with suppliers, enduring severe downturns in the Brazilian economy and its own privatization. For the Brazilian government, which had kept a golden share in the company,[13] Embraer was the only success story in its search for a slice of the high technology export market. The Brazilians were playing for keeps.

Confronted by a market in which Bombardier was a *de facto* monopolist, Embraer – with the help of the Brazilian government – decided the only way to break this stronghold was to offer customers financial terms they couldn't refuse. These subsidies – handed out under a program called ProEx – clearly contravened the WTO Agreement on Subsidies and Countervailing Measures (ASCM) and did not conform to the existing industry standard, the OECD Arrangement on Guidelines for Officially Supported Export Credits. Brazil offered a number of justifications for its actions, but the rationale matters little in face of the reality. Brazilians knew the maximum penalty for this infraction[14] – retaliation by Canada on goods imported from Brazil[15] – was insignificant, compared to the potential gains.[16] A game theory analytical framework best explains the situation: Brazil, the new entrant, kept the subsidies in place until it had captured a substantial market share. Once the game changed from monopoly to duopoly (where the two firms share the market) the subsidies were no longer needed. At that point, ProEx was brought into compliance with WTO rules. It is interesting to note that the duopoly theory predicts that dynamic equilibrium will be reached – just as we have seen in this case.

Brazil's action infuriated Bombardier, and the Canadian government. Officials – from ambassadors to Brazil to the senior bureaucrats of the Department of Foreign Affairs and International Trade – demanded that Brazil play by the rules. Incredulous Brazilians countered that Bombardier received massive support from the Canadian government and had not always played by the rules.[17] Why, they asked, are Canadians engaging in moral posturing when the dispute was actually about defending a commercial interest?

Both governments eventually appeared to comply with WTO rulings on their export subsidies. But this status is in a tenuous state of equilibrium. For almost two years, everything has been quiet, but a new controversy is about to erupt. This time around, Embraer has taken the lead with a new series of airplanes – the 170/190 Ejets, with seating capacity of 70 to 110 – developed without government support.[18] In an attempt to catch up, Bombardier has announced the development of the C-series, with seating capacity of 110 to 130. There are a number of sticking points, including: the announced $350 million and $110 million research-and-development assistance from the federal and provincial governments, respectively (plus $340 million from the UK government, in return for a promise to employ the company's plant in Belfast to build component parts); the lack of buy-in from suppliers, particularly an engine manufacturer; and most importantly, no "launch customer" in sight. At the time of writing, no final decision on the C-Series has been made. In any event, there are no easy solutions to this commercial dispute. A fresh approach is required to ensure the two companies' acrimony does not contaminate the entire bilateral relationship, as it clearly did when Canada decided to ban imports of Brazilian beef in February 2001.

THE MAD COW EPISODE

A Canadian ban on Brazilian beef over fears of possible Bovine Spongiform Encephalopathy (BSE or mad cow) contamination caught both the Brazilian and the Canadian public by surprise. Under the provisions of NAFTA, the US and Mexico had to follow suit with their own bans.

For Brazilians, the ban was a huge issue – especially since not one BSE-infected cow had been found. While it sold Canada a mere US$5 million a year in beef, sales to the United States were US$95 million (Lafer, 2001). Having its reputation as a safe producer tarnished was

costly and potentially devastating. And, in political terms, there is significant representation of the agricultural sector in Congress; in fact, a
number of congressmen are also cattle producers.

Not surprisingly, they were furious, but the Brazilian population at
large was livid. Canadian whisky was being dumped in the streets,
public rallies mocked Canada and the iconic Mounties, and a cow
named Bombardina was delivered to the Canadian embassy. Canadian
officials offered convoluted and unconvincing explanations. Brazilians
believed the ban was retaliation for their lack of compliance with the
WTO ruling on ProEx and Embraer.[19] The WTO ruled Canada had the
right to retaliate against Brazilian imports; it was obvious Canadian
officials couldn't figure out how to do so effectively.

Canada maintained that Brazilian authorities for months had failed
to respond to an animal health risk assessment questionnaire. The
assessment was among the measures taken by the NAFTA partners in the
aftermath of Europe's mad cow crisis, to prevent infection in North
America. The partners had looked for ways to harmonize import standards and regulatory frameworks, so they divided the world into
regions. Canada became responsible for South and Central Americas
and South Asia (Evans, 2005). Given the low volumes of trade in this
sector between Canada and Brazil, there was no urgency to get the
appropriate documentation until a new wave of BSE cases was detected
in Germany and a report that Brazil had imported live cattle from that
country as recently as 1999. This heightened concern in the Canadian
Food Inspection Agency (CFIA).

But bureaucratic righteousness and political insensitivity is a toxic
mix. Early in the process of trying to get the papers filed, faced with a
Brazilian bureaucrat who did not speak English, Canadians turned to
their multilingual American counterpart to act as a go-between. From
then on, the Americans pre-empted every move Canada made by being
the first to tell Brazilians what was about to happen.

At the same time, there was incredibly poor co-ordination and communication among Canadian departments. The CFIA was not aware of
the aircraft dispute between Brazil and Canada; the interaction with
the departments of Agriculture and Foreign Affairs was almost non
existent, and Canadian officials in Brazil barely learned of developments before they were reported in the media.[20]

Finally, when the ban was brought to Cabinet for approval, it is
reported that only one minister – Pierre Pettigrew – spoke of the harm
the measure could cause.[21] Everyone else around the table still had
Ontario's Walkerton water tragedy on their minds, and feared a fallout
if they were seen not to be aggressive on a public safety and health
issue.[22]

These missteps once again led Brazil and Canada to confrontation and ongoing trade malaise. The ban lasted only three weeks – but the effects were felt for years. Worse still, it reinforced the Brazilian view that Canadian and US interests were irretrievably linked – a perception it holds firmly in FTAA negotiations.

THE FTAA NEGOTIATIONS

No sooner had the North American Free Trade Agreement (NAFTA) come into effect in 1994, then the push for a hemispheric agreement was on. The first Summit of the Americas was held in Miami in December 1994 and leaders of the 34 democracies of the hemisphere agreed to negotiate a Free Trade Agreement of the Americas with a goal of concluding it by 2005.[23]

Brazil approached the negotiations with caution and reluctance. It couldn't afford not to be at the negotiating table, but it needed time to consolidate its position as regional leader of the four-nation Mercosur[24] trading alliance to help it negotiate with the United States from a position of strength. Brazil had no appetite for a NAFTA-style agreement for the hemisphere, with an investment chapter and side agreements on labour and the environment. To be able to impose its own agenda, Brazil understood it would have to consolidate its leadership and strengthen its market power.[25]

Canada, on the other hand, took the opposite approach. It saw in the FTAA an ideal mechanism to protect its preferential access to the US while gaining far deeper entree into the Brazilian and Mercosur markets than it could have gotten through bilateral negotiation. As an initial strategy, it strengthened its relationships in the hemisphere through a series of measures: it signed Trade and Investment Cooperation Arrangements (TICAS),[26] which, in essence, are not about trade and investments at all. Instead, Canada used TICAS to get to know and become known by others as an independent player; it reached a trade agreement with Chile in 1997 that provided a model for FTAA objectives, and worked diligently with the Organization of American States (OAS). It strengthened the OAS in a variety of ways, including the creation of the OAS Trade Unit, which provided technical support for the FTAA negotiations (Jubany, 1998: 17). Moreover, it used every opportunity to act as a coalition builder and to support any proposal that would accelerate the conclusion of the FTAA.[27]

With the countries having such divergent strategies and visions, it should come as no surprise that there isn't much harmony between Canada and Brazil on hemispheric negotiations. Although the differences were barely visible in the beginning of talks, by early 1998, they were clearly noticeable. Brazil cancelled the signing of the Mercosur-Canada TICA scheduled for then-Prime Minister Jean Chrétien's visit to Brazil in January 1998 after Canada's Bombardier rescinded a contract with Embraer to build airplanes for its NATO pilot training centre. However, as Florencia Jubany (1998) explains in her brilliant Master's thesis, this was only one of the reasons Brazil stalled the negotiation process. By the time offers were to be presented, Brazil was under a new government which had even less appetite for the FTAA than the previous one. It successfully forced a new negotiating architecture in November 2003, at the Miami Trade Ministers' gathering. This had little to do with Canada and everything to do with the US's concessions and demands.

Moreover, Brazil prefers a weaker OAS to avoid having a forum in which it might be brought into direct confrontation with the United States over sensitive hemispheric issues. It has preferred, instead, to bypass the organization and deal with situations requiring intermediation either alone (when it can take advantage of its own size) or through other multilateral venues (where US power might be somewhat diluted). This strategy is apparent in the case of Peru and embattled President Alberto Fujimori, who resigned in November 2000;[28] in the recent case of using the South American Community to help resolve the crisis associated with the ousting of Ecuadorian President Lucio Gutierrez in April 2005; and in the evolving situation in Bolivia.

This "hands off" approach to intervention almost belies Brazil's leadership aspirations. This learned behaviour has an almost visceral quality derived from living for 20 years in a military dictatorship. While Canada is much readier to accept the US's renewed love for democracy at face value, Brazil tends to be much more leery and likely to seek to ensure its actions are seen as thoughtful and independent.

Finally, as this chapter is written, FTAA discussions are at a standstill.[29] However, one issue is clear – Canada does not control the agenda – the US and Brazil do. Canada will have an increasingly difficult time influencing the agenda, and creative thinking will be needed if there is to be a renewal of productive Canadian-Brazilian relations.

PUTTING IT ALL TOGETHER

In the end, the first question that comes to mind is, why bother trying to overcome such difficulties? Does a healthy trade relationship with Brazil matter that much to Canada? The answer is categorically yes, for several reasons. Because the US is our most important trading partner, the relationship that other nations or groups of nations have with the US could have an impact on Canada. Equally importantly, we need to build our own place and space in the world. Brazil comes into play in both cases. Moreover, the argument can be built from a strictly commercial/trade angle as well as from a much wider political perspective.

In terms of trade, the US clearly wants into the Brazilian market. The question is what concessions it will have to make and when it will have to offer them. The timing is dependent on the outcome of the Mercosur-EU trade talks (so far, stalled) and the perennially shifting agenda of domestic politics. At the moment, the US administration is focused on securing congressional approval for the free trade agreement with Central America (CAFTA) and on the ongoing Doha Round at the WTO. The FTAA is definitely on the back burner, and with that, almost any chance of a US and Brazil (or Mercosur) trade agreement being negotiated. The present circumstances present a golden opportunity for Canada – a "first-movers" advantage in the market deemed the "potential jewel of the hemisphere." Most importantly, out of all the "emerging giants" Canada has identified, Brazil is the only one aggressively seeking an agreement with Canada.

That is because, from the other side, Brazil needs to secure an agreement with a developed country. So far, the Lula government has managed the South–South agenda quite well, but has not delivered any concessions with industrialized countries – a fact that is undermining Lula's support from the business sector. An agreement with Canada would send the right message. The Canadian market may be too small to command a great deal of attention, but the impressive surge in Brazilian investment suggests we should be capitalizing on attracting more of the same. Important Brazilian companies have chosen Canada as a beachhead for their North American market entry strategy and they are succeeding beyond any expectations. For instance, Gerdau Ameristeel (one of Brazil's leading steel manufacturers), with Canadian headquarters in Ontario was singled out by *The Globe and Mail* Report on Business as one of the "Biggest moves up the top 1000" for having moved from 931 position in 2004 to 43 in 2005 with a 1,276 percent gain in profits.

From a geopolitical perspective, a closer and positive relationship with Brazil would provide the hemisphere with a better balance to the US. It follows from the rationale that, in spite of constant and vocal opposition to Brazil's leadership by Argentina and Mexico, the country is increasing its relevance and weight in the region and on the world scene. The best evidence is the fact that it is often called upon by its smaller neighbours to mediate in bilateral disputes – such as was the case in the conflict between Peru and Ecuador and recently between Venezuela and Colombia – or in internal matters such as in the recent events in Ecuador and Bolivia. Brazil has been able to act as a moderate voice and influence in the hemisphere. This is particularly important to the US, which needs trusted partners who can deliver messages credibly in places where its own presence is viewed with hostility.

Brazil is considered such a partner, and Canada has the opportunity to be one as well. However, our inability to define our own direction and policies has resulted in a decline in our influence in the region and an increase in the doubt that we do have an independent voice from the US.

Clear and definitive partnership with Brazil on different files, from Haiti to the delivery of HIV-AIDS programs in Africa; from help in strengthening democracy, respect for human rights, and election monitoring to different approaches to maintaining sovereignty from the US with the commonality of vast unpopulated territories (the Amazon and the Arctic), would go a long way in helping Canada re-establish its space in the world.

But, one question remains: is Canada likely to seize this opportunity? If we are to judge by the past and also recent developments, the answer is ... not likely. Change will have to come with a clear and determined shift in attitude in Canada. It is critical that Canadian officials and the public at large understand that Brazil deserves respect and should be treated as an equal. There is no room for positions of moral superiority. A new attitude, combined with an effort to build new links, could maximize the benefit of shared lessons. This might help ease leadership pressures on Brazil, help strengthen the existing hemispheric multilateral organization – the OAS – and assist Canada in consolidating its independence from the US. On the last point alone, a renewed Canada-Brazil relationship would be worth its weight in gold.

NOTES

The author would like to acknowledge the financial support from IDRC, CIGI, Agrium and Brascan and the unbelievable warmth and the hours and hours that dozens of Canadian and Brazilian officials, scholars, journalists, and friends spent recalling their experiences, sharing their thoughts, and ultimately trusting me to tell a story with candor and passion – and no betrayals.

1 The Mercosur members are: Brazil, Argentina, Paraguay, and Uruguay.
2 The two-day meeting in early February in Ottawa followed the commitments that Prime Minister Paul Martin and Brazilian President Luiz Inácio Lula da Silva made in November 2004 to pursue bilateral market

access negotiations in goods, services and investment between Canada and Mercosur within the framework of the FTAA.

3 At this time neither the Martin government nor the provincial governments have made any formal announcements of forthcoming support. Moreover, chances of a spring election are very high. However, regardless of what party forms the new government, domestic politics – particularly in Quebec – will most likely force this support to materialize.

4 The language was repeated in the *International Policy Statement* (Canada, 2005).

5 Brazil through Mercosur is currently engaged in negotiations with the European Union and with the US (in the FTAA context). To date, both EU/Mercosur and the FTAA have not shown any positive results.

6 As of 29 April 2005, the next round of negotiations is set to take place in Asuncion, Paraguay on May 17–18.

7 For more on Brazil's economic stagnation, see <http://www.country-studies.com>, where you will find on-line versions of books previously published in hard copy by the Federal Research Division of the Library of Congress under the Country Studies/Area Handbook Program sponsored by the US Department of the Army.

8 Throughout the 20 years of military dictatorship, presidents changed almost regularly, and, towards the end of this period, a process of election through a congressional "electoral college" was established.

9 The Canada Visiting Research Chair in Brazilian Studies is a collaborative project of York University, University of Western Ontario, L'Université du Québec à Montréal and University of Calgary.

10 Trade figures from Statistics Canada and the Brazilian government, Investment data from UNCTAD, GDP Deflator from the World Bank, and Exchange Rates from the Bank of Canada.

11 This purchase was a result of Belgium's Interbrew merger with Brazilian AmBev in August 2004. AmBev acquired Labatt from Interbrew for C$7.3 billion. This amount was paid through the assumption by AmBev of existing debt at Labatt of C$1.3 billion plus C$6.0 billion in newly issued shares of AmBev in favour on Interbrew.

12 Although a plebiscite regarding a parliamentary versus a presidential system took place in 1962, the last directly elected president in Brazil was Jânio Quadros in 1960.

13 Brazil has a very different and interesting model of reform of state enterprises. In both cases of Embraer (which has been privatized) and Petrobras (the Brazilian oil company which has remained state owned), the federal government maintains a golden share which gives it final control over key decisions.

14 Note that almost every Brazilian Foreign Affairs Minister in the last twenty years has been posted to the GATT or to the WTO at some point in

their career. Consequently, the level of understanding of the powers and limitations of the international trading system is deep.

15 The link between the two accords is that in one of the annexes of the WTO ASCM there is a provision that authorizes certain export credits that are compatible with the interest rate provisions of the OECD Arrangement. Brazil contends this is a 'back-door' entry of a provision agreed to by a limited number of countries into the WTO rules.

16 In a series if decisions dating July 2000, August 2000, and February 2001 Canada was given the right by the WTO to retaliate against Brazil by first imposing tariffs on Brazilian goods worth US$230 million a year until a bilateral accord was concluded and then on February 2001 Canada was authorized to impose restrictions on imported goods to a maximum value of US$233 million a year for six years (Goldstein and McGuire, 2004: 544; and Lafer, 2001).

17 In 1999 a WTO panel found that the Technology Partnerships Canada research fund and the Canada Account were inconsistent with the ASCM rules but did not constitute an export subsidy. Also, in February, 2003 the WTO gave Brazil the right to retaliate against Canada in the amount of US$247,797,000 for subsidies given to Air Wisconsin and Comair for the purchase of regional jets from Bombardier (WTO, 2003).

18 Embraer managed to secure partnerships with its suppliers in sharing the development costs of this series and expects to recover these costs by imbedding them into the price of the aircraft.

19 And they still do! Every single Brazilian I interviewed on this subject as I was writing this chapter – from executives of Embraer to Brazilian officials – still believe that the motivation behind the ban was linked to the Bombardier-Embraer dispute.

20 At least from this disaster a lesson was learned. An interdepartmental group on Brazil was created and meets regularly to coordinate activities.

21 Cabinet meetings are secret – consequently, I can not confirm this is what happened. However, I have this assertion has been confirmed by more than one source who were at the meeting.

22 In May 2000 seven people died and at least 2,300 others became ill when Walkerton's water supply became contaminated with E. coli bacteria. The blame rested on the shoulders of the Walkerton Public Utilities Commission's operators and the Ontario Provincial government for their hasty privatization of public water testing labs. See <http://en.wikipedia.org/wiki/Walkerton,_Ontario>.

23 Cuba remains the only country in the hemisphere not included in the negotiations.

24 The Tratado de Asuncion which established the Mercosur dates back to 1991.

25 "The Mercosur creates a potential market of over 200 million people,

with a GDP in excess of a trillion dollars, making it among the fourth largest world economies, just behind NAFTA, the European Union, and Japan." Translated from Portuguese. For the original, see <http://www.mre.gov.br/portugues/politica_externa/mercosul/mer cosul/mercosul_02.asp>.

26 It signed a similar agreement with Central America (Costa Rica, El Salvador, Guatemala, Honduras and Nicaragua) in March 1998, a TICA with Mercosur in June 1998, and one with the Andean Community (Bolivia, Ecuador, Colombia, Peru, and Venezuela) in May, 1999. See <http://www.dfait-maeci.gc.ca/tna-nac/tieca-en.asp>.

27 Such a proposal was brought forth at the Ministerial meeting of April 2001, in Buenos Aires. Brazil, with the support of Venezuela, was able to defeat it.

28 Brazil was instrumental in defeating a proposal brought forth by the US at the OAS General Assembly in Windsor, Ontario, in June 2000, to impose harsh sanctions against Peru over purported irregularities in the country's 28 May 2000 presidential election. Canada managed to secure a compromise with an agreement to send an OAS delegation to Peru to explore ways to strengthen democracy.

29 Brazilian foreign affairs Minister, Celso Amorim, and the newly appointed US trade representative, Robert Portman, met in early May in Paris and confirmed their commitment to continue the FTAA negotiation process. However, they did not set a date for talks to resume. Further, the US point man for the FTAA – Peter Algeier – has just been appointed US representative at the WTO in Geneva.

REFERENCES

Amorim, Celso. 2004. "Brasil, politica externa e comércio internacional," *Brasil International Gazeta*, 21 December.

Bell, John. 2005. Interview with Author. Vancouver, 27 February.

Canada. 2005. *Canada's International Policy Statement: A Role of Pride and Influence in the World*. Ottawa: Department of Foreign Affairs and International Trade (DFAIT), 19 April. Available at: <http://www.dfait-maeci.gc.ca/cip-pic/ips/ips-en.asp>.

Chrétien, Jean. 1995. Address by the Prime Minister of Canada to a Dinner Hosted by President of Brazil. Brasilia, 27 January. Available at: <http://www.pco-bcp.gc.ca/default.asp?Language=E&Page=pmarchive>.

Cooper, Andrew F. 2004. *Tests of Global Governance: Canadian Diplomacy and United Nations World Conferences*. Tokyo: United Nations University Press.

Data Communications. 1984. "Two Home-Owned Satellites Will Soon Orbit over Brazil," vol. 13, no. 3: 58–61

Daudelin, Jean. 2002. "Trapped: Brazil, Canada, and the Aircraft Dispute," in Norman Hillmer and Maureen Appel Molot, eds, *Canada Among Nations 2002: A Fading Power*. Toronto: Oxford University Press, 256–79.

Dosman, Edgar J. and Kenneth N. Frankel. 2002. *Brazil and Canada: What Is To Be Done?* Ottawa: Canadian Foundation for the Americas.

Dwyer, Augusta. 1990. *Into the Amazon: Chico Mendes and the Struggle for the Rain Forest*. Toronto: Key Porter Books.

Evans, Brian. 2005. Chief Veterinary Officer of Canada, Canadian Food Inspection Agency (CFIA). Phone Interview with Author, 8 April.

Goldstein, Andrea E. and Steven M. McGuire. 2004. "The Political Economy of Strategic Trade Policy and the Brazil – Canada Export Subsidies Saga," *The World Economy*, vol. 7, no. 4 (April): 541–563.

Hadekel, Peter. 2004. *Silent Partners: Taxpayers and the Bankrolling of Bombardier*. Toronto: Key Porter Books.

Instituto Socioambiental. 2003. "A polêmica da usina de Belo Monte." Available at: <http://www.socioambiental.org/esp/bm/index.asp>.

Jubany, Florencia. 1998. "Canada and Brazil in the 1990's: The Aircraft Dispute and the Free Trade Area of the Americas," Master's thesis, The Norman Paterson School of International Affairs, Carleton University.

– 1999. *Shall We Samba? Canada-Brazil Relations in the 1990s*. Ottawa: Canadian Foundation for the Americas.

– 2001. *Getting Over the Jet-Lag: Canada-Brazil Relations 2001*. Ottawa: Canadian Foundation for the Americas.

Lafer, Celso. 2001. "Notas Taquigr'aficas do Depoimento do Ministro Celso Lafer no Senado," Ministério das Relações Exteriores, Assessoria de Comunicação Social, Informação à Imprensa, no 92, in *RelNet, Relatório no 015/2001*, 15 March.

Lake, David. 1989. "Going Down in Rio," Canadian Business, vol. 62, no. 3 (March): 42–50.

McDowall, Duncan. 1988. *The Light: Brazilian Traction, Light and Power Company Limited, 1899–1945*. Toronto: University of Toronto Press.

MacKinnon, Mark. 2001. "Scientists rip mad-cow 'ruse'," *Globe and Mail*, 9 February.

Mallan, Caroline. 1995. *Wrong Time, Wrong Place? How Two Canadians Ended Up in a Brazilian Jail*. Toronto: Key Porter Books.

Runnalls, David. 1993. "The Road from Rio," in Fen Osler Hampson and Christopher J. Maule, eds, *Canada Among Nations 1993–94: Global Jeopardy*. Toronto: Oxford University Press, 133–53.

Silcoff, Sean. 2005a. "Embraer jettisons its 'jungle jet' roots – Brazil takes flight," *Financial Post*, 26 March.

– 2005b. "Embraer pulls off mission impossible," *Financial Post*, 28 March.

– 2005c. "Embraer cracks new markets," *Financial Post*, 29 March.

Tachinardi, Maria Helena. 1993. *A Guerra das Patentes: o Conflito Brasil X EUA Sobre Propriedade Intelectual.* Rio de Janeiro: Paz e Terra.

Valle, Henrique. 2003. "Brazil of Today and Brazi-Canada Relations." Remarks by the Ambassador of Brazil to Canada to the Inter-Departmental Group on Brazil. Ottawa, 24 April.

Vasconcelos, Paulo Cesar Meira de. 1996. "A Inserção do Canadá nas Américas. Reflexões sobre as Relações com o Brasil," Executive summary. Brasilia: Instituto Rio Branco.

Vincent, Isabel. 1995. *See No Evil: The Strange Case of Christine Lamont and David Spencer.* Toronto: Reed Books.

World Bank. 2004. *World Development Indicators Online.* Washington: World Bank. Available at <http://publications.worldbank.org/ecommerce/>.

World Trade Organization (WTO). 2003. "Decision by the Arbitrator: Canada – Export Credits and Loan Guarantees for Regional Aircraft," Recourse to Arbitration by Canada under Article 22.6 of the DSU and Article 4.11 of the SCM Agreement. Geneva, WT/DS222/ARB (17 February).

PART THREE
The Ottawa Game

13 Trade, Commerce, or Diplomacy? Canada and the New Politics of International Trade

LOUIS BÉLANGER

The very first foreign policy decision made by Paul Martin as Prime Minister in December 2003 – to create, a Department of International Trade, separate from the Department of Foreign Affairs – was roundly criticized. Since the announcement of this imposed divorce (after twenty-one years of happy marriage), a significant number of Canada's foreign policy observers and experts have vehemently spoken out against what quickly became a symbol of the new government's lack of judgment and vision in the field of international policy. As a result, the two bills that would have formally provided the framework for the creation of two distinct departments were defeated on first reading in the House of Commons on 15 February 2005. Nevertheless, the government appears to have no intention of backing down and while waiting for a new election, is pursuing the work of dismantling the Department.

The invective and condemnation provoked by this decision of the Martin Government have not been driven by serious analyses of its consequences. Indeed, in itself, the creation of an independent agency responsible for international trade is far from sacrilegious. Our American neighbours are quite happy to entrust the conduct of their trade diplomacy to the US Trade Representative, who reports directly to the President, rather than to the State Department. Moreover in several other countries, for example, France and Germany, this responsibility is entrusted to ministries with economic missions and not to their foreign ministries (Bayne, 2003b: 68). Rather it is the complete lack of, or even the hint of an explanation on the part of the government to justify its decision that fuelled the indignation. The fact that no one seems to want to defend this decision or claim responsibility for it inspired Jeffrey Simpson (2005), columnist for *The Globe and Mail*, to say that it would take skills such as those of the great detective Hercule Poirot to find the guilty party.

In a way, this whole fuss has first and foremost revealed Ottawa's complete lack of strategic thinking on the linkage between trade policy and foreign policy.[1] The decision to free the Department of Foreign Affairs and International Trade (DFAIT) of its responsibilities for international trade could also be interpreted as the logical outcome of a ten-year effort to free Canadian foreign policy from a trade reality considered to be too "continental" by the Liberals in power in Ottawa. In recent years, Canadian diplomacy has in fact done its utmost to mark Canada's difference from the United States by giving priority to fields of activity that are the furthest away from the trade sphere, as if it were trying to atone for the expression of continentalist faith that led Canada to sign the Canada-US Trade Agreement (CUSTA) and the North American Free Trade Agreement (NAFTA).[2] Subjects such as the banning of landmines or the creation of the International Criminal Court dominated the Canadian diplomatic agenda during the Chrétien era, relegating trade issues to the sidelines.[3] This trend does not appear to be challenged by Paul Martin's *International Policy Statement* (IPS). In fact, a step forward in distancing trade from diplomacy is taken with the introduction of a new conceptualization of trade policy. By renaming it "international commerce" policy, the implication seems to be more of a domestic economic policy orientation rather than one of foreign policy.[4] This raises the question: On what reasoning and interpretation of the evolution of world trade policy and the Canadian national interest is such a reconceptualization based?

HOW MUCH DIPLOMACY IN YOUR TRADE POLICY?

A recent book on the practice of economic diplomacy, edited by Nicholas Bayne and Stephen Woolcock, suggests that states organize their trade policy by trying to reconcile certain fundamental tensions: the tension between economic rationality and political rationality; the tension between the priority attached to domestic pressures and that given to international constraints; and finally, the tension between legitimization founded on the arbitration of individual interests and the client-centred approach on the one hand, and legitimization based on the greater good and the national interest on the other.[5] Based on these three types of tension, each specific trade policy organization can be situated along an axis, the extremities of which are represented by two ideal-type models. Thus, at one end of the axis (the Low Politics Model), trade policy is conceptualized as economic development policy, placed under the authority of a home department, negotiated between interest groups at the national level and carried out by bureaucrats. At the other end (the High Politics Model), trade policy is conceived of as foreign policy, placed under the authority of a department responsible for diplomacy, the subject to broader consultations, and defended in the international arena by elected politicians. With the creation of a department charged solely with responsibility for international trade and investment, Canada is moving from a High Politics towards a Low Politics Model.

As this departmental split has been rejected by Parliament and is proceeding only on Orders in Council, the wisdom of this decision and its implications for national interests are open for debate. In order to properly assess the current situation, the profound changes in global trade policy in recent years in terms of both substance and practice must be understood. In substance, the scope of international trade negotiations has been considerably broadened beyond the domain of low politics. Prior to the conclusion of the Uruguay Round, the subject of negotiations was still essentially limited to the traditional issues of tariffs, access to markets and export subsidies. For a variety of reasons, with the signing of regional agreements like NAFTA, services, intellectual property, agriculture, investment, government procurement, trade facilitation, labour and environmental standards, as well as competition policies, have since dominated the agendas. This broadening of negotiations to the inclusion of non-tariff issues has brought new interests into play. These new interests are of a different nature and are more related to national debates concerning domestic regulatory systems – thus substantially changing the politics of trade.

Governments cannot hope to tackle these new issues effectively by relying on a technocratic approach limited to close consultation of corporate pressure groups with concentrated interests, as they were able to do for tariff issues (Evans, 2003). The new trade policy must now address social and moral issues that mobilize both political parties and social movements, such as environmental groups, consumer rights groups and NGOs. Indeed, in recent years this has led parliamentarians to go beyond simply ratifying trade agreements and to actually getting involved in trade policy-making. Civil society groups have demanded and sometimes obtained more transparency and consultation at both the national level of policy development and the international level of negotiation. Given this evolution, it is reasonable to question whether it is an appropriate innovation to try to conceptualize trade policy as a "commerce" policy mainly concerned with economic competitiveness rather than as a foreign policy defined more broadly in terms of national interest.

Another way of considering the relationship between trade policy and foreign policy is to approach it from the more practical perspective of diplomacy. In a state like Canada, what role does diplomacy play today – or will it be called upon to play in the future – in the conduct of trade policy? If needed, would the Department of Foreign Affairs even have the capacity to redefine Canada's role in trade negotiations?

The level of sophistication and diplomatic means with which a government chooses to conduct its trade policy largely depends on its approach to the various institutions set up by states to regulate global trade flows. A state that prefers to use a bilateral approach does not need a highly developed trade diplomacy because bilateral trade institutions are normally not very complex and keep the level of shared sovereignty to a minimum. Additionally, bilateral negotiation issues are often less complex and easier to explain to the national political actors, and the management of bilateral affairs is rarely contaminated by other issues of high politics (Bayne, 2003a). Conversely, the level of diplomatic resources required for the conduct of trade policy will be more considerable for a state that relies more on regionalism and multilateralism. More particularly, middle powers like Canada are thought to be able to reap special benefits from the diplomatic resources put at the disposal of their trade policy when they can take advantage of a highly structured institutional environment. This would explain why, based on the typology described above, states with power similar to that of Canada generally opt for an approach that is closer to the High Politics Model than to the Low Politics Model. Thus, middle powers tend to entrust their foreign ministry with the responsibility for trade issues (for example, this is the case in Australia and New Zealand), or make it a joint responsibility by creating a trade policy branch within their foreign affairs department (as is done, for example, in Norway) (Bayne, 2003b: 68; Moses and Knutsen, 2002).

The assertion often heard – and sometimes referred to as "the orthodoxy" – that a multilateral-type environment is the most beneficial institutional environment for a middle power like Canada, is not entirely true.[6] In fact, it would be more accurate to say that middle powers profit most from their diplomatic action in a "plurilateral" environment, that is, in organizations, such as the ones detailed by W. Andy Knight in this volume, that have exclusive membership based on a functionalist vision of the international system. For example, the G8 and the OECD are exclusive forums made up of members who assume certain regulatory and innovative functions in the world economy. Plurilateralism is often grafted onto multilateralism, the most obvious example of this cohabitation being the United Nations Security Council. In the area of trade, the Quadrilateral, the group of four international trade ministers from the United States, European Union, Japan and Canada, or even the OECD are good examples of plurilateral bodies that strive to fulfill structuring functions within a field which is governed by what is today a multilateral body, the World Trade Organization (WTO). Middle-sized powers benefit from this hybrid environment because it provides enough rule-based institutions to balance their own power deficit vis-à-vis the great powers without, however, reducing the diplomatic transaction costs and information asymmetry which give them an advantage over weaker states — an advantage which could be rebalanced through stronger multilateralism.[7] In this way, plurilateral functionalism legitimizes the role assumed by certain middle powers in international forums based on their diplomatic skills and technical competences in a specific domain of co-operation, such as trade (see Cooper, 1997a: 5).

The international mode of trade governance has provided Canada with just this type of favourable institutional environment. Following the failure of the plan to create the International Trade Organization (ITO) in the late 1940s, which was intended to be a truly multilateral body modeled after other specialized United Nations agencies created during the same era, efforts to regulate world trade were based on a plurilateral approach. The General Agreement on Trade and Tariffs (GATT), with a rather informal structure, a membership which was initially limited to the twenty-odd countries most directly involved in international trade and concerned by fragile institutional foundations, worked and developed as a member-driven organization (see Hart, 1998: 27–53). It did not take long for Canada to realize that the GATT's lack of formalism and institutional foundations offered ideal conditions for it to assert its influence and pursue its interests. As Andrew F. Cooper (1997b: 76–7) asserts, thanks to its diplomatic activism,

Canada won a form of 'insider' or 'core' status within the GATT ... This 'insider' presence, in turn, allowed Canada to have an influence 'above its weight.' Although Canada's stature as a commercial power should not be underestimated, it seems clear that the Canadian 'leading' role in trade diplomacy was out of proportion to its place in the international hierarchy and owed much to skill and reputational attributes.

If these conditions change, it then follows that the style, if not the pertinence of Canadian trade diplomacy is open to question. If the evolution of the institutional form of trade governance, and its impact on the ability of middle powers to successfully push their agendas, no longer provides Canada with the benefits to which it was previously accustomed, we must be able to create policy to address these evolutions.

THE NEW INSTITUTIONAL FABRIC OF INTERNATIONAL TRADE GOVERNANCE

The creation of the WTO in 1995 reinforced the multilateralist nature of the GATT. In many respects, however, the WTO inherited the institutional design of the GATT whose weaknesses proved, by and large, to be favourable to Canada's diplomatic action. Its rather informal decision-making system, linked to the technical complexity of the rules and issues negotiated, still constitutes a framework that lends itself to the expression of the Canadian functionalist doctrine. In particular, the WTO negotiating rounds, like those of the GATT, take place for the most part outside of the formal framework of the General Council. The ministerial meetings, which in accordance with the statutes are held every two years, constitute the strategic core of the negotiations, alongside the very informal "Green Room" meetings,[8] or invitation-only mini-ministerials. Part of this core also includes consultations between regional groups or coalitions concerned with particular sectoral issues. This informal structure of participation is becoming even more and more complex. This is evident in the increasingly important role played by the mini-ministerial meetings, which have all the characteristics of regular ministerial meetings but to which only a limited number of countries are invited (see Wolfe, 2004). Unheard of before the creation of the WTO, seven of them were convened during the new organization's first seven years of existence and eight during the two years between the Doha and Cancún ministerial meetings (ibid: 48).

Such informal modes of operation maintain the costs of participating in the negotiations at a very high level and exacerbate the asymmetry of information among states. This gives disproportionate power to the states that do not necessarily have the economic weight to warrant being "fully-fledged" participants, but have the diplomatic means and technical capacities to ensure their presence at summits/meetings. In the past, Canada has benefited greatly from this institutional framework, first and foremost through its status as a member of the Quadrilateral (or Quad). From its creation in 1981 until Seattle, the Quad formed the core of the GATT/WTO informal decision-making structure by initially negotiating compromises among themselves and later imposing them on smaller countries. Canada has also been one of the most regular participants in the mini-ministerial meetings,[9] which it can claim to have created since the first mini-ministerial was convened by Minister Roy MacLaren in 1995. Interestingly, this Vancouver mini-ministerial brought together a combination of "select middle-size economies."[10]

Canada has also been able to increase the relative advantage conferred by the institutional framework of the trade system by uniting with other middle powers such as Australia, Argentina, and Brazil, each members of the Cairns Group which supported the liberalization of agricultural trade. The technical complexity of the issues negotiated combined with the weakness of the organization's central secretariat also gives an enormous advantage to states that are able to mobilize skilled human resources and generate for themselves the information on which to base their negotiations. For example, during the Cancún ministerial conference, the size of the United States and European Union official delegations was each estimated to be in excess of 800, whereas Nigeria, the most populous country in Africa with approximately 130 million inhabitants, could only mobilize 12 people for the occasion (Narlikar and Wilkinson, 2004: 452). For its part, Canada arrived at Cancún with an official delegation of 103 people.[11]

However, in the wake of the failed ministerial conferences in Seattle and Cancún, it appears not only that the institutional design of the WTO is being increasingly opposed, but also that Canada's capacity to take advantage of the current structure is shrinking. With the arrival of several developing countries within the organization, but especially several regional powers such as Brazil, India, and China, it was clear that the traditional mode of centralized management of trade negotiations could not endure. In Cancún, India and Brazil reacted to the attempt by the United States and the European Union to impose the result of their own bilateral negotiations regarding agriculture by jointly drafting a detailed counter-proposal around which they formed a coalition of about twenty developing countries representing at least half the world population – the famous Group of Twenty developing countries (G22).[12] This affirmation of leadership outside the Quad, as well as the quality of the preparation and organization demonstrated by the G22, suggested a radical transformation of the basic conduct of trade diplomacy. According to Alec Erwin, South Africa's Minister of Trade and Industry and one of the coalition's leaders, the emergence of the G22 is not merely an act of posturing on the part of the developing countries, but rather is the sign of a new balance of competences: "There is absolutely no possibility that we merely pontificated or made political statements. The hallmark of this new group is its technical competence. I think this is a change in the quality and nature of negotiations" (cited in Palley, 2003: 17).

Two other coalitions also emerged at Cancún. With the technical support of the NGO Oxfam, a group of four small African countries (Benin, Burkina Faso, Chad, and Mali) successfully imposed a proposal regarding the gradual elimination of cotton production subsidies on the negotiating agenda. In addition, the Coalition on Strategic Products and Special Safeguard Mechanism brought together 33, mainly African, states around the idea that developing countries be allowed to define what the special product was for each country and be granted special treatment on it. As Amrita Narlikar and Rorden Wilkinson (2004: 458) observed, these recent coalitions are superimposed on existing alliances which can rely on each other for certain issues.

All of this clearly shows that in the current institutional framework, the golden age of Canada's relative advantage is on the wane. Other countries with technical competences and diplomatic skills similar to those of Canada have appeared on the trade diplomacy scene and know how to profit from the WTO's "informal multilateralism." These countries are not only capable of intellectual innovations and of being effective in the art of building coalitions, but also several of them simply have more economic and political clout. However, perhaps more fundamentally, Canada is suffering from the adverse effects of the structural response to the arrival of a new set of players. We have in fact evolved from a pyramidal decision-making structure to one based on blocs, that is, the bloc of developed countries led by the United States and the European Union, the bloc of emerging trade powers that took the lead in the G22, and while less influential, the bloc of less developed countries that joined forces in the Group of Ninety developing countries (G90).

Previously, most of the negotiations were carried out between the developed countries within coalitions to which Canada belonged, like the Quad or the Cairns Group. However, this is no longer the case. As Ailish Johnson and Dan Ciuriak (2004) point out, within the whole Doha Agenda, "the Cairns Group was in the background and the Quad was not in play at the ministerial level; [the General Council of]

Geneva seems to have sounded their death knell." New informal groups formed to meet the needs of the new structure, for example, the "Five Interested Parties" (FIPs), which initially included the United States, the European Union, India, Brazil and Australia, and was also joined by Kenya, thus giving a voice to Africa (Johnson and Ciuriak, 2004: 24–5). The centre of power in terms of trade policy shifted and Canada found itself further removed from it. During the Uruguay Round, Canada was still able to act as a classic middle power. As Michael Hart (1998: 183) explains: "Canada, trading on its status as a member of the Summit and the Quads, proved an indispensable link between the smaller countries and the big three and learned to play the 'honest broker' card with great skill, pursuing its traditional role of enthusiastic cheerleader for any agreement that advanced the cause of international rule making." However during the Doha Round, Canada became invisible. Unable to use its level of expertise to serve its own interest, Canada allowed it to serve everyone, with the Minister of International Trade Pierre Pettigrew agreeing to act as one of the "Friends of the Chair," or so-called "Facilitators," on the Singapore issues.[13]

However, the top-down, institutional design of the WTO may soon change. The deadlocks at Seattle and Cancún have led more than one observer to denounce the shortcomings of the trade organization's institutional design. The current debate on this subject both inside and outside the WTO, as well as the position taken by Canada in this regard, shed considerable light on the challenges it faced in terms of the evolution of international trade policy. Aware of the disadvantages of maintaining the status quo, the developing countries, supported by several NGOs (Third World Network, 2003), are demanding an institutional reform of the WTO aimed at greater formalization of the negotiating rounds. The main protagonist of this position is a coalition of 15 African, Asian and Central American countries, the Like Minded Group (LMG).[14] Essentially, the LMG believes that the uncertainty created by the lack of clearly established formal rules for the negotiating rounds penalizes countries that do not have the resources to deal with a demanding negotiating process, not only because of its scope and high level of technical sophistication, but also because of its unpredictable nature and frequent lack of transparency. Their proposals are intended in large part to shift the centre of negotiating activities from the Ministerial Conference, where it is currently located and which they consider to be too anarchical, to within the more formal and permanent confines of the General Council. Thus, a WTO reformed according to the plan proposed by the LMG would give more weight to the preparatory process carried out at the Geneva headquarters by the General Council and its Trade Negotiations Committee (TNC). The Ministerial Conference would only intervene at the end of the decision-making process, once maximum consensus has been reached on the draft ministerial declaration and everyone has agreed on the procedure to be followed at the conference (Narlikar, 2004: 7–11). In short, the goal is to increase the multilateral character of the organization, while marginalizing its plurilateral components.

It is revealing that Canada, along with seven other countries which can definitely be described as diplomatic middle powers (Australia, Hong Kong, Korea, Mexico, New Zealand, Singapore, and Switzerland), were sufficiently concerned about the LMG's plans for reform that they attempted to neutralize them in order to maintain the status quo. In a 2002 statement that openly referred to the LMG's proposals, these eight delegations reaffirmed the supreme authority of the Ministerial Conference (WTO, 2002). In addition, they defended the need for informal consultations in order to facilitate consensus decision-making, and although they recognized the usefulness of an efficient Geneva-based preparatory process, they nevertheless maintained that it "should leave space for the Ministerial Conference to take up those issues which call for resolution at [the] ministerial level" (ibid: 4).

Since any institutional reform of the WTO must be decided in accordance with the principle of consensus, no major changes will occur overnight. However it is possible that, faced with the impasse in which the Doha Round finds itself, the multilateral framework for trade decisions, which the new Director General Pascal Lamy described as "medieval" when he represented the European Union, will one day have to be redesigned. When this takes place, the most predictable outcome will be an institutional environment which is less advantageous to middle powers like Canada. Moreover as mentioned earlier, even within the current institutional context, Canada is losing a part of its relative advantage due to the appearance of new influential players on the trade diplomacy scene which are able to play the alliance game and mobilize considerable technical competences. Must the Canadian government therefore throw in the towel and opt for the low-profile approach to a low-politics commerce policy? For the time being, this would amount to disqualifying itself: even though it should not expect to profit as much as it used to from its investment in trade diplomacy, Canada still faces an international trade system which requires significant investment in diplomatic resources from those who wish to have their voices heard.

THE BRIC AND THE POLITICS
(OR POLITICIZATION?)
OF TRADE LIBERALIZATION

The final element that should be considered in determining the relevance for Canada of conceptualizing its trade policy as commerce policy rather than foreign policy is the evolution of the discourse of trade diplomacy. Trade policy, by definition, implies dialogue. Thus, it is crucial to know whether the dominant discourse of trade diplomacy will be that of high politics or low politics. Several observers have referred to the politicization of the trade agenda since the start of the Doha Round, not only because of the emergence of anti-globalization movements, but principally because of the discourse used by several leaders of developing countries to communicate and legitimize their negotiating positions. Thus, many observers have attributed the failure of the Cancún conference to the fact that politics had "contaminated" the trade negotiations. A relatively optimistic interpretation of this shift attributes this politicization to momentary posturing by "too many third-world politicians [who] got carried away by the thrill of saying no" (*Economist*, 2003). The tendency of these leaders was to engage in a North-South rhetoric popular on the domestic front and backed by anti-free-trade support from numerous NGOs. It could therefore be assumed that once third-world leaders regain control of their emotions, they will adopt a more "realistic" approach and put politics aside. If that were the case, by distancing its trade policy from its foreign policy, Canada would certainly do something useful and help to "decontaminate" the trade agenda. However such a short-sighted analysis conceals a much more complex reality.

In fact, if the analysis of this phenomenon of politicization is extended beyond certain purely ideological positions, which have been taken in particular by small countries, the most remarkable element is without a doubt the complete integration of trade policy into the geostrategic doctrine of the BRIC countries. Thus, Jeffrey Schott (2003) was partly wrong when he wrote in *The Economist* that, "At Cancún, it was clear that some countries wanted to push geopolitical objectives rather than trade reforms." Indeed, for several of these countries, there is no contradiction between trade reforms and geopolitical objectives as the two are intrinsically linked. Although the example of Brazil, which actively uses Mercosur to defend its regional power status and to promote its aspirations of a permanent seat on the United Nations Security Council, quite naturally comes to mind, this phenomenon is actually more noticeable in Asia.

Take the case of India, for example. The Indian government's involvement in the trade diplomacy scene is far from minor. Beyond its lead role in the organization of the G22, New Delhi has played a central role in establishing coalitions of developing countries within the WTO since the 1996 Ministerial Conference in Singapore, and before the launch of the Millennium Round (Narlikar and Odell, 2003: 6). Thus, it led a group of 8 countries to oppose the inclusion of the Singapore issues and labour standards in the WTO agreements. This group became the LMG, which initially made its mark by raising issue with what are now called implementation problems on different negotiating fronts. Basically, the LMG's argument is that the commitments made at the close of the Uruguay Round have not been adequately implemented and this has hurt developing countries. Furthermore, the LMG's diplomatic action cannot be dismissed as mere posturing. As Narlikar and Odell state, it has relied mainly on technical competences.

In raising implementation problems, the LMG went beyond simply opposing. They developed technical expertise and presented detailed proposals on a diverse set of WTO issues including TRIPS, TRIMS, agriculture including the Net Food-Importing Developing Countries, accelerated integration of textiles, customs valuation, and implementation of recommendations of completed reviews and WTO disciplines. (2003: 9)

For BRIC countries such as India, the discourse of high politics cannot mask an inability to articulate an effective technical discourse. India has been mixing styles since 1991 when it radically transformed its foreign policy by abandoning its status of champion of the Third World and non-alignment in favour of the role of aspiring manager of the international economic system (Hathaway, 2003). One of the fundamental elements of the reorientation of Indian foreign policy during the last ten years has consisted in a radical shift of focus from political to economic issues. "A new emphasis on trade and foreign investment," writes Robert Hathaway, "replaced the begging bowl as a symbol of Indian diplomacy" (ibid: 3). According to Kripa Sridharan, this diplomatic shift towards trade is profoundly linked to the liberal economic reforms undertaken during the same period:

Apart from the purely domestic economic objectives that the reforms were expected to achieve, there was a recognition that reform was imperative if India wanted to become an economic power of consequence within and beyond its region. This had important foreign policy implications. Official pronouncements reflected the concern that the balance of fiscal power was the key factor in determining a country's international standing. This called for an integrated strategy to bring economic and foreign policies closer. The implementation of a vigorous foreign policy could not be undertaken without sharpening the commercial diplomatic tool. (2002: 57)

New Delhi's involvement in the Doha Round, at the head of the LMG and the G22, made it realize that in addition to contributing ultimately to the success of its economic liberalization program, its trade diplomacy in itself could enhance its status and power (Perkovich, 2004).

Like India, China is increasingly integrating its trade policy into its global geostrategic action. In no less than fifteen years, from 1986 to 2001, the economic reforms in China have been largely structured and paced by the negotiations of its entry into the WTO.[15] Trade policy has thus become an important element of China's strategy to position itself as an economic power. Although China did not hesitate to become part of the G22, it kept a relatively low profile during the Doha Round negotiations, being careful not to adopt Brazil or India's militant tone. Moreover, China demonstrated its pragmatism by presenting itself as a credible intermediary between the G22 and the developed countries and largely freeing itself of its image as an ineffective multilateral player. According to Yong Deng and Thomas G. Moore, the diplomacy conducted by Beijing in Cancún and since should be seen as a sign of its ambition to achieve a strategic positioning:

Presumably, this is why WTO Director General Supachai Panitchpadki called on Beijing to "use its influence to be a bridge between developed and developing countries" in the wake of the collapse of the Cancún meeting. This direct appeal to Chinese leaders, in which Supacahai acknowledged that China is both a "developing nation" and an "emerging superpower," reflects the growing influence of Beijing in shaping the economic order from which it already benefits handsomely. (2004)

Like that of Brazil, China's diplomatic activism also has a regional variant. Indeed, Beijing has taken many initiatives to promote the constitution of an East-Asian trading bloc whose *pièce de résistance* is without any doubt the project to create a China-ASEAN (Association of Southeast Asian Nations) Free Trade Area. The latter is currently being negotiated and should be created in 2010.

Thus, there is an unmistakable trend on the part of the emerging economic powers to treat trade policy as high politics. This trend reinforces the already strong movement of politicization of the global trade agenda. One has only to observe the ongoing debate on the ratification by Congress of the US-Central America Free Trade Agreement (CAFTA) to realize how much the American discourse on trade liberalization is now about defending freedom and democracy, and regional security, as much as it is about the economy. In Europe, last spring, trade liberalization has emerged as the central contentious topic that has derailed the process to adopt the proposed Constitutional Treaty. Here again, the debate has not really focused on the economic aspects of free trade, but rather on its impact on the regulatory power of the states in the social and environmental spheres. Moreover, Europeans are perfectly aware that, at the current stage of EU political development, their common trade policy remains the central pillar of its relations with the rest of the world and they run it as such. Now, the new other emerging shapers of the global trade agenda join the game with the clear objective of using their trade policies to legitimize years of liberal reforms and to advance geopolitical objectives. And it is highly likely that when Russia manages to join the WTO, against the reluctance of its bureaucracy and its new class of corporate czars, it will follow suit (Rumer and Walander, 2004). Having become a member of the G8 despite the fact that its GDP is lower than that of the Netherlands, Russia has perfectly understood how to use international economic institutions to remain an influential power (Gomart, 2003).

The inescapable result of all this is that the language of trade diplomacy and the reality of trade politics will be increasingly tinged with high politics. It is hard to figure out how the split will give Canada a significant voice in this new discursive environment, nor how it will encourage our government to develop adequate strategies to face it. Up to now, the result has been discouraging. On the one hand, the volume dedicated to "commerce" in the new *International Policy Statement* remains dead silent on any substantive key issues defining the current global trade agenda. No one would know after reading this document where Canada stands on agricultural subsidies, intellectual property, investments, etc. More generally, the document says almost nothing about this government's vision on free trade: why is it a good thing and how should it be pursued? Four small paragraphs out of 23 pages are devoted to WTO issues. On the other hand, the "Diplomacy" volume of the same policy statement offers a panorama of Canada's positions on global issues, from nuclear proliferation to HIV/AIDS pandemics, to sustainable development, to human rights, from which the trade dimension is absent. Thus, while under the pressure of the BRIC trade has become even more incorporated into the global diplomatic strategy of all our main interlocutors on the international scene; while trade issues have percolated to the summits of the worlds diplomatic circles, the most open of the globe's major economies has decided to think and voice its foreign and trade policies separately.

CONCLUSION

There is no doubt that the structural changes undergone by the international trade system represent major challenges for Canadian diplomacy. After having enjoyed ideal conditions for the conduct of a middle power trade policy, today Canada is facing a much less favourable environment: emerging powers have joined the crowd of liberalized economies and occupy a growing share of diplomatic ground; the old club culture of the GATT/WTO that has been so profitable to Canada is contested; the technical nature of trade issues, if it still plays an important role in the negotiations, no longer protect them from "high politicization" and linkages. In such a context, the decision made by the government to distance its trade policy from its diplomacy may be considered as a retreat: accepting as irreversible its relative diplomatic marginalization, Canada "realistically" lowers its ambitions and decides to focus on the domestic conditions of its competitiveness rather than mobilizing its foreign policy apparatus on the advancement of the global trade agenda. This would be a shame, considering what is at stake for an open economy like ours in the future of trade liberalisation, but it should not be a surprise. Trade would then simply be the last foreign affairs domain – after defence, peacekeeping, development assistance – where, no longer able to punch above its weight, Canada decides to more or less quit the ring rather than to put in some weight.

However, if it wishes to continue to have a voice on the international trade scene and not sink into oblivion, Canada will have to choose the High Policy road rather than the Low Policy one. This means not only reversing the split decision, but going further in the direction of the High Policy model. This would first require more, not less, diplomatic resources. It would also require a change in style: a trade diplomacy which dares favouring substance over process. As we have seen, the institutional fabric of trade governance no longer gives Canada or other "middle powers" the extra leverage to which they have been accustomed. This will not be regained and, furthermore, in trying to salvage the traditional way of doing business at the WTO, Canada will only paint itself as a reactionary force. Instead of focusing on process and looking for the next opportunity to play the intermediary or the bridge-builder between conflicting positions, Canada should forcefully articulate its own vision on the future of free trade and enter the real substantive discussion.

Canada should simply acknowledge the very existential nature of its trade relations and build on its national interest as the more open of the major economies to develop a real comprehensive and strategic trade policy. To simply say, as is the case in the recent IPS chapter devoted to commerce, Canada's trade policy will be used to increase the competitiveness of our economy and success of our businesses is no longer enough in today's context of economic trade liberalization which is giving rise to important debates here and elsewhere not only on economic issues, but also on ethical, social and environmental ones. By defining a coherent, principled position not only on topics like agricultural trade reform, investment rules or intellectual property, but also on how the government sees the articulation between trade and development, democracy, security and good governance, that will yield a clear linkage between trade policy and foreign policy, Canada could be able to remain a significant actor in the global trade arena, even if it is one of a different kind.

NOTES

1 On this point, the evidence presented to the Standing Committee on Foreign Affairs and International Trade by Pierre Pettigrew, the minister of Foreign Affairs and former minister of International Trade, speaks volumes. Mr Pettigrew's lack of enthusiasm for the decision to split up his department was ill concealed and he attempted to trivialize the issue involved in this decision by reducing it to a simple question of the exercise of the prime minister's discretionary power: "This is not the first time that the government has questioned this way of proceeding. And so I do not expect that it will be cause for much surprise. Other prime ministers have revisited this issue and have ended up keeping the 1982 status-quo, that is one department. This time, after having discussed the issue with various people, the prime minister made a different decision." See House of Commons, Standing Committee on Foreign Affairs and International Trade (SCFAIT), *Evidence*, no. 12, 38th Parliament, 1st Session, 29 November 2004.

2 For a fairly harsh opinion of the diversion created by the Chrétien and Martin governments' adoption of a "value-based" foreign policy agenda, see Dymond and Hart (2004: 39–45); and Gotlieb (2004).

3 On the low priority attached to trade issues under the last Liberal Government, Pal Stohart (2003: 23) states: "Prime Minister Chrétien has

attached low priority to the international trade portfolio over the past decade, with the result that his trade legacy will be limited to leading Team Canada trade missions and signing a free trade agreement with Costa-Rica."

4 "Commerce, as distinct from trade or investment, embraces the full range of international business activities—from exporting and importing, through two-way investment, to licensing, partnering, management contracts and more" (Canada, 2005: 12).

5 This is my own adaptation of the various typologies found in several of the book's chapters, but it is largely based on the three levels of tension identified by Bayne and Woolcock (2003: 3–20).

6 The idea that multilateralism dominated Canadian postwar economic diplomacy has been severely criticized in the last few years. See Cutler and Zacher (1992), and Cooper (1997b: 87–97). For a defence of the multilateralist thesis, see Keating (2002).

7 For a more thorough theoretical presentation of this argument, see Bélanger and Michaud (2004).

8 This refers to the closed-doors meetings of the states "that count" which are convened at the initiative of the Director General of the WTO to break deadlocks in negotiations on specific issues.

9 According to the data summarized by Wolfe (2004: 79–105), Canada was excluded from only two of the fifteen mini-ministerials.

10 The countries invited were Argentina, Australia, Brazil, Chile, Hong Kong, Hungary, Indonesia, Mexico, Morocco, New Zealand, Norway, Singapore, South Africa, Switzerland, and Thailand (Wolfe, 2004: 79).

11 Of these people, 74 were federal government officials and 29 were federal, provincial and municipal elected representatives. If the organizations accredited with the WTO (NGOs, academics, etc.) are added, the number of Canadians rises to 300. See Department of Foreign Affairs website: <http://www.dfait-maeci.gc.ca/tna-nac/WTO/canadians-en.asp>.

12 Twenty countries co-signed the counter-proposal on agriculture: Argentina, Bolivia, Brazil, Chile China, Colombia, Costa Rica, Cuba, Ecuador, El Salvador, Guatemala, India, Mexico, Pakistan, Paraguay, Perú, Philippines, South Africa, Thailand, and Venezuela. The group was subsequently joined by Egypt and Kenya.

13 The four other Facilitators came from Guyana, Kenya, Singapore and Hong Kong (Narlikar and Wilkinson, 2004: 459).

14 The LMG was made up of Cuba, Dominican Republic, Egypt, Honduras, India, Indonesia, Jamaica, Kenya, Malaysia, Mauritius, Pakistan, Sri Lanka, Tanzania, Uganda and Zimbabwe. Benin, Bostwana, Nigeria, Senegal, Sierra Leone and Zambia joined the African countries of the LMG on the eve of the Cancún meeting to submit similar proposals (Narlikar, 2004: 6–7).

15 See Zhang (2003). China became a member of the WTO on 11 November 2001.

REFERENCES

Bayne, Nicholas. 2003a. "Bilateral Economic Diplomacy: The United States," in Nicholas Bayne and Stephen Woolcock, eds., *The New Economic Diplomacy: Decision-Making and Negotiation in International Economic Relations.* Aldershot: Ashgate, 163–79.
– 2003b. "The Practice of Economic Diplomacy," in Nicholas Bayne and Stephen Woolcock, eds., *The New Economic Diplomacy: Decision-Making and Negotiation in International Economic Relations.* Aldershot: Ashgate.
Bayne, Nicholas, and Stephen Woodcock, eds. 2003. *The New Economic Diplomacy: Decision-Making and Negotiation in International Economic Relations.* Aldershot: Ashgate.
Bélanger, Louis and Nelson Michaud. 2004. "Looking for Voice Opportunities: Canada and International Security Institutions After the Cold War," in Onnig Beylerian and Jacques Lévesque, eds, *Inauspicious Beginnings: Principal Powers and International Security Institutions after the Cold War, 1989–1999.* Montreal & Kingston: McGill-Queen's University Press, 189–216.
Canada. 2005. "Commerce," in *Canada's International Policy Statement: A Role of Pride and Influence in the World.* Ottawa: Department of Foreign Affairs and International Trade (DFAIT), 19 April.
Cooper, Andrew F. 1997a. "Niche Diplomacy: A Conceptual View," in Andrew F. Cooper, ed., *Niche Diplomacy: Middle Powers after the Cold War.* London: Macmillan Press.
– 1997b. *Canadian Foreign Policy. Old Habits and New Directions.* Scarborough: Prentice Hall.
Cutler, A. Claire and Mark W. Zacher, eds. 1992. *Canadian Foreign Policy and International Economic Regimes.* Vancouver: UBC Press.
Deng, Yong and Thomas G. Moore. 2004. "China Views Globalization: Toward a New Great-Power Politics?" *The Washington Quarterly,* vol. 27, no. 3 (Summer): 124–5.
Dymond, Bill and Michael Hart. 2004. "The Potemkin Village of Canadian Foreign Policy," *Policy Options,* vol. 25, no. 1 (December/January).
Economist. 2003. "Cancún's Charming Outcome," vol. 368, no. 8342 (20 September): 11–12.
Evans, Phil. 2003. "Is Trade Policy Democratic? And Should It Be?" in Nicholas Bayne and Stephen Woolcock, eds., *The New Economic Diplomacy: Decision-Making and Negotiation in International Economic Relations.* Aldershot: Ashgate, 147–59.

Gomart, Thomas. 2003. "Vladimir Poutine ou les avatars de la politique étrangère russe," *Politique étrangère*, vol. 62, nos. 3–4 (Fall-Winter): 796.

Gotlieb, Allan. 2004. "Romanticism and Realism in Canada's Foreign Policy." C.D. Howe Institute Benefactors Lecture, Toronto, 3 November.

Hart, Michael. 1998. *Fifty Years of Canadian Tradecraft. Canada at the GATT 1947–1997*. Ottawa, Centre of Trade Policy and Law, 27–53.

Hathaway, Robert. 2003. "India Transformed: Parsing India's 'New' Foreign Policy," *India Review*, vol. 2, no. 4 (October); 1–14.

Johnson, Ailish and Dan Ciuriak. 2004. "From Cancún to Geneva: Were the Optimists or Pessimists right?" in John M. Curtis and Dan Ciurak, eds., *Trade Policy Research 2004*. Ottawa: Department of Foreign Affairs and International Trade.

Keating, Tom. 2002. *Canada and World Order. The Multilateralist Tradition in Canadian Foreign Policy*, 2nd ed. Don Mills: Oxford University Press.

Moses, Jonathan W., and Torbjorn Knutsen. 2002. "Globalisation and the Reorganization of Foreign Affairs' Ministries." *Discussion Papers in Diplomacy series*, Netherlands Institute of International Relations (Clingendael), May.

Narlikar, Amrita. 2004. "wto Institutional Reform: A Role for G20 Leaders?" Paper prepared for the conference *Breaking the Deadlock in Agricultural Trade Reform and Development*, The Centre for International Governance Innovation (cigi), Oxford, 8–9 June.

– and John Odell. 2003. "The Strict Distributive Strategy of Bargaining Coalition: The Like-Minded Group in the World Trade Organization." Paper prepared for the *Conference on Developing Countries and the Trade Negotiation Process*, United Nations Conference on Trade and Development (unctad), Geneva, 6–7 November.

– and Rorden Wilkinson. 2004. "Collapse at the wto: A Cancún Postmortem," *Third World Quarterly*, vol. 25, no. 3 (March).

Palley, Thomas. 2003. "After Cancún: An Optimistic Case," *Challenge*, vol. 46, no. 6 (November/December).

Perkovich, George. 2004. "Is India a Major Power?" *The Washington Quarterly*, vol. 27, no. 1 (Winter), 141–2.

Rumer Eugene B. and Celeste A. Walander. 2004. "Russia: Power in Weakness?" *The Washington Quarterly*, vol. 27, no. 1 (Winter): 67.

Schott, Jeffrey. 2003. "Unlocking the Benefits of Free Trade," *Economist*, vol. 369, no. 8348 (1 November): 65–7.

Simpson, Jeffrey. 2005. "Who, dear Hercule, sliced Foreign Affairs in two?" *The Globe and Mail*, 22 January, A21.

Sridharan, Kripa. 2002. "Commercial Diplomacy and Statecraft in the Context of Economic Reform: The Indian Experience," *Diplomacy & Statecraft*, vol. 13, no. 2 (June): 57.

Stohart, Pal. 2003. "Modernizing Canada's Approach to the Global Market-place - Getting Governance Right in Trade Policy and Management," *Policy Options*, vol. 24, no. 7 (August).

The Third World Network, et al. 2003. *Memorandum on the Need to Improve Internal Transparency and Participation in the WTO*, 13 July.

Wolfe, Robert. 2004. "Informal Political Engagement in the WTO: Are Mini-Ministerials a Good Idea?" in John M. Curtis and Dan Ciurak, eds., *Trade Policy Research 2004*. Ottawa: Department of Foreign Affairs and International Trade, 33–111.

World Trade Organization (WTO). 2002. *Preparatory Process in Geneva and Negotiation Process at Ministerial Conferences. Communication from Australia; Canada; Hong Kong, China; Korea; Mexico; New Zealand; Singapore; Switzerland*, (WT/GC/W/477), 28 June.

Zhang, Yongjin. 2003. "Reconsidering the Economic Internationalization of China: Implications of the WTO Membership," *Journal of Contemporary China*, vol. 12, no. 37 (November): 699–714.

14 Split Images and Serial Affairs: Reviews, Reorganizations, and Parliamentary Roles

GERALD SCHMITZ and JAMES LEE

Canada's parliament is a paradoxical actor with a split image; its powers and potential are belied by perceptions of little actual ability to effect change, especially in the traditionally executive-dominated areas of foreign and defence policy. Moreover, even as demands have increased to address "democratic deficits" and return power to Parliament, it has become more regionally fractured, with different parties holding majorities of seats in Quebec, the West, Ontario and the Atlantic provinces.

In terms of the conduct of international affairs, the formal parliamentary reviews of recent times have raised democratic expectations, yet delivered underwhelming results. The fact that such reviews have also generally not been linked to changes in the Foreign Service and departmental machinery constitutes another kind of disconnect. A decade or more has sometimes passed between these episodes, of which the International Policy Review (IPR) process begun in 2003 became both the most protracted and first to be conducted under the circumstances of minority government.

In this case, repeated delays – in part due to the attempt at a "whole of government" approach to international activities – have also for the first time coincided with an unexpectedly difficult and divisive departmental reorganization. Previously separate tracks became entangled in ways that complicated rather than facilitated the government's agenda. As a result, 14 months after Paul Martin became prime minister and 10 years after the last government statement *Canada in the World*, impatient MPs were instead debating – and, on the ides of February

2005, ultimately defeating – the bills splitting the Department of Foreign Affairs and International Trade (DFAIT) into Foreign Affairs Canada (FAC) and International Trade Canada (ITCan).¹ As we will see, these suddenly loomed as far more than an administrative "house-keeping" matter.

If there is a tide in the affairs of reviews and reorganizations, both seemed to have veered off track in early 2005. IPR "coordinator" Michael Pearson (1999) has written of the importance of "fate and will" in foreign policy formulation. By the time the *International Policy Statement* (IPS) finally appeared in April 2005, some had already written it off as fatally compromised by lack of resolve and minority jeopardy.

We begin by briefly recapping how serial reviews have raised the bar in regard to Canadian foreign policy goals and democratic processes, offering lessons for making public consultation more than a matter of mandatory genuflection. Following the 2003 *Dialogue on Foreign Policy*, and with faith in the subsequent IPR being tested, we then review how MPs took the government to task over its *unreviewed* changes to the foreign affairs machinery, drawing critical scrutiny to an area seldom subjected to parliamentary oversight. We conclude that in the wake of several years of intra-governmental frictions and overdue review, it is now in the hands of parliamentarians and the citizens they represent to press for results that will build the stronger policy and operational capacity, both domestically and internationally, needed to achieve Canada's proclaimed "role of pride and influence" in the world.

PARLIAMENT AND THE WORLD: SOME LESSONS FROM REVIEWS AND "DIALOGUES"

Commenting on the future of the Foreign Service just two days after the defeat of the government bills, *Globe and Mail* columnist Hugh Winsor lamented, "the failure of the Canadian foreign service to engage, to explain, to dialogue with the Canadian public on world issues and how they relate to Canadian interests" (2005). Such dialogue should also include Parliament speaking for citizens across the country.

A related concern, therefore, is a failure, notwithstanding the formal foreign policy reviews of recent decades, to create significant additional and sustained parliamentary and public capacity for engaging in policy analysis that is taken seriously in actual decision-making

(Draimin and Schmitz, 1997). Three main lessons could be drawn from parliamentary roles in such reviews.[2] The first would be to focus on policy options that can galvanize public interest, where there are real stakes at issue and government policy is open to at least some modification; otherwise the process becomes a pointless exercise of consultation for its own sake. The second would be to involve the permanent parliamentary standing committees from the outset, enhancing the capacity of these underutilized existing vehicles to dig deeper into policy matters and to sustain the follow up necessary to hold government accountable for its decisions and the implementation of its commitments. The third would be to avoid setting rhetorical goals without considering necessary resources, subjecting creative policy rethinking to the underlying discipline of what is deliverable in high priority areas.

Public and parliamentary outreach had very limited beginnings in the Trudeau-era exercises setting out a "foreign policy for Canadians," reflecting both a certain "domestication" of the foreign policy agenda and an emphasis on getting Canadians to think about their national interests in a global context. However the parliamentary hearings of the time were harshly criticized as inadequate by, among others, Thomas Hockin (1969), a subsequent co-chair of the Mulroney government's 1985–86 parliamentary review.[3]

That review in turn, despite its coincidence with a push for parliamentary reforms, did not alleviate scepticism about the lasting value of consultation. After a first phase in which a parliamentary special joint committee looked at the high-profile issues of Reagan's "Star Wars" and negotiating free trade with the US, interest faded in the final report and government response delivered over a year later. The special committee and its work quickly disappeared from view, with no mechanism for follow up. Initiative returned to the standing committees while the ephemeral and low-stakes nature of the review process was underlined.[4]

Looking back to the 1994 foreign and defence policy reviews – reflecting a Liberal government's turn to promise a "democratization of foreign policy" – is to see new problems added to the old. There were now two separate special joint committees proceeding on tracks that almost never intersected. *Canada in the World* came out several months after the defence White Paper; neither gave much attention to issues that were soon to be at the core of the Axworthy "human security" agenda. Moreover, the standing committees were again not involved, so that after an intensive year of multiple cross-country consultations, there was little parliamentary follow up to the review reports.

As for the scaled-down proposals on "democratizing" foreign policy that produced the Canadian Centre for Foreign Policy Development, like the national forums that disappeared within a few years, this initiative seems also to have run its course without parliamentary notice or protest. David Malone's astute 2001 evaluation of *Canada in the World* argued that its "weakest sections ... have to do with the engagement of Canadians on policy formulation and implementation" (Malone, 2001: 575). Malone's predecessor in DFAIT policy planning, Don Page, had drawn an equally important conclusion from the 1985–86 review:

Effectiveness will depend on Parliament's ability and willingness to hold the government responsible for implementing policy recommendations that arise from outside the bureaucracy. Ultimately, even limited democratization of foreign policy making cannot be effective without the strong leadership of the Minister of Foreign Affairs who is responsible for making it happen. The continued willingness of the public to participate in this exercise in populism will depend as much on the bureaucratic initiative in taking these suggestions seriously in its policy making as on the actual process used to obtain the input. (1994: 597)

What matters in the end is mobilizing sufficient support behind concrete, achievable objectives. The accomplishments of the Ottawa Process on landmines, for example, prove this point because they both embraced ideas from the outside and required focused, sustained ministerial/bureaucratic initiative. (Tellingly, Axworthy makes no reference to *Canada in the World* in his 400–page chronicle, *Navigating a New World*, which recounts his time as foreign minister.) Until reviews begin to demonstrate real impact on Canada's actual engagements in global affairs, they are unlikely to motivate, or indeed justify, greater parliamentary and public interest in foreign policy consultations.

FROM 9/11 TO "DIALOGUE" TO THE IPR

It is often said that events determine the actual conduct of foreign policy more than the preconceived notions of policymakers, much less half-remembered statements in some previous policy document. In the case of the 11 September 2001 terrorist attacks on New York and Washington, the immediate reverberations from the mega-shock next door signalled the need for a comprehensive review of international policy. 9/11 did more than trump whatever foreign policy "update" had been slowly percolating, it upped the ante and fast-tracked to the front burner the most critical concerns in relations with Washington. A number of parliamentary committees moved rapidly to pursue border-related questions.

The House Standing Committee on Foreign Affairs and International Trade (SCFAIT), which under then chair and future Foreign Minister Bill Graham had already been preparing to examine Canada-US relations, was no exception, having produced two reports within several months including the first phase of a major North American study. SCFAIT's December 2002 final report, the largest and most complex in the committee's history, in effect covered much of the ground of any larger review (House of Commons, SCFAIT, 2002a).[5] Some of the report's proposals have found echoes in government policy; indeed, it is the only parliamentary committee report explicitly mentioned in the April 2005 IPS (Canada, 2005b: 7). During 2002, at Prime Minister Chrétien's request, SCFAIT also reviewed Canada's G8 role leading up to the Kananaskis Summit, addressing terrorism, development and other important areas of foreign policy in a post-9/11 context (House of Commons, SCFAIT, 2002b). Subsequently, SCFAIT undertook a major study on relations with countries of the Muslim world that resulted in a unanimous all-party March 2004 report (read-opted by the new minority-parliament committee in October 2004); the government's broadly positive March 2005 response to that report's recommendations claimed they had been taken into account in the then still unseen IPS (Canada, 2005c: 4).

An argument could be made that, in addition to important work by Parliament's three other international committees, notably in the defence and security area, SCFAIT's body of work since the 1994 review has examined a number of key areas in far more detail than would any general review. The committee has reported on reforms to the international financial institutions, the WTO agenda, export policies, circumpolar cooperation, nuclear weapons policies, and, only several months before 9/11, the South Caucasus and Central Asia regions bordering Afghanistan.

As the new Minister of Foreign Affairs, Graham was nonetheless handed the task of delivering on a mandate for some kind of overarching "international policy review," confirmed by the September 2002 Speech from the Throne. The eventual scaled-back result, the *Dialogue on Foreign Policy* launched in January 2003, did not substantially deviate from *Canada in the World's* "three pillars" in posing broad questions. Some who had been the most insistent in calling for a wide-ranging review to re-energize the policy machinery in the wake of new challenges were obviously disappointed with what they saw as a half-hearted and likely interim measure. Much of the process, essentially ministerially driven with support from the Canadian Centre for

Foreign Policy Development in organizing a web forum and a cross-country series of "town-hall" sessions with Graham, also turned into a ventilation of views provoked by circumstances surrounding the Iraq war.

In terms of parliamentary response, SCFAIT members dutifully held a few hearings on the Dialogue paper and produced a report that succinctly addressed the need for increased resources, for strengthened capabilities and linkages across the "3Ds" of diplomacy, development, and defence, for more effective management of Canada-US relations – citing its December 2002 report – and for retaining a "margin of manoeuvre" to advance Canadian interests and values through multi-lateralist approaches (House of Commons, SCFAIT, 2003). No other committee contributed to the *Dialogue*, although a few MPs submitted reports of constituency meetings held on it.

The *Dialogue* process had innovative dimensions and afforded opportunities for ordinary citizens to interact with the minister. But it was never given a mandate to set a new direction for Canadian foreign policy. Limited to recording the views of participants, the June 2003 *A Dialogue on Foreign Policy: Report to Canadians* was released after Parliament had recessed, its impact kept to a minimum.[6] Although SCFAIT had recommended that the minister "should appear before the Committee at the earliest possible opportunity to discuss the results and implications of the dialogue process," that never happened (House of Commons, SCFAIT, 2003: 16). By the fall of 2003 the *Dialogue* seemed to have disappeared except as a prelude to the "real" IPR that was expected under a new prime minister, Paul Martin.

Again, this reinforces the lesson that consultation can only bear fruit when connected to deliverable outputs. Certainly there is merit in stimulating further public debate on foreign policy – exploring creative uses of new interactive technologies and media, e-consultations, "town-halls," more parliamentary outreach, and so on. These efforts at engagement can be unfairly discounted, with the risk that the dimension of seeking to expand the circle of democratic deliberation will be undervalued in future policy development. But participants in the *Dialogue* have to feel that their contributions are feeding into a real decision process with discernable effect on policy directions. Otherwise, they, and an already cynical media, will turn off and disengage. Parliamentarians, too, are no more interested in wasting their time than anyone else.

Considering parliamentary roles in that light means getting beyond periodic reactions to the scripted documents of managed consultation processes too easily dismissed as navel-gazing public-relations indulgences. It means recognizing that participation in policy review exercises, which may have educational or other benefits, is not sufficient justification for expending more energy and resources on increasing democratic engagement. Improving foreign policy process must also strengthen its substance and implementation.

In a final section on learning from the troubled fate of the Martin IPR, we argue that foreign policy development can be made both more democratic and more results-oriented. In addition to more regular and systematic forms of policy review, this must also mean parliamentarians giving sustained attention to scrutinizing the instruments of policy delivery, notably the departmental machinery chiefly responsible for implementing the government's international agenda.

PARLIAMENT ON DFAIT: MERGER TO "DIVORCE" AND MINORITY DEFEAT

The one instance where parliamentarians demonstrated their power in relation to foreign affairs in 2005 was in fact on a seemingly arcane question of machinery. In defeating the legislation designed to formalize the split of the DFAIT, as Don Mackay (2005: 8) observed "the forces of a minority government, an itchy opposition (all three parties), and a badly conceived policy combined to create the perfect storm and the sinking of Bills C-31 and C-32." This action – and a subsequent related reduction in the supplementary estimates for Foreign Affairs Canada – underlined parliament's ultimate check on executive action and reinforced earlier lessons related to government reorganizations. The result could also motivate parliamentarians and others to give more attention to the organization of international policy instruments in the future.

Debates over the machinery of foreign policy are not unique to Canada. Dean Acheson once said that "reorganizing the (US) State Department is like performing an appendectomy on a man carrying a piano up a flight of stairs," and other countries have adopted various approaches to managing their foreign ministries, including the merger of foreign policy and trade functions.[7] In fact, Andrew F. Cooper has argued that despite a stylized image of cautious and hesitant adaptation, "the concern with trying to get its organizational structure rights serves as the dominant leitmotiv for the Canadian foreign ministry" (1999: 40). Nevertheless, parliamentarians have – perhaps not surprisingly – never paid significant attention to the *machinery* of foreign policy-making, implicitly accepting a "black box" model that considers inputs and outputs, but rarely the processes between them.

The 2005 debate over organizational issues can only be understood by looking backwards to the 1970s, by which time it had become obvious both that the economic expertise of the venerable (1909) Department of External Affairs was inadequate, and that the government needed greater integration – or "coherence" to use the current buzzword – in its trade and broader foreign policy. It therefore basically killed two birds with one stone, taking advantage of a mainly domestically-oriented Reorganization for Economic Development in January 1982 to (finally) transfer trade policy functions to the Department of External Affairs and creating a (theoretically junior) Minister for International Trade as part of the portfolio. A further reorganization of External Affairs followed in 1983.[8]

The 1982 reorganization of External Affairs was controversial, with both constituencies and employees suspicious of grand reorganization schemes and convinced that either trade or foreign affairs, as the case may be, would be dominated by the other element. The parliamentary debate at the time touched on both the process – accusations of a Pitfield-inspired obsession with the machinery of government and criticisms of general confusion – and the substance of the change – mainly fears of trade-offs between trade and broader international and humanitarian objectives within the new department. In May 1983, New Democratic Party (NDP) member Ian Deans complained that parliament was being asked to put into law what was already in place in practice (the government had used the traditional "temporary" tool of orders-in-council). In opposing the merger and calling for the establishment of a separate ministry of international trade, he argued prophetically: "I wish that we had had an opportunity to debate this Bill before it became a fait accompli since I am convinced that it will ultimately be changed anyway. Let us not ram the thing through and then find ourselves in a position of rewriting the law again, and debating again because on the next occasion we may find that the Conservatives are on the other side of the argument, who knows" (House of Commons, 1983).

By the time of the 1985–86 review, the merger seemed to have been accepted as a fait accompli, and in the ensuing decade the evolution of departmental organization and the Foreign Service failed to excite much parliamentary attention. While parliamentarians participating in the 1994 special joint review of Canada's defence policy addressed structural issues related to the Canadian Forces, their colleagues studying Canada's foreign policy did not do so to any comparable extent in relation to foreign affairs and aid structures. The 1990s saw significant challenges to DFAIT, including a combination of budget cuts and a further perceived reduction in influence within government that contributed to a reduction in Foreign Service capabilities and morale. SCFAIT did not address these subjects directly until its contribution to the 2003 *Dialogue*. However, committee members, including long-time chair Bill Graham, were sensitive to the problems, raising questions during the consideration of departmental spending estimates.

THE MARTIN MAKEOVER
AND ENSUING PARLIAMENTARY DEBATE

On 12 December 2003, the first day of the Martin government, the Prime Minister announced a number of changes to the structure of government designed to "build a twenty-first century economy," including "creating a strengthened department of international trade to provide centralized support for integrated federal trade and investment promotion" (PMO, 2003). The split of DFAIT was made effective immediately through orders-in-council. As a result of the federal election in June 2004, Bills C-31 and C-32, the legislation designed to give the new departments formal mandates, were only tabled in Parliament in December 2004 and eventually debated in February 2005.

Under questioning at SCFAIT in November 2004, Foreign Minister Pierre Pettigrew, a former trade minister, explained the move as "a matter of profile; trade is so important in Canada, the Prime Minister wanted to give it a stand-alone department ... the idea is that International Trade is receiving new responsibilities on the investment front ... Foreign Affairs will be able to concentrate, in my view, on the coordination role for the whole foreign policy." Further, he claimed that "the 1982 decision was reviewed by several other governments ... other prime ministers have revisited this issue and have ended up keeping the 1982 status quo, that is one department. This time, after having discussed the issue with various people, the Prime Minister made a different decision" (House of Commons, SCFAIT, 2004).

Despite the allusion to pre-study, the Martin decision came as a surprise. There had been no public call for it, including on the part of the business community or other stakeholders. Indeed, the Canadian Manufacturers and Exporters (CME) noted in a July 2004 letter to the Minister of International Trade: "While this structural change is a significant development, the business community did not request it. CME members were quite pleased with DFAIT as it existed and with the integration of trade, economic and political relations and with all the 'one-stop-shopping' advantages that that integration entailed. We have received member feedback expressing concern that managing the disassociation of trade and foreign affairs may rob needed resources from delivery of programs abroad and at home, and roll back what was

254 Schmitz and Lee

achieved since the early 1980s. If this separation is to be continued, the government must get it right" (CME, 2004).

The months that followed the announcement saw significant public criticism of the decision from journalists, retired senior officials and academics, and no public support. In Jeffrey Simpson's unsparing words, the decision to split the department once again was "an idea so splendidly stupid that literally no one in Ottawa will admit to having favoured it," adding that "temporary insanity is the most probable explanation, although the deed could also have been linked to those old Ottawa standbys: empire-building, bureaucratic turf wars or ministerial rivalries" (2004, 2005).[9] Richard Gwyn observed that "our diplomatic capacity is strained, and has been strained further by the quite ridiculous – expensive and time-consuming – decision by Martin's government (it's impossible to discover who actually made it) to slice the foreign affairs department into two by detaching international trade from it" (2005). James Travers saw negative effects on the key Canada-US file: "To make the most of the Bush visit ... federal departments must be working in concert. Instead, deputy foreign minister Peter Harder is at odds with [clerk of the Privy Council Alex] Himelfarb over a disputed backroom decision to separate international trade from diplomacy." (2004).

Particularly critical of the split were retired senior officials, both former deputy ministers such as Robert Johnstone (2005) and Gordon Smith (2005) – who might be thought to have a bias in favour of the status quo – former ambassadors to the United States such as Allan Gotlieb (2004b) and Derek Burney (2005b), and, perhaps more tellingly, the association representing 270 retired Canadian heads of mission who reminded the ministers concerned that

the controversial merger of Foreign Affairs and Trade in 1982 was one of the most successful realignments of responsibility within Canada's public service. In our wide-ranging consultations on the subject, RHOMA has yet to hear a voice which explains the rationale and bien fondé of the decision. There is much to lose in undoing what has been achieved as a result of the successful integration of these two critical sectors of Canadian foreign policy." (RHOMA, 2004)

Although the defeat of the authorizing legislation arose from a particular set of circumstances, the February 2005 second-reading debate that preceded it provides lessons both for students of Canadian parliamentary government and foreign policy. Beyond the partisan dynamics of a minority House, that debate encapsulated the case for and against the December 2003 decision. In addition to arguments about lack of transparency, seeming contradiction with stated goals of greater coordination and coherence among departments, and the dubious logic of precipitating major reorganization prior to rather than proceeding from the IPS, a main criticism was simply that the government had not offered good enough reasons for undoing the 1982 merger seen by most as ultimately successful.[10]

In the House debate on C-31, trade minister Peterson contended that a stand-alone trade ministry was needed and that "the cost of separating the one department into two is going to be cost neutral." He also claimed support from a significant number of industry groups (although this support was not publicly obvious) (House of Commons, 2005a). Summing up many of the opposition arguments, then Conservative trade critic Belinda Stronach pushed back: "If the government believes that its decision to carve up the country's foreign and trade policy apparatus could simply be presented as a fait accompli before a sleepy Parliament with no interest in the implications, then it is wrong and underestimates this House." As she outlined the situation:

To oppose the legislation would mean in effect to reverse the process and re-amalgamate the two departments. The government might be hoping that since the train has already left the station, the perceived costs of such a move would be seen as prohibitive. Therefore the House has been presented with both a fait accompli and a game of chicken. This is neither an appropriate approach to this House nor an effective conduct of public policy.

While the Conservative position initially favoured allowing the bill to go to SCFAIT so that, as Stronach put it, "we might be able to have a much closer look at its origins, implications and costs" (ibid.), the Bloc Québécois (BQ) and the NDP made clear from the outset that they would oppose both bills. Bloc MP Pierre Paquette called C-31 "not transparent, undemocratic, illogical, retrograde and harmful." (House of Commons, 2005b). A number of members also raised concerns that a separate ministry of trade would bypass broader considerations such as human rights. NDP critic Alexa McDonough complained of "the absence in this debate of any clear, articulated position for why the government is doing what it is doing," giving rise to

a genuine concern that the real driving force behind this is coming from the multinational corporate friends of the government. They are saying to whisk the international trade portfolio away from foreign affairs so that they will not find themselves having these nasty questions raised about what kind of trade relationships they are entering into, without any kind of protection for human rights. (House of Commons, 2005c)[11]

Such suspicions may be reinforced by the avoidance of aid/trade linkages to human rights in the IPS despite its avowed aim of "coherence," perhaps, as Andrew Cohen suggested to SCFAIT, because the issue of human rights "gets in the way of commerce" (House of Commons, SCFAIT, 2005d). More concretely, the Canadian Labour Congress noted that licenses for the export of sensitive technology were now the responsibility of International Trade Canada, arguing that these should be "vetted more broadly" (House of Commons, Subcommittee on International Trade, 2005).

In underlining the need for an integrated approach to international policy issues, BQ critic Francine Lalonde pointedly referred to the previous parliamentary committee experience of Bill Graham

who was an excellent Minister of Foreign Affairs. He headed the Standing Committee on Foreign Affairs and International Trade, as well as a very large number of studies addressing foreign affairs, international aid, human rights and international trade. He could back me up on this: not one of those studies would have been possible without all four aspects. We would have had a wobbly table with one important leg missing. That is what is being proposed to us. (House of Commons, 2005c)

With criticisms multiplying and impatience rising over further IPS delays, the Conservatives shifted to solidify united opposition in the negative votes on 15 February. Yet the day after the defeat of both bills, Trade Minister Peterson was quoted saying that the two departments would continue to work independently. While Liberal House Leader Tony Valeri stated the government was "considering its parliamentary options" (House of Commons, 2005d), the opposition raised a question of privilege in the House arguing that Peterson's position amounted to contempt of Parliament. In an unprecedented move, SCFAIT's opposition majority then reduced the 2004–2005 supplementary estimates for Foreign Affairs Canada by a symbolic $1 in protest (House of Commons, SCFAIT, 2005a).

House Speaker Peter Milliken's March 2005 ruling on the question of contempt, while granting that the government had the procedural right to reorganize its existing functions, put the problem as follows: "How can the decisions of the House on these bills be without practical consequence? We appear to have come upon a paradox in Canadian practice ... it leaves the government and the House in a most unfortunate conflict on the matter ...." In his conclusion, Milliken recommended simply that in "reviewing its parliamentary options," the government should "have further consultations with all parties in the House to clarify events and restore the central working relationship to its usual good form" (House of Commons, 2005e).

AFTERMATH AND LESSONS
OF AN APPREHENDED SEPARATION

By the time the IPS appeared in April 2005, it downplayed the departmental split, addressing it only indirectly in the context of restructuring "to ensure that we have the right tools to deliver a coherent and effective foreign policy across government and effective representation abroad." The concession to circumstances was a commitment to "establish an advisory and consultative process to consider how these objectives can best be achieved, in light of issues raised in parliament and by stakeholders" (Canada, 2005b: 32, and 2005a: 23). Foreign Minister Pettigrew was quoted telling a press conference upon release of the IPS that the government had "taken into account the recent decision by parliament," and wanted to review the situation some more" (Sallot, 2005). In response to a question about how a Conservative government would proceed, Conservative Foreign Affairs critic Stockwell Day stated a week later that: "We have no intention of completing an initiative of the government's which was ill-conceived in the first place" (McGregor, 2005).

A number of witnesses before SCFAIT commented on the split in the months following the release of the IPS. Retired senior diplomat Paul Heinbecker went first, telling the committee that trade policy is "integral to foreign policy," and that "Nothing in the statement ... including in the separate commerce book, demonstrates to me why we need a separate department of trade ..." (House of Commons, SCFAIT, 2005c). Roy Culpeper of the North-South Institute was "agnostic" about the split, arguing that the need was less for a particular organizational structure than for coherence based on "leadership ... from the top" (House of Commons, SCFAIT 2005g). Gauri Sreenivasan of the Canadian Council for International Cooperation argued that "the key issue is ... the coherence agenda," adding that "where the issue hits the road most importantly is in the embassies on the ground" (House of Commons, SCFAIT, 2005f). David Stewart-Patterson of the Canadian Council of Chief Executives told SCFAIT in June 2005 that while his organization had never asked for nor been consulted on the split:

258 Schmitz and Lee

Given the reality that decision was made, we said we were prepared to offer our qualified support for carrying on on three conditions: one, that the split be revenue neutral; two, that the split of the department not disrupt its ability to do its job to help Canadian companies and individual Canadians; and three, that the split not undermine the morale and effectiveness of the dedicated and talented people who work there ... I have to say that on all three counts the execution of the split has failed to meet those conditions.

He added, however, "I don't want to suggest that we necessarily want to go back to precisely what we had before, because I think there was certainly a positive motivation and I think some good ideas have been incorporated into the current situation ..." (House of Commons, SCFAIT, 2005h). Likewise Derek Burney's (House of Commons, SCFAIT, 2005e) sharp criticism of the split – "I just have not heard anybody tell me what it is we're trying to fix, because I don't see anything that was broken" – had not rejected the possibility of organizational change, but had underlined that: "If you want a strong Department of Trade, this is not the way to do it." Even if such a reorganization were done properly, "you're looking at a period of at least two years of disruption, reorganizations and endless turf fights."

What then are the lessons for both foreign policy implementation and parliamentary oversight? The first and broadest is to approach reorganizations with caution. As former DFAIT deputy minister Gordon Smith (2005: 51) – who was also responsible for machinery of government issues in the Privy Council Office (PCO) for a number of years – wrote in the 2004 volume of *Canada Among Nations*, "government reorganizations are expensive, above all in time lost but also in money, and rarely solve problems without creating new ones." Gordon Osbaldeston, also a former deputy minister of External Affairs as well as clerk of the Privy Council and a major player in the original amalgamation, argued in his definitive 1992 book *Organizing to Govern*, that the first rule is to "resist proposals to reorganize unless you are certain that the benefits of the proposed change outweigh the costs." Moreover: "Decision makers should insist on a full analysis of the short-and-longer-term implications – political and operational – of any reorganizing proposal, no matter how attractive the benefits may be. They must satisfy themselves that the cost of maintaining the status quo is so high that it justifies the cost of reorganizing."

While the Martin government, then operating in majority mode, seems to have assumed that "housekeeping" legislation such as this would pass easily through the Commons, Osbaldeston had pointed out a decade before this was unlikely to be the case. "Taking organizational legislation to Parliament is often an unpleasant experience for the government," he argued. "In government, organizing is linked closely with legislation. This linkage means that the process of organizing can be subject to the same procedural and political manoeuvring as any policy bill," and that a government planning to introduce an organizational change should prepare for the same type of legislative fight as if it were introducing a new policy. Finally, "If a government is not prepared to face Parliament, it simply delays introducing the organization's legislation. The government does not have to pay the price until it is ready." If this advice held for a majority government, of course, it would be much more important in a minority one. Indeed, "an experienced parliamentarian" had warned Osbaldeston not to "expect reasoned debate if the House is in a fractious mood."[12]

The 2005 DFAIT "divorce" debate was a sharp reminder not to take either restructuring or Parliament lightly, especially when the latter was in no mood to be treated as a rubber stamp. While it was a particular conjunction of minority circumstances that shone a spotlight on these issues in 2005, the resulting legislative debate on the split and related debates over the future of the foreign service have given momentum to parliamentary interest, hopefully sustained over the longer term, in scrutinizing the instruments as well as the intentions of Canada's international policy framework.

PARLIAMENTARY PROSPECTS
BEYOND THE MARTIN REVIEW

Featured on the cover of the 6 April 2005 issue of Ottawa's weekly *Embassy* magazine was a "Crash Course on Hill Committees," carrying the subtitle "Minority Government Gives Parliamentary Committees Real Power." Yet more will be needed than temporary minority configurations if parliamentary mechanisms are to connect with citizens and to overcome the deeper "democratic deficits" of which parliamentarians themselves are acutely aware.[13]

The measures to boost parliamentary democracy introduced by the Martin majority government were at most a modest downpayment on ambitious promises of change. In foreign policy, the February 2004 Speech from the Throne announced that the IPR "will be completed this autumn and then considered by a parliamentary committee, where Canadians will have an opportunity to make their views known." The Liberal platform referred to parliamentarians and Canadians having "the opportunity to debate its analysis and implications" (Liberal, 2004: 11). However following the June 2004 election campaign, in which international issues had little influence, some commentators expected any progress to depend on "the daily drama of minority government" (Manthorpe, 2004). Having had almost a year since the publication of the Dialogue's *Report to Canadians*, many of the groups that had been involved in that process had reworked their proposals and were looking forward to a fresh Martin government approach.[14] There was no shortage of unsolicited advice from a dissonant, sometimes cranky, chorus of NGOs, academics, pundits and former diplomats waiting for the dividends to materialize from their invested hopes.

By April 2004, articles were appearing that a new, more "integrated" and "coherent" framework for international policy was starting to fall into place, and that the whole process, including parliamentary consultations could be wrapped up by the end of the year (Cornellier, 2004). At the same time, advocacy groups renewed the pressure for a full-sale public review, calling for early, inclusive, and transparent consultations. An open letter to the prime minister dated 26 April from a coalition of NGOs and activists, insisted that "civil society" be brought into the IPR as it had been into the Dialogue process, urging the government "to envision these previous consultations as the first – not the final – steps of engaging Canadians in the IPR process ... dialogue needs to be open, informed and – above all – sustained."[15]

Of course the 2004 election aftermath with its minority permutations, changes of ministers, and delayed opening of parliament put an end to any danger of a completed review being sprung on an unsuspecting public. The government's October 2004 Throne Speech reaffirmed an intention to proceed, but gone were any illusions of a smooth or expedited process. As long as the government's international policy agenda could be left officially pending, parliament's power to shape it was put on hold too. In the meantime, with confident majority timing lost, the way was also open for critics and sceptics to have a field day at the review's expense. Could the results of the final product ever justify the wait?

The minority 38th Parliament tested the Martin government's earlier reform intentions in an unfamiliar environment (only a few MPs had any experience of minority government) in which it could no longer count on being able to safely steer the agenda of change. It soon became apparent how much that agenda might be hostage to the shifting ground of parliamentary support (including within the government's own restive caucus) and to convoluted negotiations with one or more among the opposition parties claiming a collective majority of Commons seats.

Lurching from one showdown to another, opposition influence could not be denied in the House and on committees. However, the results in terms of parliamentary reform remained modest: more assertive behaviour by some MPs and small increases in resources for committee work; hardly a radical transformation in the workings of parliament. To take one foreign policy flashpoint on which SCFAIT did hold hearings, the government had agreed to opposition demands to hold a House vote on the issue of participation in ballistic missile defence. But when in February 2005 it suddenly announced, without debate or vote, that Canada would not participate in the US program, the parliamentary fallout was limited and there was more quiet applause than protest on Main Street. Political calculations easily prevailed over process promises.

At the same time, the fluidity of minority parliament required policymakers to take its role seriously – as those in charge of dividing DFAIT discovered to their chagrin when the "divorce" bills were returned to sender by an unimpressed Commons majority. The longterm significance of such skirmishes may, however, depend on a minority situation persisting long enough to entrench parliamentary opportunities for substantive policy influence being brought to bear in ways that can no longer be predictably managed from the centre.

In the case of the comprehensive IPR that morphed into an endlessly delayed IPS, Foreign Minister Pierre Pettigrew had promised SCFAIT in November 2004 that he looked forward "to hearing the views of parliamentarians and Canadians on the review's outcome and proposed directions" moving toward "more regular dialogue with members of Parliament and Canadians on foreign policy in the future" (House of Commons, SCFAIT, 2004). Of course any parliamentary role in that regard would require a genuine consensus among the parties on how to proceed. While SCFAIT waited impatiently for the IPS to be released, plans were prepared and revised for possible cross-country hearings, an e-consultation, as well as international travel. As of the summer 2005 recess SCFAIT had at least been able to hear some witnesses on the IPS and to set in motion a study program for the fall session.

Yet the irony is not lost that by the time *Canada's International Policy Statement: A Role of Pride and Influence in the World* was finally made public in April 2005, it faced the prospect of another electoral interruption, and potential reversal of fortune since it was put forward as, in effect, a White Paper. An accompanying government press release did state that "parliamentarians and other Canadians" would have an opportunity to review the IPS and that: "To increase accountability on international affairs, the Minister of Foreign Affairs will table annual foreign policy updates in Parliament." The latter was also promised in the IPS Diplomacy paper (though not mentioned in the prime minister's foreword or the overview). Only the Defence paper explicitly called for parliamentary committees to study its contents, although a letter from the four ministers to the chairs of the four parliamentary international committees asked them to "consult widely with Canadians and report their views and recommendations on the future direction of Canada's international policies." Andrew Cohen underlined the lack of any post-Dialogue public input in arguing before SCFAIT that "if this is going to be sold to Canadians and embraced by Canadians they need to be brought in" (House of Commons, SCFAIT, 2005d).

Although formal consultation had yet to take place as anticipated, the prolonged and vexing IPR episode provoked a proliferation of articles and commentaries leaving no stone unturned on the "tortuous path to a new foreign policy" (Blanchfield, 2005b).[16] These have sharpened contending schools of opinion beyond a usual contrast between the inherent caution of the bureaucratic managers and gatekeepers with the myriad good causes pressed on the politicians by concerned NGOs.

The most "realist" view, exemplified by former ambassadors to the United States Allan Gotlieb and Derek Burney, distrusts appeals to "romanticism" and populism in foreign policy matters. Gotlieb wrote that reviews "tend to embody the lowest common denominator. At best they accomplish little; at worst, they blow stale air into clichés and encourage self-congratulation. ... The Prime Minister would do well to follow in the footsteps of Lester Pearson. Don't study foreign policy. Conduct it" (2004a).[17] According to Burney: "These perpetual consultations and reviews are, in a sense, an abdication of responsibility. The purpose of government is to lead, not follow, public opinion" (2005b: 2). Although Gotlieb found encouraging elements in the IPS, he rested his case: "History shows that usually all the major foreign policy departures that are made have nothing to do with any review" (Geddes, 2005: 17). If reviews are a temptation to be resisted, Gotlieb and Burney were, as already noted, no more charitable about the costs of needless departmental reorganization, the idea for which never surfaced during the 2003 Dialogue.

Both realists and traditional "internationalists" looked back to a time when they considered that Canada was taken more seriously internationally – and especially in Washington – because of an activist record of "punching above its weight" (Cohen, 2003). The latter especially urged a major reinvestment of resources across the spectrum of international policy instruments from diplomacy to aid and defence in order to rebuild Canadian credibility.

Fresh perspectives also emerged appealing to new generations of Canadians to supply the ideas and energy for a bracing renewal of Canadian foreign policy. They would let go of the "cult of middleness" (Valaskakis, 2005) and look elsewhere than to the traditions and conventional wisdom of the foreign policy establishment. While concepts of Canada as exemplar – such as the youth group Canada 25's (2004) "model power" or Jennifer Welsh's (2004) "model citizen" – sound idealistic, they promote an action-oriented globalism (rather than a globalization critique) focused on creating the conditions of opportunity for Canadians, individually as well as collectively, to achieve international aspirations.

One senses among Foreign Affairs officials considerable sympathy with that impatience to get on with it, reading between the lines of Rob McRae's mid-course assessment that: "Reviews have rarely, if ever, presented real choices to the Canadian public. Nor have reviews been crucial to a government's decisions about how we manage our international engagement at home. ... [W]e need to be much more explicit in future as to what a review should seek to accomplish" (2005: 55).[18] The focus on outcomes also comes through in the pointed findings of Robert Greenhill (2005: 21) that the world needs not only more Canada, but more *from* Canada. As the future CIDA president told SCFAIT a few days before the release of the IPS: "we don't need an international policy statement. We need international policy actions. The world is actually tired of Canadian rhetoric."

While acknowledging that "you can't have an international policy strategy without an international policy debate," Greenhill also appealed to SCFAIT members for a "multi-partisan approach" which he saw as critical "if we're going to have the consistency that leads to credibility and impact over time" (House of Commons, SCFAIT, 2005b). Citing examples from other countries, including the British approach of annual foreign policy debates in the House of Commons, he encouraged committee members to discuss appropriate mechanisms for building public consensus around Canadian objectives. In a parliamentary democracy – particularly one that is domestically divided along regional and increasingly fractious party lines – who should establish what international goals are to be accomplished and how? By what means are Canadian interests, or "values," to be defined? While realists emphasize executive decisiveness on closer Canada-US relations, numerous NGOs demand their voices be heard early and often on putting normative aims ahead of crass state or commercial considerations. Internationalists wanting action on ambitious multilateralist agendas to inspire more public engagement and support often also demand reforms that are only realizable working with many other countries.

A diversity of perspectives, reflecting as well a growing range of multi-cultural/racial/faith communities within the changing "Canadian mosaic," deserves a thorough airing by the elected representatives of Canadians. Debate cannot happen only in back rooms, lecture halls, and on editorial pages. It should aim to be inclusive of all regions and all segments of the population. Given the experience of ephemeral consultations and "dialogues" to date, it is also apparent it should take place in a much more regular, systematic, and consequential way. That, too, is an issue calling for serious parliamentary deliberation and response.

The IPS commitment to annual updates to Parliament by the foreign affairs minister is a first step. Annual parliamentary debates would be a minimal concomitant. Beyond that, SCFAIT members might consider instituting a regular process of pre-update public hearings analogous to the pre-Budget consultations undertaken by the House finance committee. In fact all this and more had been suggested to SCFAIT by Lloyd Axworthy nine years earlier when, in his first appearance as foreign minister, he both called for undertaking a "serious considered restructuring and retooling of the mechanisms, the delivery, and the priorities" of foreign policy "to bring coherence into the international activities" of multiple departments, and envisaged the committee acting "to reinforce the role of Parliament in opening up foreign policy and bringing more Canadians into a dialogue of our role in changing times" through "an annual, revolving review of what is important on a year-to-year basis" (House of Commons, SCFAIT, 1996).[19]

We have seen how the frustrations of the Martin IPR were exacerbated by the troubled attempt to bring departments together while simultaneously splitting DFAIT apart. The shortcomings of these processes added to the baggage weighing down positive elements of the IPS. As that was delayed and then delivered into a precarious minority scenario in the spring of 2005, the potential parliamentary contribution to review was also overshadowed.

But looking ahead, this latest episode underlines a need to explore innovative, practical ideas, not least from parliamentarians themselves, on how better to incorporate ongoing meaningful public deliberation into effective international policy decision-making. Surely it is not beyond the reach of Canadians to strengthen the democratic means whereby international policies are made along with the capacities to achieve the goals of those policies. That challenge continues beyond the uncertain outcome of international policy review and reorganization in the 2005 minority parliament.

NOTES

This chapter reflects the views of the authors alone.

1 The last occasion we have been able to find of a government bill being defeated at second reading in the House was eighty years earlier – the *Dominion Elections Act* on 19 February 1925.
2 For a detailed examination, see Gerald Schmitz, "Foreign Policy White Papers and the Role of Canada's Parliament: Paradoxical but not without Potential." Paper presented to the Canadian Political Science Association annual meeting, London, Ontario, 3 June 2005 (forthcoming in *Études internationales*, Fall 2005). This paper builds on one by the same author presented to the CPSA exactly ten years earlier following the 1994 review, "The State, the Public and the Decennial Refashioning of Foreign Policy: Democratizing Diminished Expectations or Demanding a New Departure?" Montreal, 3 June 1995.
3 Douglas Bland and Roy Rempel (2004: 9) maintain that: "Parliament was hardly consulted during the so-called 1968–69 defence and foreign policy reviews."
4 Indeed the House external affairs committee, split from defence and joined to trade, produced a much more thorough examination of Canadian aid policies and programs (*For Whose Benefit?*) in 1987.
5 The committee's reports can be accessed at <http://www.parl.gc.ca/faae>.
6 The *Report* was never seen as an expression of government priorities. The Dialogue also took place separately from an internal PCO Task Force on the International Policy Framework, the July 2003 report of which, *Towards an International Policy Framework for the 21st Century*, was not publicly released.
7 Acheson is quoted in Osbaldeston (1982). On developments in other countries, see Brain Hocking, ed., *Foreign Ministries: Change and Adaptation* (London: MacMillan Press Limited, 1999).
8 For further information on the 1982 reorganization see, Osbaldeston, "Reorganizing Canada's Department of External Affairs," in Osbaldeston (1982, 1992); and, among others, James Lee, *The Reorganization of the Canadian Department of External Affairs 1980–83: A Case Study*, Master's thesis, Carleton University, 1987.
9 As questions about the "why" of the decision yielded unsatisfactory answers, many observers turned to questions about "who"?

10 In an April 2005 interview, retired senior diplomat James Bartleman reflected on the years when foreign affairs and trade were separate: "In those days there was a war going on between the two departments. It was actually very time-wasting and unproductive ... Fortunately, that ended with amalgamation in 1982, and I certainly hope that we never return to those old days, when so much energy was lost" (Leadlay, 2005: 12).

11 In fact, during the 1983 debate NDP member Pauline Jewitt had made exactly the *opposite* case in opposing the merger of trade and foreign affairs into a single department. As she explained, "I think it is better to have Trade and Commerce quite separately represented at Cabinet ... we may very seriously undermine other policy directions, whether they be in human rights, peacekeeping or whatever the Department of External Affairs ordinarily conducts." House of Commons, *Debates*, 32nd Parliament, 2nd Session, 22 June 1983, 26707.

12 The preceding citations are from Osbaldeston (1992, vol. 1: 144–5, 112, 110, 137, and 113). While much of the spectacle of the 2005 debate came from the fact that the government was undoing its own previous reorganization, Osbaldeston shows in a discussion of Industry, Trade and Commerce (37–8) that even this was not unprecedented.

13 See, for example, *The Parliament We Want: Parliamentarians' Views on Parliamentary Reform*, A report prepared by the Library of Parliament under the direction of Carolyn Bennett MP, Deborah Grey MP, Senator Yves Morin with Graham Fox and William Young, Ottawa, December 2003.

14 Going back to a major foreign policy speech that Mr Martin had given as a leadership candidate in May 2003, his pronouncements before and after becoming prime minister were eagerly scanned by all concerned for clues as to the touchstones that might at least reinvigorate Canadian foreign policy, if not provide it with a dramatically new direction. The case for vigorous leadership in shouldering Canada's international responsibilities was a common refrain on all sides of the debate as the Martin transition was being prepared. See, for example, Margaret MacMillan, "A new foreign policy? Not necessarily," *National Post*, 11 September 2003.

15 The Canadian Council for International Cooperation, Canadian Labour Congress and Amnesty International were among the 16 signatories to the letter, which argued further that the Dialogue had demonstrated Canadians' support for a values-driven agenda that should be "applied coherently" to international policy.

16 In fact, months prior to the IPS release much of its contents had already been 'pre-announced' or hinted at, and earlier drafts leaked to the press (Blanchfield, 2005a).

17 See also Gotlieb (2004c).

18 See also John Noble, "Do Foreign Policy Reviews Make a Difference?" *Policy Options*, vol. 26, no. 2 (February 2005): 41–46.

19 Axworthy explicitly suggested the committee "do something similar to what the finance committee does in pre-budget preparation, where the committee plays an invaluable role in acting as the venue for Canadians to make their views known and for Parliament to put forward its proposals and ideas" (House of Commons, SCFAIT, 1996).

REFERENCES

Blanchfield, Mike. 2005a. "Canadian 'values' form backbone of foreign policy plan," *The Ottawa Citizen*, 8 March.

– 2005b. "Canada's tortuous path to a new foreign policy," *The Ottawa Citizen*, 12 March.

Bland, Douglas, and Roy Rempel. 2004. "A Vigilant Parliament: Building Competence for Effective Oversight of National Defence and the Canadian Armed Forces," *Policy Matters*, vol. 5, no. 1 (February).

Burney, Derek. 2005a. "Adrift in the world," *The Ottawa Citizen*, 4 March.

– 2005b. "Foreign Policy: More Coherence, Less Pretence." Simon Reisman Lecture in International Trade Policy, Centre for Trade Policy and Law, Carleton University, Ottawa, 14 March.

Canada. 2005a. "Commerce," in *Canada's International Policy Statement: A Role of Pride and Influence in the World*. Ottawa: Department of Foreign Affairs and International Trade (DFAIT), 19 April.

– 2005b. "Diplomacy," in *Canada's International Policy Statement: A Role of Pride and Influence in the World*. Ottawa: Department of Foreign Affairs and International Trade (DFAIT), 19 April.

– 2005c. *Government Response to the Report of the Standing Committee on Foreign Affairs and International Trade, Exploring Canada's Relations with the Countries of the Muslim World*. Ottawa: Department of Foreign Affairs and International Trade (DFAIT), March.

Canada25. 2004. *From Middle Power to Model Power: Recharging Canada's Role in the World*. Toronto: Canada25. Available at: <http://www.canada25.com>.

Canadian Manufacturers and Exporters (CME). 2004. Letter to the Honourable James Peterson, Minister of International Trade, 27 July.

Cohen, Andrew. 2003. *While Canada Slept: How We Lost Our Place in the World*. Toronto: McClelland & Stewart.

Cooper, Andrew F. 1999. "Trying to Get It Right: The Foreign Ministry and Organizational Change," in Brian Hocking, ed., *Foreign Ministries: Change and Adaptation*. New York: St Martin's Press.

Cornellier, Manon. 2004. "Cohérence, le mot clé de la future politique étrangère," *Le Devoir*, 17 April.

Draimin, Tim, and Gerald Schmitz. 1997. "Effective Policy Dialogue in the North: A View from Canada," in David Gillies, ed, *Strategies of Public Engagement: Shaping a Canadian Agenda for International Co-operation.* Montreal & Kingston: McGill-Queen's University Press.

Geddes, John. 2005. "Q&A with former ambassador Allan Gotlieb," *Maclean's*, 2 May.

Gotlieb, Allan. 2004a. "Please, Paul, no more reviews," *Globe and Mail*, 12 October.

– 2004b. "The Right Stuff," *National Post*, 27 December.

– 2004c. "Romanticism and Realism in Canada's Foreign Policy." C.D. Howe Institute Benefactors Lecture, Toronto, 3 November.

Greenhill, Robert. 2005. *Making a Difference: External Views on Canada's International Impact.* Interim Report of the External Voices Project. Toronto: Canadian Institute of International Affairs, 27 January.

Gwyn, Richard. 2005. "Dear Prime Minister: Clarity begins at home," *Toronto Star*, 28 January.

Harder, Peter V. 2005. Address to the Canadian Institute of International Affairs on *Does Canadian Foreign Policy Need a Foreign Service?* Ottawa, 17 February.

Hockin, Thomas. 1969. "The Foreign Policy Review and Decision Making in Canada," in John Warnock and Thomas Hockin, eds., *Alliances and Illusions: Canada and the NATO-NORAD Question.* Edmonton: Mel Hurtig Publishers.

House of Commons. 1983. *Debates*, 32nd Parliament, 2nd Session, 27 May, 25810.

– 2005a. *Debates*, 38th Parliament, 1st Session, 7 February.

– 2005b. *Debates*, 38th Parliament, 1st Session, 9 February.

– 2005c. *Debates*, 38th Parliament, 1st Session, 14 February.

– 2005d. *Debates*, 38th Parliament, 1st Session, 17 February.

– 2005e. *Debates*, 38th Parliament, 1st Session, 23 March.

House of Commons, Standing Committee on Foreign Affairs and International Trade (SCFAIT). 1996. *Evidence.* Ottawa, 16 April.

– 2002a. *Partners in North America: Advancing Canada's Relations with the United States and Mexico.* Ottawa, December.

– 2002b. *Securing Progress for Africa and the World: A Report on Canadian Priorities for the 2002 G8 Summit.* Ottawa, June.

– 2003. *A Contribution to the Foreign Policy Dialogue.* Ottawa, May.

– 2004. *Evidence.* Ottawa, 29 November.

– 2005a. *Evidence.* Ottawa, 10 March.

– 2005b. *Evidence.* Ottawa, 14 April.

– 2005c. *Evidence.* Ottawa, 21 April.

– 2005d. *Evidence*. Ottawa, 3 May.
– 2005e. *Evidence*. Ottawa, 12 May.
– 2005f. *Evidence*. Ottawa, 19 May.
– 2005g. *Evidence*. Ottawa, 9 June.
– 2005h. *Evidence*. Ottawa, 28 June.
House of Commons, Subcommittee on International Trade, Trade Disputes and Investment of the Standing Committee on Foreign Affairs and International Trade. 2005. *Evidence*. Ottawa, 23 March.
Johnstone, Robert. 2005. "Fixing foreign affairs is flawed," *Globe and Mail*, 19 January.
Leadlay, Christina. 2005. "Reviving the diplomatic memoir," *Embassy*, 27 April, 12.
Liberal Party of Canada. 2004. *Moving Canada Forward: The Paul Martin Plan for Getting Things Done*. Available at: <http://www.liberal.ca/documents/platform_en.pdf>.
Mackay, Don. 2005. "The Perfect Storm: Foreign Affairs Hits an Uncharted Rock," *Focal Point*, Canadian Foundation for the Americas (FOCAL), vol. 4, no.2 (February).
Malone, David. 2001. "Foreign policy reviews reconsidered," *International Journal*, vol. 56, no. 4 (Autumn).
Manthorpe, Jonathan. 2004. "Foreign affairs will continue to suffer after the election," *Ottawa Citizen*, 4 July.
McGregor, Sarah. 2005. "Foreign Policy: What's the Tory plan?" *Embassy*, 27 April, 7.
McRae, Rob. 2005. "International Policy Reviews in Perspective," in David Carment et al., eds., *Canada Among Nations 2004: Setting Priorities Straight*. Montreal & Kingston: McGill-Queen's University Press.
Osbaldeston, Gordon F. 1982. "Reorganizing Canada's Department of External Affairs," *International Journal*, vol. 37, no. 3 (Summer).
– 1992. *Organizing to Govern*, 2 vol. Toronto: McGraw-Hill Ryerson.
Page, Don. 1994. "Populism in Canadian Foreign Policy: The 1986 Review Revisited," *Canadian Public Administration*, vol. 37, no. 4 (Winter).
Pearson, Michael. 1999. "'Fate and Will': Reflections on the Implementation of Canadian Foreign Policy," *Canadian Foreign Policy*, vol. 6, no. 2 (Winter).
Prime Minister's Office (PMO). 2003. "Changing Government: Prime Minister Announces Appointment of Cabinet." Ottawa: PMO, 12 December.
Retired Heads of Mission Association (RHOMA). 2004. Letter to Ministers Pettigrew, Peterson, Sgro and Carroll, 1 December.
Sallot, Jeff. 2005. "Liberals Pare aid recipients list China cut from program; Ottawa will rethink splitting Trade and Foreign Affairs," *Globe and Mail*, 20 April.
Simpson, Jeffrey. 2004. "A bureaucratic python is crushing this vision," *Globe and Mail*, 27 November.

– 2005. "Who, dear Hercule, sliced Foreign Affairs in two?" *Globe and Mail*, 22 January.

Smith, Gordon. 2005. "Establishing Canada's Priorities," in David Carment et al., eds., *Canada Among Nations 2004: Setting Priorities Straight*. Montreal & Kingston: McGill-Queen's University Press.

Travers, James. 2004. "Bush visit planners locked in struggle," *Toronto Star*, 25 November.

Valaskakis, Kimon. 2005. "Escaping the cult of middleness," *National Post*, 11 March.

Welsh, Jennifer. 2004. *At Home in the World: Canada's Global Vision for the 21st Century*. Toronto: HarperCollins Publishers.

Winsor, Hugh. 2005. "Does Canadian Foreign Policy Need a Foreign Service?" Remarks to a Canadian Institute of International Affairs Panel, Ottawa, 17 February.

15 New Bottles for Old Wine: Implementing the *International Policy Statement*

THOMAS S. AXWORTHY

Veterans from Canada's "Golden Age" of diplomacy would have little difficulty in comprehending and supporting the priorities of the 2005 *International Policy Statement* (IPS). As in 1950, with North Korea's attack on South Korea, 11 September 2001 was a bolt from the blue and in each case the response has been dramatically increased military spending and a new emphasis on national security. As in 1950, too, the United States is using unsurpassed military power to confront worldwide threats and the unilateralism of American decisions (led by General Douglas MacArthur in 1951 and by President George W. Bush today) worries many allies and necessitates many Canadians to think long and hard about the North American partnership. In 1951, for example, Mr. Pearson created a storm with his statement that "the days of relatively easy and automatic political relations with our neighbours are, I think, over" (Pearson, 1951).[1] Dana Wilgress, Canada's foremost trade expert in 1950, famous for negotiating the General Agreement on Tariffs and Trade, would welcome the emphasis of Paul Martin's foreword to the IPS that "we have benefited enormously from our open economy" (Canada, 2005c: 3). Escott Reid, proud of the fact that in 1950 at Colombo for the first time in its history, Canada committed resources to the poor of Asia, would be delighted that development policy in 2005 commanded equal weight with defence, commerce and diplomacy. As envoy to India from 1952–57, he would also agree with the priority accorded in the 2005 IPS to the South Asian giant: "India and Canada share a mutual commitment to democracy and the rule of law, and to the better integration of developing countries into the multilateral trading system" (Canada, 2005a: 17).

However, what would surprise the foreign policy elite of the 1950s, if they were to read the 2005 review would be the booklet on diplomacy. Why are there sections on organized crime or communicable diseases or climate change, they might ask? What do these subjects have to do with the "high politics" of foreign policy? What is this thing called public diplomacy – is it not the diplomat's job to quietly influence foreign chancelleries? Why does "achieving our international objectives require the active participation of business and civil society?" (Canada, 2005b: 29). Shouldn't foreign policy be the preserve of a generalist elite who interact with comparable elites of professionals abroad? The interests and values proclaimed by the *International Policy Statement* would be instantly recognized by the founders of Canada's postwar Foreign Service, but the implementation mechanics of the self-described "new diplomacy" of 2005 might confound even those skilled managers of the Golden Age.

My thesis is that the policy priorities of the IPS fall squarely within the Pearsonian tradition of an independent multi-lateral helpful fixer. The Martin Government has also begun to address the crucial commitments-capability gap in international policy with the 2005 budget: $12.8 billion in new defence outlays over 5 years (although the increases for 2005 and 2006 are modest at $500 million and $600 million respectively), growing to $5.7 billion in new money by 2009 to 2010; a doubling of development assistance by 2010 from the 2001 base (though not enough to get Canada to 0.7 percent of GDP); and even $42 million over five years to increase the diplomatic staff, $59 million to address security needs at missions abroad, and $40 million for public diplomacy.

Intelligent priorities are the start to good public policy and the Martin list is fine. Capacity is the second key requirement and the Martin Government has finally begun to reverse the long, slow, steady decline of investment in international policy assets. But, the third essential aspect of public policy – a sensible management structure and motivated employees to implement the priorities and use resources wisely – is missing from the Martin plan. The *International Policy Statement* asks the essential question: "how to better support the diverse interests of these many new players, while at the same time creating foreign policy coherence across and among levels of government?" (Canada, 2005b: 29). But, it does not answer it. The Martin Government is not alone in having difficulties in putting in place a management structure attuned to the needs of the twenty-first century. Robin Cook, the former Foreign Secretary of Great Britain, for example, derides those who still talk of the national interest in the language of Palmerston for "it is no longer possible to separate into neat compartments domestic and foreign policy," and therefore British foreign policy "requires a gear shift in the way we regard the relationship of our country to the rest of the world" (2003: 354–5). On the machinery of government needed to implement the IPS, the Martin Government is stuck in neutral, or even worse, by undoing the 1982 integration of the Foreign Affairs and Trade Departments, it has put the foreign policy omnibus into reverse.

THE DIPLOMATIC MACHINE

The origins of diplomacy, according to Abba Eban the former Foreign Minister of Israel, are rooted in the acceptance of rivalry as the natural condition of interstate relations. Eban approvingly quotes Ermolao Barbaro, one of the earliest commentators on diplomacy, that the duty of the ambassador is "the same as that of any other servant of a government – to do, say advise and think whatever may best serve the preservation and aggrandizement of the state" (1983: 337).[2] Bringing Barbaro up to date, Eban writes that in the modern age, "diplomacy is called upon to bridge gulfs and to defuse tensions in a world where there is no effective restraint on the policies of individual states and no development of enforceable international authority" (ibid.: 398).

Harold Nicolson's classic, *Diplomacy*, describes the origins of interstate negotiation and how the tasks invented by ancient Greek ambassadors continue to be relevant today. Diplomacy is derived from the Greek word "diploun" meaning "to fold." Passes for imperial roads were stamped on double metal plates, folded and sewn together. The metal passes were diplomas. The Greeks invented truces, conventions, alliances and commercial treaties. Arbitration was a favourite device of the Greek city-state: records of nearly fifty cases of arbitration have been found, dating prior to 100BC. As we know from Thucydides, the first requirement of an ambassador was skill in persuasion. Greek diplomacy was largely the ability to put a case before an assembly and the ability to persuade, negotiate, listen, and understand is still a primary function of modern day diplomats. The *International Policy Statement* defines the overall role of Foreign Affairs as being that of the "chief advocate of Canada's values and interests abroad" (Canada, 2005b: 30).

The Byzantines developed the second major function of diplomacy – gathering information abroad. Byzantine courts in the twelfth century used their messengers or ambassadors not only to make a case, but to report on conditions in the countries to which they had been sent. The Italian city-states logically innovated to better achieve this function by inventing resident ambassadors. Rather than continuing the practice of sending ambassadors for short visits in 1455, Milan established a permanent mission in Genoa. Florence developed an especially high standard for ambassadors – Dante, Petrach, Boccaccio, and Machiavelli (though not quite in Petrach's class, in Canada's diplomatic Golden Age, poets like Robert Ford and Douglas LePan were also senior officials in External Affairs). The qualities required for a successful diplomat evolved from advocacy to intelligence gathering and this necessitated, in turn, the personal virtues of trust, accuracy, calmness, patience, modesty and loyalty (Nicolson, 1939: 126).[3] James Bartleman (2004: 19), in his entertaining account of his life as a Canadian Foreign Service Officer, emphasized that self-discipline and keeping one's temper should be added to Nicolson's list. In 2005, the first role outlined for Foreign Affairs in the *International Policy Statement* continues to be that of the "interpreter of international events and trends for the Government and Canadians" (Canada, 2005b: 30).

The third major function of diplomacy was added by Cardinal Richelieu when he established a Ministry of External Affairs in 1626 in France to concentrate the management of foreign relations under a single roof. In *Diplomacy*, Henry Kissinger lauds Richelieu as the supreme interpreter of raison d'état. Richelieu, as an advisor to Louis XIII, developed a policy of weakening the Hapsburgs by aligning France with Protestant princes. Kissinger writes that "in an age dominated by religious zeal and ideological fanaticism, a dispassionate foreign policy free of moral imperatives stood out like a snow covered alp" (1994: 64).[4] The important point is that Richelieu developed a ministry of expert fulltime officials to permanently advise the Monarch. In 2005, the Foreign Affairs policy role is defined as the "articulator of a distinctive Canadian international policy" and the "integrator of Canada's international agenda and representation abroad" (Canada, 2005b: 30).

Advocacy, intelligence gathering and policy development, continue to be the fundamentals of diplomacy. But, these old tasks must now be accomplished in a radically altered environment.[5] Summitry, a twenty-four hour media clock, a total blurring between domestic and foreign policy, engaged mass publics, the proliferation of non-governmental organizations, instant communication, and the rise of informal networks both within governments and between governments would challenge even Richelieu. Anne-Marie Slaughter writes about the difficulty in central control, noting that "the state is not disappearing: it is disaggregating" (2004: 31). How to fulfill the traditional mandates of diplomacy, while coping with our changed world, is the great unanswered question of the *International Policy Statement.*

THE EXTERNAL AFFAIRS ACCORDION

In delivering foreign policy, the reputation and effectiveness of Canada's cadre of professional diplomats has waxed and waned. The "Dear Department," as diplomat Arthur Andrew (1993: 3) described his institutional home, was the heart of the Ottawa bureaucracy in the great days of the Mandarins (see Granatstein, 1982), but it has suffered a steady decline in resources and prestige for over a generation. "From the Golden Age to the Bronze Age" is how Andrew Cohen (2003: 118–56) describes the modern history of the Department of Foreign Affairs and Trade. From the cozy club of 1,350 at home and abroad in 1950, the Department has grown to over 9,600 and the bureaucratic norms of the Pearson building have replaced the easy informality of the East Block and the Chateau Laurier cafeteria in the good old days.[6] Money is power in Ottawa and the Department of Foreign Affairs has less of it to spend on programs (as opposed to personnel costs) than almost any other department. In the 2005–06 estimates, for example, the Department of National Defence has a budget of $13.4 billion compared to $2.7 billion for the Canadian International Development Agency (CIDA), $1.8 billion for the Department of Foreign Affairs, and $190 million for the Department of International Trade (The Department of Industry, the original home of the Department of International Trade has a budget of $1.3 billion). Most of the Department of Foreign Affairs budget (56 percent) goes toward the maintenance of 164 embassies, high commissions, and consulates in 114 countries.

In answering the question of how best to organize ourselves in promoting Canada's interests abroad, it is instructive to note that Canada originally defined its interests abroad as immigration and trade. In 1868, the new Dominion of Canada opened its first bureau abroad, the Dominion Emigration Agency in London. In 1880, Sir Alexander Galt was appointed Canada's first high commissioner in London, largely to promote trade, and in 1882 a similar office was opened in Paris. When the government of Wilfrid Laurier finally accepted the advice of Sir Joseph Pope in 1909 to create the Department of External Affairs, Canada had 30 immigration agents and close to 20 trade offices abroad. External Affairs itself began with two clerks, a secretary, and temporary offices over a barbershop, already a poor cousin compared to immigration and trade.

I first came to Ottawa in the mid-1960s as a very junior assistant to the Hon. Walter Gordon, president of the Privy Council. It was the waning years of the "Ottawa Men," but the East Block was still the nerve centre of the Privy Council Office, Finance and External Affairs. For my brief time there, I was in the neighbourhood of public servant greatness. Over sandwich lunches or just roaming the halls, I listened to and observed what was an ongoing Oxford tutorial on how to make public policy. Three groups of men (they were all men then) dominated the scene: the first was Finance (I remember to this day Simon Reisman lecturing me on the virtues of free trade), next came Trade and Commerce with a definite élan in the Trade Commissioners Service, proud of ministers like C.D. Howe, George Hees, and Mitchell Sharp, and then the holy of holies, External Affairs. The foreign officers I met a generation ago were deeply knowledgeable about the government as a whole (the functional divisions of the department kept in touch with the line departments to ensure that foreign and domestic interests converged), experts about the world (the most desired positions in the department were in the political or geographic divisions), and witty and fun to be with to boot. Officers could turn from an arcane discussion about nuclear proliferation to the merits of T.S. Eliot versus Ezra Pound with a flick of a cigarette (most seemed to smoke in those days). There is a danger in romanticizing the past, but comparing my youthful memories of the gaiety and expertise of the Foreign Service with the current results of the 2001 Foreign Service Retention Survey or the 2002 report of Price Waterhouse on comparative employment conditions of Foreign Service offices, is like following Dante on the road to hell (see William H. Mercer, 2001; and Price Waterhouse Coopers, 2002).

But, the very brilliance of the Department of External Affairs in the 1960s may have led to the eventual fragmentation of its international role. Canada had begun its foreign aid program in 1950 with the Colombo Plan and the External Aid Office was initially located in the Department of Trade and Commerce. In 1960, the office was transferred to External Affairs. There the Aid Office languished far from the centre of the action in NATO or Washington. Development in the 1950s and 1960s was not high politics. But it was soon to become so. In 1966, Paul Martin Sr, the secretary of state for External Affairs, asked Maurice Strong, the president of Power Corp., to head up the agency. Strong took an 85 percent salary cut to come to Ottawa and he was already one of the best connected men in the country. Years before, External Affairs had declined even to consider Strong for a junior position because of his lack of formal education. Prime Minister Pearson told him "lucky you didn't have the qualifications ... if we'd taken you, at your age, even if you'd performed well under our system, you could never have been more than the lower-middle ranks at this point in your career" (cited in Strong, 2000: 100–1). With the support of Pearson, Strong became chairman of the External Aid board, over the objections of the under-secretary of state for External Affairs. In 1968, Pierre Trudeau made the centrality of the developing world a major theme in his election campaign and the External Aid Office was recreated as the Canadian International Development Agency with Strong as President. Names matter and "agency" demonstrated more flexibility than "department," and "president" was a more action-oriented title than "deputy minister." Through the Trudeau years, CIDA continued to report to the minister of External Affairs – the minister having two deputies, the under-secretary of state for External Affairs and the President of CIDA – but in 1984, the Mulroney Government began its practice of having a minister responsible for international development as well as the secretary of state for External Affairs. Over the years CIDA's independence and scope have grown, so that today it has significantly more financial resources than the Department of Foreign Affairs.

In 1982 another re-organization took place, much more controversial than the creation of CIDA in 1968. Pierre Trudeau began as prime minister by questioning the value of diplomacy itself and rejecting the initial External Affairs review of NATO headed by the legendary Norman Robertson. But Trudeau had a high opinion of the individual qualities of the men and women who served in External Affairs and showed it by appointing several of them as deputy ministers of other departments. The generalist ethic of External Affairs served the Trudeau Government well. In the 1970s Michael Pitfield, the clerk of the Privy Council, was seized with the same question posed by the 2005 *International Policy Statement* – how best to structure foreign policy? Pitfield created an Interdepartmental Committee on External Relations of deputy ministers and at the minister's level, there was a Cabinet Committee on Foreign Policy and Defence. In 1979, the Clark Government appointed Barry Steer, a senior Trade Commissioner serving as consul general in New York to head a task force to improve the efficiency of foreign operations. Steer recommended the integration into External Affairs of the senior officers of the Department of Industry, Trade and Commerce, and Employment and Immigration. The returning Trudeau Government in 1980 appointed Pamela McDougall to enquire into the conditions of the Foreign Service. Her recommendations included the incorporation of the Trade Commissioner Service into a consolidated Foreign Service.[7] The clerk of the Privy Council was convinced that only integration would give the Department of External Affairs the economic expertise required to be relevant to Canada's needs. Gordon Osbaldeston, the under-secretary of state for External Affairs, candidly wrote that "the main objective of these changes is to ensure the effective action in support of government priorities both in regional and industrial development and in trade and export promotion" (1982: 453). Many in External Affairs were opposed because they feared the "commercialization" of foreign policy. Mitchell Sharp (1994: 172) was opposed for the opposite reason: he believed that the Trade Commissioner Service would lose its commercial edge because of lost contacts with exporters. Like any major re-organization, it took years of work to implement.

Then, out of the blue in 2003, the newly minted government of Paul Martin reversed the 1982 integration. In the 1980s, the debate over integration had been robust and the Clark and Trudeau Governments had appointed task forces and a Royal Commission to report on the situation. On 12 December 2003, the Prime Minister's Office, through an order in council, suddenly announced the splitting of DFAIT. The reaction was almost totally negative. Jeffrey Simpson (2005) the respected columnist for *The Globe and Mail* asked, "Who, dear Hercule, sliced Foreign Affairs in two?" He could find no answer because, it is "an idea, so splendidly stupid that literally no one in Ottawa will admit to having favoured it." Derek Burney, former Canadian ambassador to the US, having experienced the disruption of the integration effort in 1982, said that eventually "this marriage gave our Foreign Service an enviable sense of purpose and relevance," and that the split "may have more to do with the vanity and aspirations of individuals than a perceived need for more coherence and resolve on trade policy" (2005). Allan Gotlieb, former under-secretary chimed in, too: "trade policy is at the heart of foreign policy," he said, "[the split] is not consistent with any movement or arguments" (quoted in McGregor, 2005). Robert Johnson, a former deputy minister of Industry, Trade and Commerce said, "if it ain't broken, don't fix it," and Pamela McDougall defended her advocacy of the initial integration: "if you put trade commissioners and foreign service officers together, they would somehow work together" (ibid). With no defenders and a sea of critics, the two bills to reorganize the foreign relations bureaucracy were defeated in the House of Commons on 15 February 2005. The *International Policy Statement* did not mention the debacle, but blandly promised that "the Government will establish an advisory and consultative process" (DFAIT, 2005a: 23).

DELIVERING ON THE *INTERNATIONAL POLICY STATEMENT*

To achieve the three traditional goals of diplomacy – advocacy, foreign intelligence, and policy development – the Martin Government will have to be far more sure footed on implementation than it has demonstrated on splitting Trade from Foreign Affairs. As Derek Burney maintains, "the reality is that, by fragmenting further the very few real instruments of foreign policy power Canada has, we diminish our capability to play more than a peripheral role" (2005). The Martin government has begun to reduce the capability – commitment gap, now it must reduce the implementation gap.

Three ideas should be considered: First, to advocate successfully in our wired-world, public diplomacy must be central to the work of the Department of Foreign Affairs, not an add-on. Public diplomacy not only in places like the United States but at home to build a constituency for defence, diplomacy, and development. The prime task of a diplomat used to be writing insightful cables to Ottawa. Now it should be using the latest in technology to reach critical audiences through outreach activities, exchanges with think-tanks, virtual desk offices, etc. (see Copeland, 2004). Think of the difference Frank McKenna has made in Washington with his active and skilled media presence, or Pamela Wallin in New York. Canada should also use the asset of its diaspora communities abroad as intelligently as India or Greece. Having the most sophisticated public diplomacy capability in the world is like the Italian city-states of the Renaissance inventing the resident ambassador: a new and better way of carrying out an essential function.

Second, there is no substitute for the deep intelligence of Foreign Service officers who know foreign countries well. Mr Trudeau may have initially been sceptical about the utility of diplomats but in 1983, as he was thinking through his peace mission, he was educated in a profound way about the likely Soviet reaction by Robert Ford, the Canadian dean of Soviet ambassadors. There is specialist knowledge of agriculture, health, trade, and a host of other subjects honeycombed within government and society. But you still need someone to put it in context by knowing the culture well that you are trying to influence. To get deep knowledge you need good people. How are we to attract and retain good people for the Foreign Service? My idea is to give them an important job to do – too often Foreign Service officers serve as advance-men for visiting ministers or dignitaries. Foreign Affairs needs money for programs so that ambassadors and officers can make a real difference. The minister of International Development, Aileen Carroll, rightly noted in her 2005 paper that CIDA had bilateral assistance programs with 155 centers, of which only 18 receive assistance valued at more than $10 million annually. But CIDA's expanse has grown because Canada needs to be doing something in the countries we want to influence. Our ambassadors can't just hang out. The solution is two-folded

– CIDA needs to concentrate most of its resources on functions like health, education, governance or infrastructure where large investments can make a difference and be properly evaluated. But local ambassadors need resources, too, to invest in small projects, create coalitions and do some good locally. The small projects of CIDA should be transferred to the Canada Fund for Local Initiatives, so that every ambassador or high commissioner will have at least a million dollars to spend locally. CIDA should do the large functional priorities, ambassadors should do the local development and coalition building.

And third, policy development and coherence will only occur if there is someone clearly in charge. That someone should be the minister of Foreign Affairs. Trade, CIDA, and Foreign Affairs should report through one deputy to a senior minister. The splitting of Trade and Foreign Affairs should be cancelled and the minister of Foreign Affairs should be the ultimate integrator of policy, although junior ministers can direct international development and trade on a day-to-day basis. To take one example, South Korea is now a target of opportunity for a free trade pact. There should be a full court press with all our instruments of policy concentrating on creating an environment in South Korea – cultural exchanges, security in North Asia, etc. – that will help the negotiations. One of the lessons of recent years is that when the 3Ds of diplomacy, defence, and development are integrated in Canadian policy, as in Bosnia or Afghanistan, Canada's weight multiplies proportionally. One way of ensuring such integration is to ensure the primacy of the minister of Foreign Affairs.

Diplomacy is as old as ancient Athens but as current as the pressing need to persuade North Korea to forgo nuclear weapons. The need for excellent diplomacy is timeless. Canada once had it. We can have it again.

NOTES

1 Pearson gave this address in Toronto the same day that President Truman fired General Douglas MacArthur.
2 Eban's chapter 9, "Diplomacy Old and New" (330–401), is a succinct and eloquently written history of diplomacy.
3 The qualities for a successful ambassador, however, varied, from court to court. The Princess of Zerbst, mother of the Empress Catherine of Russia, writing to Frederick the Great, advised him to choose as his ambassador to St Petersburg a handsome young man with a good complexion. She knew her daughter well. Envoys to the German courts had to absorb "without derangement vast quantities of intoxicating liquor"

(Nicolson, 1939: 106). Monsieur de Callieres in his 1716 classic, *On the Manner of Negotiations with Princes*, advised that ambassadors "should entertain handsomely. A good cook is often an excellent conciliator." This is still good advice.

4 Page Urban VIII said at Richelieu's death, "If there is a God, the Cardinal de Richelieu will have much to answer for. If not ... well, he had a successful life" (Kissinger, 1994: 58).

5 To illustrate the differences between the worlds of old and new diplomacy, Eban (1983: 358) quotes Thomas Jefferson writing to the secretary of State: "We have heard nothing from our ambassador in Spain for two years. If we do not hear from him this year, let us write him a letter."

6 There are many books from former diplomats describing the rise and fall of the Department of External Affairs but one of the best accounts of life in a foreign posting is by the wife of a Foreign Service officer, Christine Hontel-Fraser, *No Fixed Address* (Toronto: University of Toronto Press, 1993).

7 The story is well told by Granatstein and Bothwell (1990: 228–33).

REFERENCES

Andrew, Arthur. 1993. *The Rise and Fall of a Middle Power*. Toronto: James Lorimer and Co.

Bartleman, James. 2004. *On Six Continents: A Life in Canada's Foreign Service, 1966–2002*. Toronto: McClelland and Stewart.

Burney, Derek H. 2005. "Does Canadian Foreign Policy Need a Foreign Service?" Remarks to the Symposium of the National Capital Branch of the Canadian Institute of International Affairs, Ottawa, 17 February.

Canada. 2005a. "Commerce" in *Canada's International Policy Statement: A Role of Pride and Influence in the World*. Ottawa: Department of Foreign Affairs and International Trade (DFAIT), 19 April.

Canada. 2005b. "Diplomacy" in *Canada's International Policy Statement: A Role of Pride and Influence in the World*. Ottawa: Department of Foreign Affairs and International Trade (DFAIT), 19 April.

Canada. 2005c. "Overview" in *Canada's International Policy Statement: A Role of Pride and Influence in the World*. Ottawa: Department of Foreign Affairs and International Trade (DFAIT), 19 April.

Cohen, Andrew. 2003. *While Canada Slept: How We Lost Our Place in the World*. Toronto: McClelland and Stewart.

Cook, Robin. 2003. *The Point of Departure: International Affairs in the Modern Age*. London: Simon and Schuster.

Copeland, Daryl. 2004. "Guerilla Diplomacy," *Canadian Foreign Policy*, vol. 11, no. 2 (Winter): 165–75.

Eban, Abba. 1983. *The New Diplomacy*. London: Weidenfeld and Nicolson.

Granatstein, J.H. 1982. *The Ottawa Men: The Civil Service Mandarins, 1935–1957*. Toronto: Oxford University Press.

Granatstein, J.H. and Robert Bothwell. 1990. *Pirouette: Pierre Trudeau and Canadian Foreign Policy*. Toronto: University of Toronto Press.

Kissinger, Henry. 1994. *Diplomacy*. New York: Simon and Shuster.

McGregor, Sarah. 2005. "Trade split causing sparks," *Embassy: Diplomacy This Week*, 16 February, 8.

Nicolson, Harold. 1939. *Diplomacy*. London: Oxford University Press.

Osbaldeston, Gordon. 1982. "Reorganizing Canada's Department of External Affairs," *International Journal*, vol. 37, no. 3 (Summer).

Pearson, Lester B. 1951. Address to the Canadian and Empire Clubs, Toronto, 10 April.

Price Waterhouse Coopers. 2002. *Comparative Terms and Conditions of Employment of Foreign Service Officers*. Ottawa: Department of Foreign Affairs and International Trade (DFAIT), 3 May.

Sharp, Mitchell. 1994. *Which Reminds Me: A Memoir*. Toronto: University of Toronto Press.

Simpson, Jeffrey. 2005. "Who, dear Hercule, sliced foreign affairs in two?" *Globe and Mail*, 22 Jan.

Slaughter, Anne-Marie. 2004. *A New World Order*. Princeton: Princeton University Press.

Strong, Maurice. 2000. *Where on Earth Are We Going?* Toronto: Alfred A. Knopf.

William H. Mercer Ltd. 2001. *Foreign Service Retention Survey Report on Findings*. Ottawa: Department of Foreign Affairs and International Trade (DFAIT), 26 July.

Contributors

AGATA ANTKIEWICZ is a project officer currently working on The BRICSAM Project at the Centre for International Governance Innovation.

THOMAS S. AXWORTHY is chairman of the Centre for the Study of Democracy, Queen's University. He was principal secretary to Prime Minister Trudeau from 1981 to 1984.

LOUIS BÉLANGER is an associate professor at the Department of Political Science and Institut québécois des hautes études internationales (HEI), Université Laval. He is currently Public Policy Scholar at the Canada Institute of the Woodrow Wilson International Center for Scholars in Washington.

BOGDAN BUDURU is a lecturer at the Institute for European and Russian Studies and the Department of Economics, Carleton University.

DEREK H. BURNEY, O.C. is an adjunct professor of International Affairs at The Norman Paterson School of International Affairs and a senior distinguished fellow at the Centre for Trade Policy and Law, Carleton University.

ANDREW F. COOPER is a professor at the Department of Political Science, University of Waterloo, and the associate director of the Centre for International Governance Innovation.

DANIEL DRACHE is professor at the Department of Political Science and the associate director of the Robarts Centre for Canadian Studies, York University.

PAUL EVANS is a professor and acting director of the Liu Institute for Global Issues, University of British Columbia.

FEN OSLER HAMPSON is a professor and director of The Norman Paterson School of International Affairs, Carleton University.

ANNETTE HESTER is a special research fellow at the Centre for International Governance Innovation.

JOSEPH T. JOCKEL is a professor and director of Canadian Studies, St. Lawrence University.

W. ANDY KNIGHT is a professor at the Department of Political Science at the University of Alberta and the editor of the international journal *Global Governance*.

RAMESH C. KUMAR is a professor at the Department of Economics, University of Waterloo.

JAMES LEE is an analyst in the Parliamentary Information and Research Service, Library of Parliament.

NIGMENDRA NARAIN is a lecturer at the Department of Political Science, University of Western Ontario, and a doctoral student in the Department of Political Science, York University

KIM RICHARD NOSSAL is a professor and head of the Department of Political Studies, Queen's University.

DRAGOŞ POPA is a doctoral student in the Department of Political Science, Carleton University.

DANE ROWLANDS is an associate professor and associate director of The Norman Paterson School of International Affairs, Carleton University.

GERALD SCHMITZ is principal analyst for international affairs in the Parliamentary Information and Research Service, Library of Parliament.

JOEL J. SOKOLSKY is a professor of Political Science and the dean of Arts of the Royal Military College of Canada

JENNIFER WELSH is University Lecturer in International Relations at the University of Oxford, and a fellow of Somerville College.

JOHN WHALLEY is a professor at the Department of Economics and the director of the Centre for the Study of International Economic Relations, University of Western Ontario. He is also a distinguished research fellow at the Centre for International Governance Innovation.

Index